Archie Robertson,

a native of Louisville, Kentucky, is well qualified to report on the "old-time religion." His father, the Reverend Dr. Archibald T. Robertson, was professor of New Testament Interpretation at the Southern Baptist Theological Seminary, and his grandfather, the Reverend Dr. John A. Broadus, was an early president of the Seminary and a Baptist preacher well known throughout the South.

Educated at Harvard and Duke University, the author began work as a newspaper reporter on the Louisville *Courier-Journal* and then edited small weeklies in North Carolina before going to Washington in 1935 as an information specialist. He has recently been employed at the National Cancer Institute in Bethesda, Maryland.

For *That Old-Time Religion* Robertson traveled 10,000 miles visiting hundreds of churches and several seminaries. He went up into the "plain people" country of Pennsylvania, and Northern Virginia to look at the subject with a "detached and sympathetic eye." He also did research in the Library of Congress, visited Dayton, Tennessee, scene of the Scopes trial, and spent time with the snake people at Chattanooga. The material he gathered included many jokes and stories which he has recounted — without jeers — in *That Old-Time Religion.* "I think the origins of the book were in my childhood," Robertson explains, "for my father and mother each had a remarkable gift of gaiety and humor, along with deep religious convictions — a combination so unusual that it made a profound impression on me as a child. As I became older, I grew sick of seeing 'that old-time religion' utterly misrepresented by others. Being essentially a person curious about American life, I could not rest until I had a stab at describing it myself. Once I had defined the subject in my own mind as the personal search, under freedom, for 'real Christianity,' all the material shaped itself up on the scaffolding of religious liberty. I have always felt a vague conviction that in America religion is the unseen balance wheel among the people as a whole, helping to keep us from swinging too far left or right; these travels confirmed this impression."

THAT OLD-TIME
RELIGION

BOOKS BY ARCHIE ROBERTSON

The Government at Your Service

Slow Train to Yesterday

That Old-Time Religion

THAT OLD–TIME

Religion

BY
ARCHIE ROBERTSON

HOUGHTON MIFFLIN COMPANY BOSTON

The Riverside Press Cambridge

1950

IN MEMORY OF MY PARENTS

The Riverside Press
CAMBRIDGE · MASSACHUSETTS
Printed in the U.S.A.

CONTENTS

PART I. ROOTS

PART II. SOME BRANCHES

PART III. THE FRUIT OF THE TREE

ACKNOWLEDGMENTS

IN THE TEXT I have tried to be objective, but I shall let go one glory shout here for the Reverend G. Y. Burgin and his Free Will Baptist friends in the North Carolina mountains. By their kindness to a stranger, they opened my eyes to the existence off the beaten path of a true old-time religion, as orthodox as the Ten Commandments yet wholly alien to the bitter arrogance of many self-styled defenders of the faith.

For critical help I am especially indebted to the insight and patience of Professor William M. Blackburn, of Duke University; Mr. and Mrs. Joseph Kovner, of Washington, and Messrs. Paul Brooks and Austin G. Olney, of Houghton Mifflin Company. The manuscript was read in whole or in part by two Baptist ministers, the Reverend Edward H. Pruden and the Reverend J. A. Easley; two Episcopalians, the Reverend Charles G. Leavell and the Reverend Spence Dunbar; and other friends of varied backgrounds, including Mr. and Mrs. A. D. Stefferud, Cary Robertson, Misses Sara Turlington and Sarah Leslie, Mr. and Mrs. Charles K. O'Neill, Mrs. Elizabeth C. Blackburn, Terry Mitchell, Mr. and Mrs. David Reeder, Mrs. Jean Maury, Miss Henriette Herz, and many others. By working part of the time my wife helped the book to completion. It began in 1946 on Mr. and Mrs. William McGovern's back porch.

I am grateful to *The Baltimore Sun* and Mr. H. L. Mencken for permission to use his Dayton, Tennessee, dispatches; to Dodd, Mead & Company for quotation from *More Mellows;* to the University of Pennsylvania Press, for quotations from *Black Gods of the Metropolis;* and to Fleming H. Revell Company for extensive use of *The Life of John Jasper,* by W. E. Hatcher.

Thanks are due the editors of *Life* for permission to reprint part of this material which appeared in their columns.

PART I

ROOTS

Some of these notes on Old-Time Religion go back to the Reformation in Europe, and some go back to the nineteen-twenties in Louisville, Kentucky

I. THE INTERPRETER'S HOUSE

*Wherein a secular reporter tries to define a
sacred subject, and turns to childhood mem-
ories for assistance*

T HE FIRST STIRRINGS of a religious revival are in the air,
and the time is ripe for a survey of America's most deeply
rooted and fundamental faith. And so, because I have always been interested in the subject, I set out to write a
reporter's book on the Old-Time Religion in the United
States as it is today. I found it was easy to describe the
outward forms of this religious movement, especially in
the countryside where on Sunday morning the cars are
parked by Beulah or Mount Zion, with its mossy gravestones and white steeple or small unpainted belfry.

At the back of the church the pulpit, flanked by two
tall chairs, is in the center of the platform. If it is winter,
a big iron stove glows red-hot in the middle aisle. In
summer the stove is settled in a corner, and the clear glass
windows are open to the breeze. Hand-made pews still
show the ancient bites of the axe. The hymns are by Watts
and Wesley; the preacher is from the country, and his
sermon is from the Bible. Other details will occur to anyone: the ladies' hats are from Sears Roebuck or Mont-
gomery Ward; the heads of the men are weatherbeaten;
babies cry, and the Estey organ is out of tune.

City visitors are always noticed the moment they enter the church, and immediately following the benediction a truly gratifying reception is held outside. At the door the minister offers a friendly handshake, not too professional, and mentions his name. Upon telling him your name, you are introduced to the next person, and the next, until a little ring has formed and you feel like a celebrity.

"Stranger in these parts, aren't you? Thought I noticed a Washington license tag."

"Some people with the same name live down the road, but they're no kin to you, I reckon. Not that it makes any difference. Proud to have you."

"Come again when you're out this way. I've got a cousin works in the Patent Office in Washington. Maybe you can look him up sometime. You must get lonely living in a big place like that."

Your visit will be long remembered. A year or so later, Mr. Quisenberry, a retired farmer, will help himself to another biscuit and say to his wife, "Wonder what happened to that Washington man that stopped here one Sunday?"

"The one that put a dollar in the plate?"

"Deacon Pfitz said it was only two quarters. Nice car, but the tires was worn smooth. Maybe the church ought to put up a sign on the highway, like the Campbellites. Might catch a few more tourists now and then."

"Hardly worth it. So few city folks goes to church these days. They're headed for the mountains."

"Reckon so. Still, you can't tell. There's a heap of good in most people, if you just know how to draw it out."

But the times were too serious and the interest in religion too great for travels which had nothing to offer but nostalgia. I found it necessary to examine my own purposes and define the subject.

The phrase "old-time religion" is from a nineteenth-century revival song, "Give me that old-time religion, it's good enough for me!" It has come to mean all things to all men — a cheap radio racket, a guilt complex to be treated by the psychiatrist, or the means of grace and hope of glory. Depending on the circumstances, I am inclined to believe that it can be any of these things, although naturally it cannot be all of them at once.

For the purposes of these travels, the old-time religion is traditional Protestant Christianity with a special emphasis which the popular American churches have given it: belief in the right of the individual to interpret the Bible according to his own conscience; in religious liberty and separation of Church and State; and especially in the "competence of the individual," the ability of each soul to deal directly with its Creator. Perhaps this one belief sums up all the others.

As I understand it, the old-time religion is also distinguished from other forms of orthodox Christianity by its attitude toward Jesus. In this tradition, the Saviour is not made known to the worshiper primarily through the official interpreters and custodians of religion, nor by creeds and rituals, but through "personal experience." It is first of all a personal religion, and despite its hundreds of sects and churches, there is in it a constant drive toward unity through simplification. Maybe it is oversimplification; but I came to the conclusion that the rank and file of the church people are always looking for what Americans call "real Christianity."

The institutions of the old-time religion are not "holy" or "sacred" to its followers, in the sense that Catholic institutions are sacred to a Catholic. They are open to self-criticism and every other kind of criticism. I have never heard of a zealous Protestant who tried to keep out of the newspapers any item of news which reflected discredit on his own church or its ministers. There may have been such occasions, but certainly they are exceptional. If the preacher runs off with a deacon's wife, the reporter will have no trouble in getting, and printing, the story. Jokes abound in the old-time religion; the best and juiciest, I found, were told me by the preachers themselves.

In a word, this is democracy in religion. I happen to like it, but in these travels I have not tried to put its best foot forward. This is not a work of piety, but an effort at greater understanding.

In the first part I have explored some of the roots of this religious movement, first in my boyhood recollections, then in American history. In the course of this study I encountered some interesting contrasts. It was surprising to learn, for example, that Christianity was only a small, weak minority in early America — quite unlike the dominating, highly organized movement it became later. In wave after wave of nation-wide revivals the churches became rich and strong, until what had begun as a religion of protest became itself almost a sort of "established" religion, wielding vast political and social power.

The nineteen-twenties were a turning point in the history of the old-time religion. I have described the Scopes trial of 1925 (and Dayton, Tennessee, as I found it a quarter-century afterward) because this memorable collision between science and the literal view of the Bible had tremendous consequences. For many an American the churches lost their iron rod of spiritual authority; and with the collapse of Prohibition, they lost their political influence also. For a while, to some observers Protestant Christianity seemed in danger of being laughed out of existence.

But it seemed to me during these travels that the churches have shifted their grounds of appeal since 1925. The chip-on-the-shoulder attitude of Fundamentalist and Modernist alike was being forgotten. The old-time religion appeared to be closing its ranks in a quieter, less controversial faith which speaks to the heart rather than to the head. It was my impression that a sort of cycle had run its course, so that we are back, in religion, to a time not unlike that of two hundred years ago — a period of uncertainty and danger, when religion was generally discredited among the educated, but had begun to stir in fresh life among the masses of the people, along with the political ferment of democracy.

Historically, the old-time religion has been an effort to combine faith and freedom: Whoever believes in God and human liberty shares to some extent in this experiment. Our country is the first great nation in which the churches rose to power among the people by rejecting power for themselves.

For this reason, I chose to visit some of the branches of the religious liberty tree which are very close to the historical stem. It is not a picture of "Protestantism today" that we are after, but something more casual and more interesting — the uncomplicated faith of ordinary people, crossing the lines of churches, underlying the seekings of intellectuals and the subtleties of theologians. The selections have been made more or less at random; the Salvation Army is left out, for instance, because it is al-

ready so very well known. Certainly it is the old-time
religion, and so are many others not included. This tradition has long since invaded nearly all the American
churches, and is very strong among those who recite
creeds and kneel at the altar rail.

The contemporary Fundamentalist movement, which
claims a copyright on the phrase "old-time religion," isn't
what we are looking for either. Now and then we shall
cross its trail, but no matter; we are in search of something
older and more enduring.

First, we visit some of the "plain people" who are so
numerous in Pennsylvania, then a few small congregations
of mountain Baptists. In the tongue-talkers and snake-
handlers of Tennessee the fire of the Great Revival breaks
out among the people afresh, long after it has departed
from the latter-day Methodists. In the life of the Reverend John Jasper we span a century of Negro religion,
before visiting some contemporary Negro churches. They
belong in the tradition for many important reasons, one
of them being that the Christian Church and the Communist Party are the two most active organizations today
which are concerned with racial injustice in the South.
Their motives are different and their methods are different; and if the United States should ever become involved in active conflict with the Soviet Union, it will be
important for Americans to recognize the distinction.

Next I report briefly on some of the more exotic offshoots of the old-time religion in Los Angeles.

But I do not want to leave the impression, as some
books on this subject have done, of a meaningless variety
and confusion. There seems to be a force always at work
pulling the churches together as well as a constant splin-

tering. Here in America is something really new under the sun, a multitude of sects which have bred not only an inevitable amount of bigotry and discord, but also an amazingly widespread tolerance and something better than tolerance. At the heart of our subject is charity, the sign of faith which (secure in the inner citadel a reporter cannot reach) laughs at its own outer forms and differences.

I should call this charity the choicest Fruit of the Tree, and in the last section, called by this title, I have reported, first on some offshoots of the great revivals in New England and Chicago, and then upon a contemporary example of the crusading spirit in a Georgia county. We also describe two American Sunday mornings in cross-sections — first in a rural Virginia county, then in Washington, D.C. And still as a reporter, in the final pages I have written briefly about the meaning of the old-time religion for our own times.

But first I should like to present my own qualifications as a reporter on this subject. My father and grandfather were shining lights of the Southern Baptist Theological Seminary at Louisville, Kentucky; and here, despite these advantages, during the stormy nineteen-twenties I grew up as one of the most unregenerate Sunday-School pupils in Christian annals.

At our house, on Sunday morning, Hattie, the cook, also a Baptist, was summoned to stand at the dining-room door, while at the table Father, still tense from urging the younger children to breakfast on time, read a chapter from the Bible, and briefly prayed. Waffles and honey partly restored my ten-year-old good humor, and I looked

at the theatrical section of the *Courier-Journal* from which
my Aunt Eliza had extracted the Katzenjammer Kids as
hostages until Monday. Then Mother called us to "hunt
quarterlies," brush hair, and put on overshoes.

The Sunday-School building, a block away from home
on the Oak Street side of the Birch Avenue Baptist
Church, had been the original house of worship; its quaint
frizzled stone looked more churchly than the new auditorium. On the left of the vestibule a small green-carpeted
parlor, formerly the pastor's study, now smelled deeply
and thickly of ladies; on the right winding stone steps led
to a dungeon toilet. However, as the lot of us came in,
four children and three adults, usually a trifle late, the
children were supposed to make straight ahead into the
assembly room for Opening Exercises. These were much
like the Closing Exercises and the elapsed time in between.

There was a song — "Saved, by His love divine,
S-a-a-v-e-d, to new life sublime, Life now is sweet and
my joy is complete, for I'm Saved, *Saved,* SAVED!" Miss
Lucy Augur played the piano with a strong, unvarying
beat. She wore a blue silk dress with a narrow white
neckline, and above gold-rimmed spectacles her coils of
brown hair seemed made of some plain, sensible, Baptist
material that would never wear out or change. She was
ageless, but I also sensed that she was youthless, and
understood the hints of indignation which my parents let
drop because "Miss Lucy just won't let loose of the young
people's services." Mr. Smith, our bald-headed, genial
superintendent, now asked Brother McNamara to lead us
in prayer, and God was thanked either for the good
weather which had enabled us to meet together in this

opportunity for service, or because, despite the inclement weather, so many had gathered. There was a Bible reading, announcements, another song, and we were dismissed for classes.

In the Closing Exercises the burning public curiosity about the morning's attendance and offering was satisfied, with comparative data for the previous week and a year ago; and blue silk class banners of supremacy, made apparently of the same material as Miss Augur's dress, changed hands listlessly while we sang "Bringing in the Sheaves." I was not the only one who felt something was lacking, for a deacon, Mr. Gresham, once drilled us in a lively chant for use in a city-wide, Protestant celebration involving a parade and ball game: "We are Baptists through and through, People from Birch Avenue!" On another occasion, Mr. Gresham, an aggressive real-estate operator of the early nineteen-twenties, prayed, "O Lord, give us pep, O Lord give us *punch*, O Lord give us SPIZZERINKTUM!"

I can never forget this petition for the effect it had upon my parents. During dinner my mother's thin shoulders shook with light convulsions until at last Mr. Gresham's interesting new word exploded from her clenched lips, after which she laughed until she cried. Father, whose degrees ran all the way out across the page after his name, wore the grim look which meant that humanity, or some part of it, was hopeless. He was Professor of New Testament Interpretation at the Baptist Theological Seminary. Mother was the daughter of the Reverend Doctor John A. Broadus, who had preached in Lee's army and served as the second president of the Seminary. She wrote Sunday-School lessons, and articles on how to bring up children, for which I forgave her, and poetry, of which I approved.

We *were* Baptists through and through. But in early adolescence, I discovered an oversight in the arrangement of the Sunday-School. Before the Opening Exercises, the adults left us in the vestibule and moved on to their own Bible classes, in the main church auditorium. It was of course not possible to duck out again on the street, which swarmed with late-coming friends of the family; but after a moment's rest in the toilet dungeon or the Ladies' Parlor, while my older brother and sisters went ahead, I climbed the stairs to an open gallery running around the assembly room. As the heads below were bowed in the Weather Report, it was possible to walk quickly and decorously around the building to the back stairs. From the dark rear hall, doors opened into the pastor's study, the choir-loft, and a vestry-room where the candidates for baptism undressed, dried, and dressed again. But a fourth little door went out into the alley, which as in all the "nice parts" of Louisville, was lined with tumbledown, whitewashed ex-stables, lit by kerosene lamps and flavored with horse manure, and inhabited by Negro household servants whose earnings averaged three to five dollars a week. Early in Prohibition times some of the alley-dwellers undertook, in a modest way, to increase their income by making whiskey from the garbage so conveniently at hand; and within fifty feet of the Sunday-School a hospitable Baptist for twenty cents supplied a slug of white mule, flavored with lemon juice and sugar.

In the small upstairs classrooms, each with its worn green carpet, parlor organ, folding chairs, and gaily colored literature, little Gothic windows opened on the alley, where flies and warm Negro voices buzzed in freedom. In a pleasant intimacy we repeated the pattern: a hymn, "Yield Not to Temptation" (a parlor organ was made for this melody); a prayer, collection, Scripture lesson, closing song and prayer. We sensed the underlying desire of our teacher — a young married woman who wore a peek-a-boo blouse — simply to avoid spit-balls at any price until the bell rang for her deliverance; and we co-operated obligingly by suggesting why God allowed Shadrach, Meshach, and Abednego to be put into the fiery furnace. It would not have been playing the game to advance the *right* reason; the teacher was there for that. Year by year as the earth turned, we followed the familiar stories on the great slow wheel of "uniform lessons" adopted by the International Sunday-School Convention in 1872.

Sensing in the peek-a-boo lady a certain hesitation to harp unduly upon Hell, I pressed my advantage to the utmost. Would those in China who had never even heard the Gospel be consigned to the everlasting lake of fire? She hesitated, her tantalizing shirtwaist fluttering in the warm breeze from the alley; the sympathies of that soft bosom, I felt, were on my side, but fearing lest the urgency of the missionary lesson be lost, she refused a clear-cut yes or no.

Father was firm about attending both Sunday-School and church, and the whole Robertson family paraded down the center aisle to a forward pew. As the youngest, I led the way, followed by Cary, Charlotte, and Nell. "Sister," my Aunt Eliza, was next, establishing her heavy acousticon on a small tower of hymnbooks, for she was very short. During the preliminaries she fidgeted with the cords of this primitive hearing aid to get the wavelength for the sermon; alarming pig-squeals from the instrument punctuated "Praise God from Whom All Blessings Flow." At her side Grandmother — who had never set foot in Sunday-School — adjusted a small carpeted footstool. Before marrying the late Doctor John A. Broadus she had been a Virginian and an Episcopalian; her coiffured white head and small square shoulders made a formal, military surrender. Mother alone had no fixed position; she often came tripping hurriedly behind the rest of us, having stopped to leave a sprig of lemon verbena in the lap of her friend Mrs. Hedges; her hair was blown in silvery haste, while Father stood waiting none too patiently in the aisle. He then entered, removed his overshoes and placed them with his umbrella next to Grandmother's prayer-stool; his heavy-set figure doubled in bulk with his seating and the gate was now officially closed. Mother often sat next to me, fetching from her nested pocketbook, after powder-box, handkerchief, and gloves, paper and pencil for the small fry. In later years, her gloved finger shyly touched my arm as we sang, and pointed in the hymnbook to the name of Beethoven or Haydn, as if to make me feel better about being a Baptist.

Without Mother's assistance, I sensed a difference in quality, as a child, between Sunday-School and Church. The hymnbooks were different. In our Sunday-School book each song had a chorus, with some of the words repeated in fine print underneath, for the bass or baritone, while the ladies and tenors followed the larger type. Thus, while the alto inquired, "Will there be any stars in my crown?" the bass drummed along in a carefree, irresponsible manner, repeating "any stars, any stars." Nobody explained this to me at the time. I tried singing "upstairs" and "downstairs," uncertain which the Lord favored.

This arrangement dated from the eighteenth century "fuguing tunes," devised in New England after our forefathers rebelled against singing nothing but the psalms. As for the songs themselves, by Moody and Sankey, Fanny Crosby, E. O. Excell, G. S. Stebbins, and others, they were mostly products of the great revival waves of the late nineteenth century. They were all about saving souls. That was their one idea.

In Church, there was no "upstairs" and "downstairs" music. We sang from a fat old-fashioned book, with stately words and music; vague and beautiful thoughts formed in my mind, of Greenland's icy mountains and India's coral strand, of Jerusalem the Golden, the spacious firmament on high, and every creature, every tribe, on this terrestrial ball. I do not think the old-time religion can be understood without the hearty congregational singing. To the people in the pews the language of the Bible and the music form mental pictures so bright that they are quite unaware of tabernacles dreary to outward view and services flat and tedious. The beauty of our subject, lying almost wholly inward, shows only now and then to outward view on the faces of the people as they sing. But as a child, I was far from having such appreciation.

Only the often counted organ-pipes relieved the fumed oak and white plaster; the stained-glass windows carefully avoided anything so popish as pictures. There was nothing else to look at except the pulpit, the three chairs, and the heavy Communion table, on which a mountainous white cloth once a month telegraphed ahead the bad news of a long service. Not yet a member, I sat in miserable awe while the elements were passed.

Small, childhood puzzles helped to pass the time. What,

for example, was the consecrated, "cross-eyed bear"? What, indeed, was the Holy Ghost — something unspeakably awful, draped in a sheet? And when the minister said, "The doors of the church are now open," why couldn't we go home?

In our second-floor bedroom, over my brother Cary's bed, hung a picture of Virginia's Christian Soldier; it was entirely natural that he should ask if General Lee was in the Old Testament or the New Testament. The night sounds mingled adventure and security; the watchman's stick beating its tattoo against the gate; the early-morning clopping of the farm wagons; and once at least each night the whistle of a freight train chuffing lazily on the outer fringes of time and space. It was not that I so much denied the Sunday-School explanation of the universe as that I sensed the existence of other worlds beyond worlds.

Having lately graduated from Tom Swift and the pious adventures of Doctor Grenfell into the first flush of promiscuous reading, I set forth on roller skates for an armload of books. It was a pleasant half-mile skate past the Christian Science Church, and the Reformed Jewish Synagogue — meteorites from those other planets which I meant some day to explore — through a block of neighborhood bakeries and shoemakers, to the Library plaza, across from the Unitarian Church. Here the true city magic began; ten-story apartment buildings in Broadway were in view, and just a block away began Downtown, with its book and music stores, soda fountains, and the glamorous Seelbach Hotel.

During my high-school days I became a devout follower of H. L. Mencken. I used to bring home his old

Smart Set magazine, with its raffish devil on the cover, and later the acid-green *American Mercury,* in which Mr. Mencken continued to say unkind things about the Baptists. Common observation confirmed some of Mr. Mencken's Prejudices. It was simple truth, for instance, that a Baptist church was usually the ugliest in town, and the more prosperous, the worse. I did not wish my parents to lose their religion — they would have been inconceivable to me without it — but I often wished earnestly that they had just a little less. Why couldn't they have been Episcopalians? Or even Methodists?

At such moments I was probably thinking of people like the Trotters. They were family friends of not quite the first order of intimacy; it was said that Doctor Trotter drank a little at the Pendennis Club, but was a fine man. He was of middle height, with a Vandyke beard, pleasant twinkling brown eyes, and a habit of asking questions, but seldom committing himself.

Just once he received his come-uppance, from Grandmother Broadus. After she broke her leg at seventy, Doctor Trotter asked her age, one of the most closely guarded secrets in the city.

"Young man," said Grandmother, "you set, and I'll knit."

Doctor Trotter went out on calls twelve to fourteen hours a day, absorbing social and intellectual currents on the run. He knew all about H. L. Mencken, for example; and was not shocked by my dislike of schoolteachers and preachers, pointing out only that doctors weren't much better. "We don't always know how to leave people alone either," he said.

Mrs. Trotter was motherly, although not in the baking-powder sense. She was about as worldly as a Methodist can be. She went to the races once a year, on Derby Day. I learned afterward that she was a gentle but persistent modifying influence upon my own upbringing, so that eventually I was able to go to dances like anyone else. She and Mother were on committees together in the Woman's Club. Our own church ladies or the Seminary wives came right into the library which was our family living room; but when Mrs. Trotter came to ask us to a Methodist oyster supper — *noblesse oblige* after she had been to the Baptist rummage sale — she was always received in the front parlor. She called one evening as we were having family prayers, and brought even into this occasion her own slightly formal aura, by suggesting that we say the Apostles' Creed. Baptists do not say creeds or catechisms. But Mother, who knew everything, recited with vigor, while Father looked nonplussed, and I wondered at the kindly, malicious gleam in Mrs. Trotter's eye.

The Trotter and Robertson children were close, to the point of pillow fights. If I spent the night at Bill's, on Sunday morning, of course, Mrs. Trotter hustled us both off to his Sunday-School. I did not mind. It was a welcome change from Birch Avenue; for although the lesson was about the same, it didn't seem necessary to be saved exactly, in order to be a Methodist — just christened and received. Furthermore, Bill did not have to go every Sunday. (Eventually, he entered the ministry.)

Doctor Trotter's private beliefs were a vague, half-humorous mystery. He went sometimes with his wife to hear Doctor Doolittle at Parkwood Methodist, but he never told us what church he belonged to. Once he said that his mother had been a Methodist who switched over to the Baptists.

"My grandmother told her that she'd left the Army of the Lord and joined the Navy," he said.

At Sunday dinner he asked a long, thorough blessing, as if to take the curse off one or two slightly racy medical stories to follow. On Temperance Sunday, for example, he remembered the Dry lecturer of his student days, who made an elaborate demonstration with a worm.

First he dropped the worm into a glass of water, where it wiggled happily, then into a glass of whiskey, where it died.

"And what does this clearly prove, gentlemen?" asked the man from the Anti-Saloon League.

A black sheep spoke up from the rear. "If you drink enough whiskey, you'll never have worms."

Or Mrs. Trotter recalled the day when Patsy, their youngest, set off for Parkwood Methodist with two nickels, one for chewing-gum, one for the collection. She lost one on the way, and returned with the gum. "The Lord's nickel rolled down the drain," she explained.

Wonderful Trotters! I thought — to love the Lord in such a lighthearted way. Through adolescence I defended them mentally against all adversaries. A revivalist at our church, having made few converts, was engaged in probing or reconverting the faithful. In words which seemed directed at people just like the Trotters, he denounced the lukewarm Christians of our worldly city. Jesus, he said, would spew them out of His mouth. I refused to believe it; there might be some big surprises on Judgment Day, I thought, keeping my fingers crossed and my eyes on the blue sky outside the window.

The Trotters were somehow impervious to assaults from either side. During my college years, when religion

was highly unfashionable, I stayed with them after a
dance during the holidays; they served an eggnog of
prescription whiskey, told a new story, and slipped out
quietly on Sunday morning to hear Doctor Doolittle's
Christmas sermon.

Not only from the Trotters, but from many visitors to
our house, I sensed the existence of a vast, strangely separated family, bound together by an invisible tie. There
was not a sectarian bone in either of my parents. I remember one Sunday afternoon when, skating home from
the Public Library under an armload of books, I found a
fire in the grate and cocoa being served for a Catholic
lady, Miss Anna Blanche McGill, who wrote book reviews
for the *Courier-Journal* and encouraged my own literary
ambitions. She had called with a small present for the
family, a book containing one long poem. Reading an
Oz book by the fire, I overheard scraps of conversation:
the author, Francis Thompson, was a Catholic (good! I
thought), a drunkard (fine!) and a dope-fiend (admirable!).

"Perhaps the children might enjoy it later on," said
Miss McGill, and departed. My parents remarked, as they
occasionally did, that some Catholics were wonderful
Christians — my mother sighing a little. I soon explored
the *Hound of Heaven* and found an approach to faith far
more poetic than that of Birch Avenue Sunday-School, if
not wholly unrelated. And many others came and went;
Doctor John R. Mott, of the Y.M.C.A.; a rugged African
missionary named Dan Crawford, who left a copy of his
book, *Thinking Black*. Bound in heavy black leather to
emphasize his point, it was a landmark in the growing
struggle of Christian missionaries to understand native
cultures and points of view.

Perhaps it was Doctor J. F. Fraser, a pleasant Scot, who told us of the jingles which children tossed at each other on the streets of Aberdeen, when the Episcopal Church of Scotland was under pressure from the dominant Presbyterians. The Episcopalian children were greeted with "Pisky, pisky, boo and bend, up and down and up again." After a while they retorted, "Presby, Presby, dinna bend, sit thee down on man's chief end."

So there were vast extensions of the subject! Not all the humor, not all the poetry, belonged to the enemies of religion. I slipped away for an occasional Sunday to visit the Episcopal Church, suffering vaguely and helplessly on the fence while the nineteen-twenties rolled on to their climax of revolt against the Baptists and Methodists.

The famous Scopes trial, in which Tennessee Fundamentalists placed a schoolteacher on trial for teaching evolution, did not touch our own household because Father held no truck with extremists. But the *American Mercury* documented other *gaucheries* of the churches in the Jazz Decade. It was in 1924 — to pick a few examples — that the Mayor of Springfield, Massachusetts, said publicly that Coolidge had become President in accordance with a Divine plan, and that his opponents thwarted the Divine will; that the Mayor of Pomona, Kansas, warned that anyone pitching horseshoes near the public streets or alleys on Sunday would be prosecuted; and that the Honorable Noah W. Cooper, candidate for Senator from Tennessee, declared that opening the gasoline stations of Nashville on Sunday would be "a step towards Hell." Ku Klux Klan leaflets were distributed at a Dallas revival conducted by the Reverend Doctor Bob Jones; and after a revival held in New Jersey by one Charles Winter, a

group of women sang hymns by the incinerator while they
burned the publications of the Christian Scientists, Unitarians, and Russellites.

I writhed inwardly at the frequency with which Baptists made the *Mercury* honor roll. Birch Avenue sent me
to a "youth rally" at a small Kentucky college; on my return, I stood up at a church supper with the courage of
youth and told them how much I had disliked the whole
proceedings — the banner inscribed MAKE CHRIST CAMPUS
COMMANDER, the slick song-leader, the ready-made cheers
and pep slogans from denominational headquarters. To
my amazement, the church people, led by Mrs. Hedges
and finally including even Mr. Gresham, began to laugh;
at first quietly, then in rebellious, happy gales.

But they did not like criticism by outsiders.

No one suffered more than my parents from Mencken's
exposures. Father endured the presence of the enemy's
literature within his household for years, but at last he
exploded.

"Mencken's pro-German!" he shouted angrily one day.
"He's for the anti-Christ Nietschze! Don't you see that
he's opposed to everything I stand for? I want you to
promise not to read him any more."

This was difficult. I murmured that I didn't agree with
everything Mencken wrote, and Father subsided; but I
could not adequately express my belief that my father
and the Baltimore skeptic were in some ways much alike.
Each was honest and opinionated, and delighted in ex-
posing shams and hypocrisies. Father's lectures at the
Seminary overflowed with blunt country humor, directed
at Deacon Skinflint and the frauds within religion as well
as at the enemies without. In his interpretation of the

Greek New Testament he fought against "radical" criticism, but never at the sacrifice of truth and accuracy. He was a great scholar and a modest man, and I think that his faith, at heart, was mystical. But as a youngster I liked him best in his country setting.

Toward the end of each summer we visited Cool Spring, North Carolina, where the Robertsons, after losing their Virginia plantation at the end of the Civil War, had moved to a tobacco farm. Uncle Martin met us at the train with the buggy for the twelve-mile drive. He wore a farmer's wide straw hat; beneath sandy whiskers, his smile was broad and slow. He and Father promptly plunged into a deep discussion of the dry spell and the corn. My uncle, who never married, and his sister Josephine treated us like the children of royalty; Aunt Josephine stood to wave a huge peacock-feather fan against the flies, so that we could enjoy slabs of ham, chicken, giant tomatoes, and her mashed-potato salad, made with boiled dressing and celery-seed, and which kept sweet for days in the cool depths of the well.

After the Civil War, Father explained to us carefully, his brother Martin had come home early from Washington and Lee College to raise tobacco so that Father — who had already served his time at the plow-handle — could study for the ministry. The whole story was implicit in the earnest, half-humorous attention which the two men now gave, under the lamp after supper, to peeling peaches for preserves, or criticizing plans for a new sanitary privy drawn up by the county agent. Later, they sat on the porch where Uncle Martin smoked his pipe and pointed out the distant outline of the Brushy Mountains, or they settled down with the *Literary Digest* and, later, *Time,* like tolerant onlookers at an amusing world. They seldom talked about religion. His brother Martin, Father once told me, was a Secret Disciple; that is, he had never joined the church, but it was impossible to believe that so good and kind a man was not in his heart a Christian.

Father did not take steps about my own conversion until our hell-fire pastor from the Deep South was relieved by a more cheerful sort from the Middle West. The Reverend Doctor Everson, a combat veteran of the First World War, was called the Fighting Parson, but he never talked of soldiers dying without Jesus, and we got on nicely. His favorite pulpit slogan was "God and I can do *anything.*"

One day he took the Robertsons to attend an all-day "association meeting" at a country church near Louisville. I fooled around happily in the sunshine of the churchyard, reading old gravestones. It was, I remember, the Long Run Association. Long Run Creek, for which the association was called, received its name from the long flight down the valley of settlers who escaped an attack by the red man. I learned afterward that not all the settlers made the long run safely. Abraham Lincoln, a Baptist who had moved from Virginia to Kentucky between 1782 and 1784, was killed by the Indians and is buried beneath a wing of the old Long Run Church. His son Thomas escaped, however, and lived to father another Abraham.

Inside the plain old meeting-house delegates from each of the Missionary Baptist churches in the association were now conducting their interminable business, broken now and then by a snatch of hymn-singing. Local Baptist churches, bound to each other even more loosely than the United Nations, meet in "association" only once a year.

I peered under the Communion cloths covering the long dinner trestles on the lawn, taking advances of country ham and chocolate cake, and feeling more respect for the Baptists than at any previous time; it was pleasant to find that Birch Avenue Church had these country cousins.

And thus, when Doctor Everson appeared on the lawn, surprisingly, and said, "I promised your father I would speak to you today about joining the church," I was in the best of humors and even sympathized slightly with his predicament. My brother and sisters had gone through the waters, and I knew that my time had come.

"What do I have to do?" I asked, however, stalling.

"You won't be asked about Hell," said Doctor Everson, smiling. "You'll have plenty of time later on to make up your mind about that point — and others."

No one at Birch Avenue commented upon the decision except a curly-headed deacon's son whom I had always disliked, who said loudly after Sunday-School, "Yah, yah, I know what you're going to do!" I flushed violently, but, as in some subsequent assaults, felt uncertain just what action was called for. So I "went forward" during the "invitation hymn," feeling no emotion except timidity; Doctor Everson announced to the congregation that I had presented myself for baptism on profession of faith, and all in favor would please "signify by saying 'Aye,' and raising the right hand." There was the usual moderate murmur, Father's voice being just a shade stronger than usual. I was in, the pastor extended the right hand of fellowship, and after the benediction family friends did likewise. In the grasp of old Mrs. Hedges' hand and the twinkle of her eye was the admonition not to take myself too seriously before the Lord.

Doctor Edgar Young Mullins, president of the Seminary, and at other times of the Southern Baptist Convention and the Baptist World Alliance, came to supper the next Sunday night. Irreverently called "The Pope," Doctor Mullins was a tall, suave gentleman with beautifully trimmed gray whiskers, who lived on Cherokee Drive in the Highlands, then coming to be the fashionable part of town. His wife, Isla May, wrote novels — distinctly worthwhile fiction for young girls, but still a great advance in worldliness, I thought, over a mother who wrote for the Sunday-School Board and a father who wrote in Greek.

I had already encountered Doctor Mullins's diplomacy on my first visit to Father's office, in the red-brick Victorian Gothic barns on Broadway. These looked, smelled, and sounded exactly as a Southern Baptist Theological Seminary constructed in the eighteen-nineties should. The solemn thunder of students tramping from upstairs classrooms echoed ominously in the dark lower halls. After exhibiting the big dictionary with its colored plates of birds, beasts, and fish in his own dusty jungle, Father took me to the President's office. I liked Doctor Mullins, although he was a head-patter. He showed me a bottle of water from the River Jordan, produced Jordan almonds, which I have ever since considered vaguely holy, and proposed a trip to see the mummy, a gold-encrusted Egyptian lady, very worldly indeed.

After supper Doctor Mullins now patted me again, said, "Well, well, Archibald," and gave me a Bible. He preached that night — without reference to the awful event to follow — and I walked alone and shivering through the side door into the pastor's study, where Mother had placed dry clothing and a towel. The kindly Pope was secure in his rubberized baptismal robe and trousers.

I remember a last desperate pang of conscience; for it is Baptist doctrine that one must be converted *before* baptism, and I had no feeling of being saved. It was too late now; I should have to straighten out the deal as best I could afterward. But under any circumstances immersion is an awesome experience. I can sympathize with the rural brother who found as he rose from the river that he just couldn't face the public, and plunged quickly back and swam away downstream.

This was my formal entry into the largest group of American Protestants, second only to the Roman Catholic Church in the United States, and in many ways its direct opposite. For the Baptists, properly speaking, do not constitute a Church at all. Historically, they are individualists and arch-heretics. Circumstances of course have shaped them into something else, and for the greater part of the succeeding years I lived in earnest protest against the Baptists, with little effort to understand their origins or peculiarities.

Yet thus early, on the following Communion Sunday, I was permitted to realize that when the Baptists are plainest, they can reach a great dignity. After the last hymn I now stood with my family and read aloud, from a battered piece of cardboard, the Covenant which most local churches use:

> *Having, as we trust, been brought by Divine Grace to receive the Lord Jesus Christ, and to give ourselves to Him, we do now, relying on his gracious aid, solemnly covenant with one another that we will walk together in brotherly love . . .*

Now the minister stood by the table, with a deacon's help lifting and folding the white cloth. He began to read, "And on the night that Jesus was betrayed, He took bread . . . " breaking unleavened wafers into small bits as he did so. The deacons, twelve real-estate salesmen, auto dealers, hardware clerks, and schoolteachers in their Sunday suits, now came forward to pass the bread and grape-juice for the Communion, which is made simultaneously by the whole congregation.

Then there was an offering for the poor, and we sang for once without musical accompaniment. All the familiar voices — Father's strong baritone, Mother's sweet, earnest tones, Brother Gresham's loud bass off-key, Miss Lucy Augur's sharp knife-edge, the Hedges and Smiths — rose surprisingly naked and intimate, without the protection of the organ:

> *Blest be the tie that binds*
> *Our hearts in Christian love . . .*

Beneath the official Baptist version of being "true to Christ" — which seemed to mean not going to dances, drinking, smoking, or having any fun — beneath all the follies of the churches itemized by Mr. Mencken, this occasion seemed to expose a bedrock of true religion. What was it? An old, vain dream of human brotherhood, having its origins in the mind of infancy and the fears of primitive man? Or, conceivably, a glimpse of ultimate reality, toward which by Divine leading, against the willfulness of human hearts, the whole Creation moves?

Despite these rare moments of grace, I was slow to associate the church as I had known it with human liberty; and perhaps it was true that by the nineteen-twenties the old-time religion had grown into a great and powerful institution, quite different from its humble origins.

2. SOME SEEDS AND TRANSPLANTING

From Europe seeds are carried on the wind,
to start the roots of the Religious Liberty Tree

Even America as a whole was not at all sober and God-fearing. Of the hundred and one colonists on board the *Mayflower*, only a dozen belonged to the first New England Church, and scarcely a fifth of the Massachusetts Bay settlers, in the earliest years, were professing Christians. By 1731, Boston was making a million and a quarter gallons of rum a year. Most of it, as church historians note sadly, was for home consumption, although much was used in the slave trade.

All sorts of reasons have been advanced for early American wickedness. Common people were angered by the tyranny of the Congregationalists in New England and by lazy and drunken pastors among the established Reformed and Episcopal churches to the South. The eighteenth century was a time of skepticism among the educated.

In 1760 only one New Englander out of eight was a church member. In the Middle Colonies the ratio was one to fifteen, and in the South, with its slave population, no better than one to twenty. The organized, official churches, transplanted in various European and English

29

forms up and down the Atlantic seaboard, made very little appeal to the popular imagination. With varying degrees of severity, the New England Puritans being the worst, they punished dissenters and taxed the public for their support of the legally established religion.

It was the stirrings of a "free religion," outside the official churches, which began the American Protestant tradition many of us know best. Its origins are hard to trace. It is all the more puzzling because it broke out also *within* the established churches; the first great revival waves in America, as a matter of record, started in the Dutch Reformed and Anglican Churches. Certainly no existing denomination in the United States can justly claim a monopoly on the old-time religion; historically, it is the common product of them all.

The first seeds of the "free religion" came from Europe, where the Reformation itself, say the historians, early began to develop in two quite different directions. There were both an "official" Reformation and an underground movement. The great reformers, Luther, Calvin, Zwingli, and Knox, and their followers built new churches on the old Roman foundations, frequently using the same buildings, parts of the same liturgy and creeds, sometimes the same priests and government payrolls. Such was the origin of the various Lutherans, Reformed Churches, and Presbyterians, while the Church of England at first made no shift at all, except to reject the authority of the Pope. There were doctrinal differences among all these churches and their offshoots; they were all swept by such tidal movements as the controversy between Calvinism and Free Will, but all of them were originally alike in using the established machinery which they took over.

On the other hand, the "underground" included a multitude of free spirits who wanted to break completely with the old organization, placing the primary emphasis upon "communion of the soul with God," taking the Bible as their sole authority, and rejecting official support or recognition. They were the first to believe in complete religious liberty and the separation of Church and State.

They were all sorts of people. In Pennsylvania, for example, are still found Schwenkfelders, less than two thousand in number at the last census, followers of one Kaspar Schwenkfeld von Ossig, born in 1489. A friend of Martin Luther, he fell out with him over the question of the sacraments, which he believed were purely inward and spiritual. Fleeing from place to place in Germany to avoid persecution, he refused to found a church and advised his followers "to worship in the existing churches so far as liberty of conscience was not jeopardized."

But most of the parents of the old-time religion were anonymous, their names lost to history, their influence working through others. We learn of some "Familists," at the dawn of the Reformation, who were against established churches, forms, and ceremonies, and believed that all Christ's followers should be one family, united in the bonds of love. The "Seekers," first reported in England in 1617, were described by William Penn as people who "left all visible churches and societies and wandered up and down as sheep without a shepherd, and as doves without their mates," seeking the Lord.

Behind all such people was a long, pre-Reformation tradition — the Bohemian followers of John Huss, the still earlier Waldensians of France and Italy, the Lollards in England.

They claim a line of descent not only from early

heretics, but from mystics within the bosom of the medieval Catholic Church, Saint Francis of Assisi, Meister Eck-
hart, Thomas à Kempis, and from early associations of
humble people with touching names: The Brothers of the
Free Spirit, the Brethren of the Common Lot, or the
Friends of God.

I am not concerned here with the detailed efforts of
many Protestant Churches to trace their pedigrees back
to the New Testament; we are citing, more or less at
random, a sprinkling of names to show the great diversity
of our English and European sources. The largest, and
perhaps most important, group first came to public notice
at Zurich, Switzerland, in 1523. It was only six years since
Martin Luther had fired the opening gun of the Reformation. Calvin was not yet active in Geneva, Switzerland,
but his famous colleague Zwingli had taken over the
churches at Zurich. He had persuaded the local government to order the priests of the city to preach "only what
could be proved by the Bible."

But some of the Zurich citizens, taking these revolutionary orders quite seriously, searched the Scriptures for
themselves, and could find no warrant therein for any
established church, Catholic or Reformed, nor for such
accepted practices as christening infants. They insisted
on baptism for "believers only," by immersion, and were
therefore called the "Anabaptists" or twice-baptized.
Almost immediately they became unpopular. To this day,
the Thirty-Nine Articles speak unkindly of Anabaptists,
and the authorities at Zurich soon began to drown them
as a fitting punishment.

But the movement, loose and ungoverned, spread over
Europe through many generations and had all sorts of in-

fluences. The Puritans and Pilgrim Fathers of New England were affected by their doctrines of congregational freedom. The sort of Baptists among whom I was born and bred came to America by way of England, where in John Bunyan they had produced their one great writer and in *Pilgrim's Progress* their one great book. On the other hand, in Northern Italy before 1550 some of the Anabaptists met with humanist scholars and became thorough Modernists, from whom the present-day Unitarians can trace as clear a line of descent. The individual's right to interpret the Scriptures as he saw fit was a doctrine common to them all.

A large number in Germany ran amok. Taking literally both the Book of Revelation and the social teachings of the New Testament, they preached an immediate sharing of the wealth, expecting the Second Coming at any moment. Inflamed by these fanatical leaders, the impoverished peasants revolted. They were vigorously suppressed by the Lutheran authorities, but not before an uprising at Munster in 1553 which ended in an orgy of communism, free love, and massacre.

In the calmer air of Holland, the surviving Anabaptists were salvaged and placed on a firm basis by an able Dutchman named Menno Simons, a former priest. From Holland their influence continued to cut across the world in various ways.

A minority of the followers of Menno Simons took the name Mennonites, and held to the strict doctrines of plain dress, pacifism, and "separateness" from the world. Often persecuted in Europe for their refusal to knuckle under to established religion, they and others of like views flocked to America where they are found today.

But there is no one seed-bed, no one source. The belief in "free religion," in an altogether unofficial Christianity which does not seek to force its views on anyone, is something that crops up again and again. In New England, for example, after the principle was denied by the Puritans (who, as the schoolboy boner says, came in order "To worship God in their own way and make everybody else do the same"), Roger Williams promptly revolted. In 1636 he set up the new Colony of Rhode Island on the principle of religious liberty. Nobody has stated it more clearly than Williams: "It is the will and command of *God*, that . . . a *permission* of the most *Paganish, Jewish, Turkish, or anti-christian consciences* and *worships*, be granted to *all* men in all *Nations* and *Countries*." His books were burned by horrified Christians in England and Massachusetts, but he went on to develop his ideas. In 1652 he wrote as follows to the Governor of Massachusetts and to four classes of clergy (which he called "Popish, Prelatical, Presbyterian and Independent"):

> *Yea, if they refuse, deny, oppose the doctrine of Jesus Christ, whether Jews or Gentiles, why should you call for fire from heaven, which suits not with Jesus Christ, his Spirit and ends? Why should you compel them to come in, with any sword but that of the Spirit of God?*

Under his leadership, Rhode Island became the only place in the world where Jews were welcome without restrictions of any kind whatever. A Hebrew congregation was organized there in 1658.

The American Baptists claim Roger Williams as a founder, although after being immersed he soon left their fellowship and became a Seeker — for the Seekers had come over, too. He continued friendly with the Baptists; and when they built a great new church at Providence in 1774, with a steeple a hundred and ninety-six feet high and a bell weighing more than a ton, they engraved into the bell their pride in all these glories, temporal and spiritual:

For freedom of conscience, the town was first planted;
Persuasion, not force, was used by the people;
This church is the oldest, and has not recanted,
Enjoying and granting, bell, temple and steeple.

But a movement called "pietism," which sprang up within the Lutherans of Germany, a century after the great Reformer's death, was more influential than Roger Williams in building the old-time religion.

These Germans objected against too much dogmatism, ceremony, and state control within the Church that Luther had founded. They stressed the importance of "personal religion," of direct relationship between the individual soul and God, and freedom of worship; and like the Mennonites, they took to pacifism, to "separateness from the world," and "dressing plain." Many of them believed like the Baptists in total immersion for believers only, and revived another practice of the early Church: triple baptism, three times forward, once for each person of the Trinity. In 1701 they formed the first congregation of the Church of the Brethren, ever since called Dunkards, because they dunk.

In England the "pietist" movement also influenced the new sect of Quakers, who taught the doctrines of nonresistance and obedience to the "inner light," and wore simple clothes of gray.

The early Quakers were persecuted, too; some were hanged on Boston Common, others banished on threat of being fined, imprisoned, and having their ears cut off if they returned. Nevertheless, by 1750 there were said to be fifty thousand in the Colonies.

In Europe and America, pietism crossed denominational lines and took many forms throughout the world. Persecuted for their beliefs, many pietists sought shelter where William Penn had set up a colony on the basis of religious freedom. One group of pre-Reformation Protestants called Moravians — spiritual descendants of the fifteenth-century heretic John Huss — came to the New World under pietist leadership.

An accidental shipboard meeting between these Moravians and a Church of England clergyman named John Wesley shows the seeds of the old-time religion as they were carried on cross-currents back and forth. As a student at Oxford, John Wesley, with his brother Charles and a friend named George Whitefield, had already become notorious for their piety. They were called "Methodists," because of their methodical habits of Bible-reading and prayer. Wesley took Anglican orders, and was sent to Georgia in 1735 on a preaching mission by a Church of England missionary society.

During a storm, John Wesley was much impressed, and privately troubled, by the cheerful courage of the Moravians. They seemed to have a practical faith which he lacked.

One of the Moravian pietists asked him, "Do you know Jesus Christ?"

"I know that he is the Saviour of the World," answered the minister.

"True," said the German, "but do you know that He saved you?"

Meanwhile, in the Colonies the evangelistic spirit of the pietists spread among the established churches, and started the first great American religious revival. By 1726 a revival was at high tide among the Dutch Reformed in New Jersey; meetings soon began among the Presbyterians; and an Episcopal priest named William Tennent, who had emigrated with his wife and four sons, joined with the Presbyterians and set up a seminary in a cabin at Neshaminy, Pennsylvania. It was ridiculed as the "log college." Here generations of revivalists were trained in the classics and theology.

The fire spread rapidly to New England, where the movement was first called "The Great Awakening." Already the Congregationalist Jonathan Edwards was scaring the daylights out of sinners with his pictures of Hell. Edwards had a powerful, trained mind, a literary gift and a better nature; but the rank and file will always remember him for Hell, and Hell alone. Strong men rolled helpless in the aisles, screaming "For God's sakes, isn't there any hope?" He was a specialist in infant damnation.

In New England, some fifty thousand new Calvinists were added to the churches. In the South, Baptist farmer-preachers, unlettered but powerful orators, took over the revival. From time to time they were jailed for preaching without a license, but persecution only added to their following, and they carried The Great Awakening to the remote frontier.

George Whitefield, the friend of the Wesleys, traveled up and down the land for thirty years and made The

Awakening a continental revival. Although an Anglican priest, he visited the Tennents in their log college, preached in Baptist and Quaker meeting-houses, in Jonathan Edwards's church and at Harvard and Yale.

"I love those who thunder out the word," Whitefield once said; and he had one of the remarkable voices of history. David Garrick observed that Whitefield could make an audience weep by uttering the word "Mesopotamia," and Benjamin Franklin, who heard him preach out-of-doors at Philadelphia, estimated that he could be heard by twenty-five thousand. Franklin had resolved to give the evangelist nothing; but as Whitefield warmed to his plea for a new orphanage in Georgia, Ben began to shell out first the pennies, then the silver, "and he finished so admirably that I emptied my pockets into the collector's dish, gold and all." A friend of Franklin, at this same meeting, had taken the precaution to attend with empty pockets. Overcome like Ben, he now applied to a Quaker neighbor for a loan so that he could make a donation.

"At any other time, friend Hopkins, I would lend to thee freely," the Quaker answered. "But not now, for thee seems to me to be out of thy right senses."

Whitefield seldom finished a sermon without taking up a collection for some worthy cause — to repair damage done by a fire at Harvard, or to feed the hungry among the Lutherans and German Reformed in Europe. He helped the Tennents raise funds for Princeton University, which succeeded their rude "log college," and for the Indian charity school which became Dartmouth.

In the backwoods meetings, among masses not reached by the established churches, multitudes for the first time were reported roaring on the ground, wringing their hands, weeping, screaming or cursing under conviction of sin. Some historians consider that a more important result was political, 'and that democracy in The Great Awakening struck deep emotional roots. Although in their books Edwards and other preachers defended with great learning the Calvinist doctrine of predestination, in The Awakening they proceeded on the assumption that every man had his destiny in his own hands. They stressed the doctrine of equality before God, and made a point of preaching to slaves as well as masters, rich as well as poor.

The Baptists soon began to insist on religious liberty, supported loyally by some other churches and by Jefferson; and as the revolutionary storm gathered, a committee reported to Parliament in 1774 that the chief opposition to His Majesty's Government came from "Congregationalists, Presbyterians, and smugglers."

The rank-and-file Americans were opposed to institutions of *any* kind.

People were taking religion into their own hands; there was a rebellion, not only in politics but in music. For the first century of American settlement, the people, like most of the Protestants in England and on the Continent, had sung only the psalms — lined out by the preacher or "clerk," for the benefit of the congregation, and then sung one line at a time. It was a slow and tedious way of singing, still followed in some remote rural churches, where hymnbooks are scarce and some of the worshipers may have "trouble in reading without their spectacles."

The *Bay Psalm Book,* the first book printed in the Colonies, was published at Cambridge, Massachusetts, in 1640, and held sway for a century, while the art of singing rapidly declined. Meanwhile, English Noncomformist churches began to sing the new hymns of Isaac Watts, who had rebelled against psalm-singing. Ben Franklin published Watts in this country in 1729. The hymnbooks didn't sell at first; the people had forgotten how to sing.

A Massachusetts minister, the Reverend John Tufts, started singing-schools to revive the art. He imported from England a convenient system of four shaped notes, the shape of each note indicating its position on the scale; this was popularly called "fasola" music.

Mr. Tufts issued his first book of instructions and tunes about 1742, "a plain and easy method of learning to sing psalm tunes." The full musical scale of course had long been used; the "shaped notes" were just a short-cut to learning.

From New England the singing-schools — popular social occasions, although with a pious purpose — were taken up by the Pennsylvania Dutch who spread them rapidly through the Shenandoah Valley and into the Southern highland region, where "shaped-note" music flourishes today and singing-schools are still held in country churches. Later in the century, when three more shaped notes — "doremi" — were added, the innovation was violently resisted, the "fasola" singers claiming that theirs was "God's music."

During the period of The Great Awakening, many resisted the new printed notes and tunes. "The names given the notes are bawdy, yea blasphemous," wrote a New England worthy. "It is Quakerish and Popish and introductive of Instrumental Music."

Even today in one small American sect of Presbyterians, called Covenanters, they will sing nothing but the psalms.

But the Lutherans, the Moravians, and many of the German pietists had an old tradition of hymn-singing. It was known that in England the great John Wesley had said that he saw no reason why the Devil should have all the good tunes; his brother Charles wrote six thousand hymns, many set to rousing tavern airs.

Whitefield himself was partial to the psalms. But the new hymns of Watts and Wesley spread rapidly throughout the Colonies, and in many places were accepted as Gospel. When an early edition of Watts by one Joseph Barlow took some liberties, a Congregationalist divine objected in verse:

> *You've proved yourself a sinful cre'tur;*
> *You've murdered Watts, and spoilt the metre.*
> *You've tried the Word of God to alter,*
> *And for your pains deserve a halter.*

The Americans began to write their own songs; the Apple-Tree Hymn was printed in an early New England songbook, its authorship forgotten:

> *The tree of life my soul hath seen,*
> *Laden with fruit and always green;*
> *The trees of Nature fruitless be*
> *Compared with Christ the apple-tree.*

The Baptists, suspicious at first of hymnbooks used by the established churches, met their own requirements. As they stood on the river's edge near Philadelphia they sang:

Jesus Master, O discover pleasure in us, now we stand
On this bank of Schuylkill River to obey Thy great command.

Or at another ceremony, still followed in the back country:

> *Obedient to Our Lord's commands*
> *We now together meet*
> *With humble hearts and cleansed hands*
> *To wash each other's feet.*

The first known American hymn-writer was Joseph
Humphreys, born in 1720. He wrote a song describing
the progress of The Great Awakening.

> *Britain's Isle has catch'd the flame,*
> *Many know and love the Lamb.*
> *Both in England and in Wales,*
> *And in Scotland grace prevails.*
>
> *Many Germans walk with God,*
> *Through the virtue of Christ's blood . . .*
>
> *Likewise in Americay*
> *Shines the glorious Gospel-Day . . .*
> *Pennsylvania has been blest*
> *With an Evangelick feast.*
> *On South Carolina too*
> *Christ distills his heavenly dew.*
>
> *Thousand Negroes praise thy name,*
> *And New England's in a flame . . .*
> *And we hear the Hottentot*
> *By Our Lord is not forgot . . .*

With this song the seedling which had sprung up on
American soil showed already the effects of its environ-

ment. It was a popular religion, "anti-institutional," and wildly enthusiastic. Cutting across the lines of churches, nations, and races, it placed a deep religious fervor behind the drive for human liberty.

The Baptists were fierce about freedom, and so were the smaller sects which under religious liberty were already springing up left and right, so that by the time of Washington's administration, there were twenty-five religious denominations in the young Republic. A ridiculed sect called The Shakers — Holy Rollers of their time — included in an early hymnbook four lines of gratitude:

Rights of conscience in these days
Now demand our solemn praise;
Here we see what God has done
By his servant, Washington.

3. GROWTH

*From a minority position, the Great Revival
and "practical Christianity" help the old-time
religion to grow into a dominating force*

FOR THE NEXT ONE HUNDRED AND FIFTY YEARS the old-time religion grew and changed with the country. At each succeeding stage, some group or other would branch out to recover an element which they felt was in danger of being lost; or a prophet would receive a new revelation and launch a new church. But, as the United States moved from the frontier to an industrial civilization, the churches as a whole took on something like the form and shape I remembered as a boy. What the English call "dissent" became, with us, the "established" religion. The wonder is not how greatly the churches had changed, but how much of the frontier spirit remained alive in them.

After The Great Awakening, there was a lull during the Revolutionary War. Whitefield had died in 1770, and was buried in the vault of the Old South Presbyterian Church at Newburyport, Massachusetts, amid the weeping of ministers and people. He had reached the common people with his religion, incidentally stirring up all sorts of excesses, and arousing the anger of many in the more sedate churches. The Reverend Timothy Cutler complained that, although "regeneration and conversion is the whole cry," nevertheless, "Our presses are forever teeming with books and our women with bastards." His best epitaph was written long after by Austin Dobson, an English poet; for in the old country he had aroused the same sort of indignation for preaching to miners:

> *Whitefield preached to colliers grim;*
> *Bishops in lawn sleeves preached at* him.

Up and down the eastern seaboard, religion settled back into more comfortable ways; people said the ground was burnt over. The Methodists for a while became highly unpopular, because John Wesley sided with the King. Many of the American leaders who had helped the popular churches win religious liberty were themselves deists or skeptics, admirers of Voltaire like Jefferson and Franklin. Tom Paine, the one-man OWI of the Revolution, was against organized Christianity.

A short while after the Revolution, virtually all the students at Harvard and Yale were said to be atheists.

The organization of the Methodist Church touched off the next wave of excitement, known as The Great Revival. More than any other single event in our history, The Great Revival, which lasted for years and spread around the world, gave the old-time religion the outward forms and shapes which many of us know best. The revivals started an impulse to rescue the perishing which has taken all sorts of twists and turns and has certainly been one of the most powerful elements in American life. An historical connection can be traced, for example, between foreign missions and the "One World" concept of the late Wendell Willkie. It is not a question of being "for" or "against" revivals, but of understanding some of the roots of our common life.

In 1784 John Wesley, who never left the Church of England, nevertheless founded his own Church. Without authority, he consecrated Doctor Thomas Coke a Bishop, and sent him to America to lay hands on Francis Asbury, who had been Wesley's General Assistant in America since 1772. Here the Methodists broke entirely with the Church of England and were separately organized under the leadership of Bishop Asbury. He was an indefatigable man of genius who inspired his followers with a terrific zeal. The Methodist circuit riders gave rise to a new description of the worst kind of weather: "There's nobody out today but crows and Methodist preachers."

A great change in theology underlay their zeal. Until about this time nearly all Americans had believed in "predestination," holding that God had chosen or "elected," since before the foundation of the world, those whom He meant to save. John Calvin had erected this belief into a formidable theological system. In a simpler and older form it was held by the rank and file of the Baptists, who might never have heard of Calvin. Predestination had been the belief of their earliest forebears, the English peasant heretics of the Middle Ages called Lollards, followers of John Wyclif.

In the sixteenth century a great Dutch Reformed theologian named Arminius had rebelled against predestination, teaching instead that Christ died for all men, and that by exercising his own free will, any sinner could repent, believe and be saved. The controversy, which spread gradually throughout the world until it swept all the churches, has been classically reconciled in the United States by a Negro preacher:

"You see, it's this way. There's an election goin' on all the time. The Lord votes for you, the Devil votes against you, and you casts the decidin' vote."

John Wesley became a strong believer in "free will." Over this issue, he broke with Whitefield; and the Methodists as a natural consequence felt a personal responsibility for extending the opportunity of salvation to all.

The Methodist Revival began in Virginia among some Low-Church Episcopalians about the middle of 1787, and two years later Baltimore was on fire. Mobs of Methodists swept through the city streets by night, shouting and singing, holding prayer meetings which overflowed from the homes of new converts and blocked traffic on the sidewalks.

The urbane Episcopalians as a rule stayed calm. On his departure from the metropolis of South Carolina, Bishop Asbury wrote, "I now leave Charleston, the seat of Satan, dissipation and folly." (His curse seems to have lingered. A century and a half later, when a tornado tore a hole in old Saint Michael's Church, the local Methodists remarked that "God Almighty's been trying to get in that church for a hundred and fifty years and at last He's succeeded.") The Episcopalians had suffered severely from the Revolution, many of their ministers having sided with the Crown and fled to England.

But the Baptists and Presbyterians, although still believers in predestination, were promptly ignited, and all up and down the expanding frontier they competed with the Methodists. All the evangelical churches held a nation-wide "Concert of Prayer" in 1795. New England caught fire again, and President Timothy Dwight at Yale started a revival in which seventy-five out of two hundred and thirty godless students were converted. From New England a current swept through western New York and Pennsylvania, where the pietists had settled, onward across the Ohio Valley and into Kentucky and Tennessee. Here it encountered a hot blast coming up from the South.

The Reverend James McGready had begun preaching, when in his late twenties, under a Presbyterian license. In North Carolina he quickly won fame for his Hell-fire, Calvinistic warnings. McGready had a way of reaching out with a mighty swing of his arm from the pulpit and dangling a figurative sinner over the brink of the blazing pit. He was soon accused of "running people distracted," his pulpit was burned, and he received a note written in blood warning him to leave the State.

In 1796 McGready came to Rogues' Harbor in Logan County, Kentucky, a pioneer nest of murderers, horse-thieves, highwaymen, thugs, and bankrupts from all over the East. Even among the respectable pioneers, "French infidelity" was strong and preachers were hooted at. Kentucky required strong medicine and McGready supplied it; by the summer of 1799 a revival had engulfed all of Logan County.

Methodists, Baptists, and Presbyterians swung the axe side by side to clear a brush arbor. Families came and stayed until their food gave out. In the cool of the evening, after the day's preaching and before the services began by the light of flaring pine torches, they called good-natured challenges through the forest. The Baptists, even then noted for a high standard of open-air eating, sang:

Baptist, Baptist, Baptist,
Baptist till I die.
I'll go along with the Baptists
And eat that Baptist pie.

To which their rivals might reply:

The World, the devil and Tom Paine
Have tried their force, but all in vain,
They can't prevail, the reason is
The Lord defends the Methodist.

Under the preaching of McGready, the hard-bitten characters of Rogues' Harbor were converted — often violently. Because some were likely to be seized with the "jerks," bodily convulsions which might last for days, a stand of small saplings waist-high was left on the edge of a clearing, for the victims to hold on to.

It was in August, 1801, that the greatest outburst occurred, an historic occasion which lasted for years, at Cane Ridge in Logan County. Here the Reverend Barton W. Stone, another Presbyterian, was pastor of the Cane Ridge meeting-house, built of squared logs in 1791 by pioneers of Scotch-Irish descent. He began a local meeting to which swarms came from all over Kentucky, Ohio, and Tennessee. All the churches joined in. By day, hundreds of preachers exhorted in the forest clearings.

James B. Finley, who was converted after attending Cane Ridge as a boy, gives us an idea of the enormous emotional power which was released by the new teaching, that every man had his eternal destiny in his own hands.

His father, a Presbyterian minister who had established

the first high school in Kentucky, one Sunday afternoon asked young James to repeat the catechism. Afterward he asked his son if he prayed.

"No," James said. "Because I do not see any use in it. If I am one of the elect, I will be saved in God's good time; and if I am one of the non-elect, praying will do me no good, as Christ did not die for them."

Soon young Finley fell under the spell of the opposite extreme, the heretical doctrine preached along the frontier by the Universalists, that *everybody* would be saved. This he found a comforting thought. "It represented God as being so merciful that it inspired a love for Him." James soon began to play cards, enjoy the giddy mazes of the dance, and take an occasional spree.

In this interesting phase of his young manhood, he first heard of the sights at Cane Ridge, a day's walk distant. The hair of the women, it was reported, "would crack like the lash of a driver's whip." He set out for Cane Ridge with a friend, purely from curiosity. "As I prided myself upon my manhood and courage, I had no fear of being overcome by any nervous excitability, or being frightened into religion." But he did not know what lay ahead of him.

Some twenty-five thousand people were gathered in the forest, and the noise was like Niagara. James counted seven ministers, all preaching at one time, from stumps, wagons, or fallen trees.

At no time, other witnesses have reported, was the ground at Cane Ridge less than half covered with the victims of religious experience. "Some lay quiet, unable to move or speak." For these, rescue squads known as "bearers of the slain" were organized, to move them out of the way, where they would not be hurt, until they came to. "Some talked but could not move. Some beat the floor with their heels. Some, shrieking in agony, bounded about like a live fish out of water. Many lay down and rolled over for hours at a time. Others rushed wildly about over stumps and benches, and then plunged, shouting 'Lost! Lost!' into the forest." Many "talked in tongues," as at Pentecost. Upon some, the "holy laugh" descended. In "the barks," the votaries fell upon all fours, forming groups which loped and gathered at the foot of a tree, yelping, barking, and snapping like dogs; this exercise was called "treeing the Devil."

Young James Finley did not observe all these phenomena in operation at one time, but what he did take in was sufficiently unsettling. His knees trembled, his lips quivered, and he felt as though he would fall.

"A strange supernatural power seemed to pervade the entire mass of minds there collected. I became so weak and powerless that I found it necessary to sit down. Soon after, I left and went into the woods, and there I strove to rally and man up my courage. I tried to philosophize in regard to these wonderful exhibitions, resolving them into mere sympathetic excitement — a kind of religious enthusiasm, inspired by songs and eloquent harangues."

Soon he felt strong enough to go back for another look. But alas! At one moment he saw at least five hundred people swept down, "as if a battery of a thousand guns had been opened upon them, and then immediately followed shrieks and shouts that rent the very heavens. My hair rose up on my head, my whole frame trembled, the blood ran cold in my veins . . . a sense of suffocation and blindness seemed to come over me, and I thought I was going to die."

James crept off for home, "a ruined man," spending a

miserable night under the hay in a barn. Near Maylick, Kentucky, he was wholly overcome and fell flat on the ground, crying aloud for mercy and salvation.

An old German settler from Switzerland, no doubt one of the pietists who had emigrated earlier, saw the fallen boy and had him carried to his house and laid on a bed. James tells us that "The old Dutch saint directed me to look right away to the Saviour. He then kneeled at the bedside and prayed for my salvation most fervently, in Dutch and broken English. . . . Suddenly my load was gone, my guilt removed, and presently the direct witness from Heaven shone full upon my soul." At the opposite extreme of emotion, he now felt that he should die from an excess of joy.

Finley now cast around for a church to join. Since he had rejected predestination, he could not sign up with the Presbyterians. He tried visiting a number of "New Light" camp meetings, as the left-wingers of the day were called. Among them were the "Shaking Quakers," who seemed too ridiculous. For about eighteen months he tried to get to Heaven alone; but after backsliding at a dancing-party, he joined the Methodists, who hauled him up at last to firm ground. Later, he became a famous circuit rider, and from his memoirs, and those of his colleague, Peter Cartwright, these accounts are largely taken.

It was quite an experience to get religion in those days.

Finley, we notice, did not bark like a dog or fall on the ground at the meeting. The mass hysteria which swept the great crowd in the forest was the wild foam on the surface of the old-time religion — not the essence of the thing itself. Having swung from the extreme of predestination to the extreme of "Universalism," he found himself back — unexpectedly — face to face with the central problem of salvation; and, with some helpful prompting from the old Dutch settler, he solved the issue alone with his God.

Unquestionably, he was afraid of Hell. The fear and dread have been an element in Christianity at all times, from the beginning until now; and perhaps those of us who latterly feel the actual dread of an atomic lake of fire and turn our thoughts more seriously to religion, are not wholly exempt either. But the feelings of fear and guilt, by themselves, are not sufficient to account for the growth and power of the old-time religion. In the book which, next to the Bible, anyone should read who wants to understand the subject, Mr. Great-Heart discusses the sad case of Mr. Fearing. "The first string that the musician usually touches, is the bass, when he intends to put all in tune. God also plays upon this string first, when He sets the soul in tune for Himself. Only here was the imperfection of Mr. Fearing; he could play upon no other music but this, till towards his latter end."

The churches, even the revivalists, would learn to play on other strings. But The Great Revival set a pattern of being converted the hard way, which lasted for many years and is by no means forgotten yet.

As of 1800, it has been estimated, only seven per cent of the people were church members. The early preachers were often tarred and feathered and sometimes killed. In St. Louis, as late as 1817, it was boasted that "the Sabbath never had crossed and never should cross the Mississippi"; and one of the first preachers to venture over reported that the Anglo-Saxon settlers held nightly drunken orgies at which they burned Bibles and celebrated a mock communion. There were men and women of quiet piety, like Daniel Boone, who said, "I always did love God ever since I could remember," and let it go at that; or the useful frontier preacher, Johnny Appleseed, who planted orchards throughout the Middle West. But in general, belief and disbelief both ran to violence.

The circuit rider had to be a man of wit and courage. The Reverend Lorenzo Dow, who labored mightily for the Methodists in the Natchez Country, is a good example. He arranged for a small Negro boy to illustrate a sermon on the Judgment Day. He instructed the Negro to climb a tall pine behind the congregation, and at a signal from the pulpit, to blow loud on a horn. The plan went off without a hitch, and the people were frightened to a gratifying degree. Panic set in. Then the frontier people, seeing the black boy up in the tree, reacted violently and surged toward the pulpit in anger.

Dow kept right on preaching. "And now, brethren, if a little colored boy blowing a tin horn in the top of a pine tree can scare the daylights out of you, what will you do when the great day really comes?"

Huge numbers in early America, despite The Great Awakening and The Great Revival, had never heard the Gospel. While missionaries labored with the Indians, others found heathen at home. Freeborn Garretson, an early Methodist who preached to the soldiers of the Revolutionary Army, once asked a stranger riding along a Delaware road if he "knew the Lord Jesus Christ," and was answered politely and sincerely, "Sir, I know not where the gentleman lives." Wilson Lee, another Methodist pioneer, preached in Kentucky on the text, "Except a man deny himself, and take up his cross, he cannot be my disciple." As the minister explained that the cross might be any sort of personal hardship, the literal-minded frontier people were moved to tears; and in one case to direct action. After the meeting Mr. Lee passed a Dutchman, a notoriously henpecked citizen, who had picked up his wife and was carrying her home.

The knowledge that the unsaved abounded all around and that now — since "salvation was free" — they waited only for the preaching of the Word to be rescued from eternal damnation, spurred the efforts of the ministers and laymen. Upon being converted, one set to and converted everyone else; it was as simple as that; and since no more effective device has ever been hit upon for building the membership of any organization, the evangelistic churches flourished mightily. The Methodists and Baptists were far in the lead, with the Presbyterians and Lutherans and Congregationalists coming along after.

There were differences in theology; but the rank and file, perhaps then as now, paid more attention to other things. The Methodists offered a tight knit organization and systematic classes of instruction. They continued to make good use of the camp meeting, which came to have dining-halls and other conveniences and, by the present century, had deteriorated into a sort of pious summer resort. After Peter Cartwright noticed an increase in the bastardy rate following the more spectacular outbreaks, the camp meetings were purged of their wilder symptoms.

As to the Baptists, they offered, besides total immersion,

the attraction of complete independence, for each local church was a law unto itself.* Without central organization, they multiplied amoeba-like; the First Baptist Church of Washington, D.C., established in 1802, is said to have two hundred descendants. Along the frontier, community churches and interdenominational Sunday-Schools were not uncommon, and the preachers of different churches co-operated — and fought.

Peter Cartwright, most famous of the Methodist circuit riders, once preached in the church of a Baptist minister who had a "dreadful rude set of children, one of whom they called Betsy. She would stand on the seats, point and laugh and when any would fall under the power of God, she would say it was nothing but a Methodist fit."

Just at the close of his next moving sermon, several hundred sinners fell down all through the assembly so that they had no need for a mourners' bench. As Peter went through the crowd ministering to the fallen, he came across Baptist Betsy, who was now under conviction of sin. She cried out, "Oh, do pray for me! I am afraid I am lost and damned forever!"

"Betsy, get up," said the hard-hearted Methodist. "You have only got a Methodist fit."

---

* The minutes of monthly business meetings of the Forks of Elkhorn Baptist Church in Kentucky from 1800 to 1820 show us a congregation managing its own affairs. "Bro. Blanton complains against Bro. Red Major for playing Carnal plays. . . . Bro. Edward Roberts is Excluded from this Church for playing fives and for offering to bet One Hundred Dollars," and "Mr. Asa Bolls Caty is Excluded for the sin of a Dultery." The slaves belonged. Sister Esther Boulware's Winney was given a hearing on charges that since the Lord converted her, "She had never believed that any Christians kept Negroes a slave, and that she believed There was thousands of White people wallowing in Hell for their treatment of Negroes — and she did not care if there was as many more." Winnie was excluded.

He did not relent until her father was himself crying and shaking in every joint. Peter then took mercy on Betsy, and exhorted and prayed with her. She struggled all night until sunrise, when "she rose and went over the camp-ground like a top," afterward joining the Methodist Church.

All his long life Peter Cartwright thundered against Baptists, the Devil, slavery, and whiskey. Peter ran for Congress once; and in a debate confronted a clever young frontier lawyer who shared only one of these beliefs, but who knew how to handle preachers. "Where are you going?" asked Cartwright, meaning, of course, to Heaven or Hell. "I'm going to Congress," said Lincoln, and did.

The Great Revival never really stopped for a hundred years. It came and went in waves. In 1812 an earthquake shook the West to its knees and started a new cycle of camp meetings. (A Kentucky evangelist at this time lost some of his following when he was seen taking off in a hurry during the quake, calling back to his wife, "O Tabby! It's Jesus and I can't wait for you!") By 1831 the burnt-over ground had grown up again, and a revival swept fifteen hundred towns, with more than one hundred thousand added to the churches.

Upper New York State at this time was the spawning-ground of new religions, like Southern California today; all sorts of New Lights flourished, the Mormons, the Shakers, the Spiritualists, and the Adventists — who were the followers of William Miller. All of these held revivals of their own.

William Miller, born in 1782 on a farm near Pittsfield, Massachusetts, was a great reader in his youth, buying the works of Voltaire, Paine, Hume, and other rationalists with his wood-chopping money. But at a Baptist revival in 1816, he was drawn into the waters; he emerged with a private determination. All the evangelists had preached that Christ was coming again. William Miller wanted to know *when*. He searched the Scriptures and made honest, if labored, calculations from the Book of Daniel. For reasons which no longer concern us greatly, he convinced himself by arithmetic that the end of the world was coming in 1843; and in 1831, a general revival year, he began to preach the news. Many churches held aloof, but thousands flocked to hear him, and other free-lance preachers joined in.

The brush-arbor days were passing; great tents and tabernacles were erected. At Concord, New Hampshire, it is still remembered that the center pole of the Advent tent was fifty-five feet high. In Boston, Millerites built a tabernacle near Scollay Square, which later became a church in which Henry Ward Beecher held forth, and by the time of my student days, a dramatic institution known as the Old Howard.

The prophet Miller went to Washington to advise calling off preparations for the 1844 elections as a waste of time. Where he could not go, the paper *Signs of the Times* went for him. This was one of the most moving of the great revivals, for it held the added note of immediate urgency: There was very little time to lose.

As 1843 passed without event, Miller discovered that he had mixed the Jewish and Roman calendars. There could be no doubt about 1844. It would be on the twenty-first of March. Hundreds of revivals throughout the nation reflected a frightful anxiety; but the sun rose on March 22.

It is a well-known characteristic of the "premillennial" belief, which has recurred throughout the history of Christianity, that it can stand almost any amount of disappointment; and after a few months excitement rose again. The day would come on October 22. A fever of excitement arose; and in the long aftermath of resentment, fables were invented which greatly exaggerated the amount of damage. It is true that here and there a few devout souls gave away their earthy possessions and had to be cared for during the coming winter by their neighbors, and that expectant throngs met and sang a requiem for the world. But large portions of the populace did not climb trees and windmills, as has often been alleged, nor were white "ascension robes" generally worn. The Adventists survived as a sober-minded body, carrying on medical and educational work as well as evangelism throughout the world. Miller published a frank *Apology and Defence,* in which he acknowledged that it was a mistake to try to set a date. He held, however, to the belief that "Jesus is coming soon"; and in times of crisis, this slogan still appears on rural fenceposts across the nation.

The Great Revival sent a backwash all over the world. Lorenzo Dow carried it to England, where his enthusiastic followers were known as "ranters"; and it swept back from Kentucky and Tennessee into the older States where it had begun. In Seneca County, New York, the Methodists were especially fervent; protracted meetings with the "jerks," the "unknown tongues," and other phenomena were frequent. Joseph Smith, the impressionable son of a poor family of the neighborhood, united with the Methodists at the age of fourteen. A strong young man,

he became a powerful well-digger, gifted in the use of the
"divining twig"; he began to search also for hidden riches,
and then for hidden relics. In the spring of 1830 on the
hill of Cumorah, near Palmyra, New York, Joseph un-
earthed a volume of golden leaves inscribed in "Reformed
Egyptian," and with it a pair of spectacles named re-
spectively "Urim" and "Thummim," by which the finder
was able to translate them.

There was much wildness in the early Mormon revivals,
and the "tongue-talking" included many words in Indian
dialect, for in the Mormon belief the American aboriginals
were linked with the Ten Lost Tribes of Israel. Viciously
opposed by other churches, the Mormons traveled west;
their story has often been told; but a chance contact with
the old-time religion is interesting. From Nauvoo, Illinois,
then the Saints' headquarters, Joseph Smith had risen to
dominate Illinois and even announced his candidacy for
the Presidency of the United States. Then he crossed
swords with old Peter Cartwright, the Methodist circuit
rider. He told Peter of the mighty works done in Nauvoo,
of faith healings and the gift of tongues, and of saints
who could drink deadly poison without being hurt. Peter
replied that the Mormons had tried to break up his camp
meetings and that he had been forced to throw them out
with a threat of lynching.

According to Grover C. Loud, in his entertaining history
of American revivals,* Joseph Smith then declared "I will
show you, sir, that I will raise up a government in these
United States which will overturn the present government, and I will raise up a new religion that will overturn
every other religion in this country!"

* *Evangelized America!* The Dial Press, 1928.

Peter Cartwright answered, "Yes, Uncle Joe, but my Bible tells me 'the bloody and deceitful man shall not live out half his days,' and I expect the Lord will send the Devil after you some of these days and take you out of the way."

The new popular churches took up the work of founding colleges which the older churches had started; from 1830 to the Civil War, the Methodists planted thirty-four permanent colleges, the Baptists twenty-five and the Disciples five. Alongside the churches they built common schools; until gradually religion civilized first the frontier, and then itself.

Before the Civil War, the leading churches in cities and towns were becoming much alike. They adopted each other's business methods and forms of worship. The Baptists and Methodists quieted down, and their services of worship were such that the ministers no longer had to ask for "order on the grounds." The bitterness of the days of "established religion" and the wildness of Cane Ridge were quickly forgotten in most places, and as education advanced and the church people intermingled, their differences became more of a pleasant topic of conversation than anything else.

Yet at every stage, groups broke away, remembering the past. The Baptists, for example, as they grew rapidly in numbers, had modified their pure frontier democracy. They were becoming a Church in spite of themselves, and felt the need of organization. They would not have bishops, like the Methodists and Episcopalians, nor even a republican form of government with synods and presbyteries, like the Presbyterians and Lutherans; but they established "boards" to direct their foreign missions, colleges, seminaries, publications, and other church business. Early in the nineteenth century these innovations provoked strong words between the "Missionary" and the "Anti-Missionary" Baptists, who held to the simplicity as well as the strict Calvinism of the early days.

There were likewise Primitive Methodists, and any number of Primitive Presbyterians, although they did not call themselves that.

Disputations over music were involved in many of these offshoots which looked to the past, and the fact is highly significant. For music had been important in the birth of the old-time religion; and in The Great Revival as in The Great Awakening, people loved to sing. The Americans had taken the great hymns of eighteenth-century English writers, "Rock of Ages" or "O Happy Day!" and often added choruses of their own. "On Jordan's Stormy Banks I Stand" is best known to most of us for its revival chorus, "I'm Bound for the Promised Land." Early revival songbooks were sold far and wide; and so long as the churches themselves remained simple, there seems to have been no popular objection.

The organ aroused widespread resentment, however. It was a symbol of citification, of the institutionalizing of religion. A New Light sect which had broken off during the time of The Great Revival, variously called the Christian Church or Disciples of Christ or Campbellites after one of its founders, had the noble purpose of being a simple New Testament Church without creeds, designed to end all sectarian differences. But even as the Disciples became a large denomination, and a church like other churches, a most serious split arose within them, largely

over the use of the organ. The purists could find no
Scripture for it. Sentiment grew very heated, windows
were broken, organs stolen. Will Carleton has captured
the Anti-Organ sentiment in one of his Farm Ballads:

> *I've been a Sister good and true,*
> *For five and thirty year;*
> *I've done what seemed my part to do,*
> *And prayed my duty clear.*
> *But Death will stop my voice, I know,*
> *For he is on my track;*
> *And some day I to church will go,*
> *And nevermore come back.*
> *And when the folks get up to sing*
> *Whene'er that time shall be —*
> *I do not want no patent thing,*
> *A-squealin' over me.*

Now the organ had long been established in the New
World. The first Protestant organ belonged to a group of
German pietists in the Wissahickon Valley, near Philadelphia; when one of their number was ordained as minister of the Lutheran Church of Gloria Dei in 1703, they
brought their organ with them. The Episcopal Church,
the Dutch Reformed, and many others had used organs
without objection. In a very large part the story of the
old-time religion is the attempt of one group after another
to freeze things just where they are — whether an objection to church organs or a specific attempt to recover the
presence of the Holy Ghost. The fear of change is understandable; so is the jealousy of country people at seeing
city ways take over. But I think we do our subject an injustice if we dismiss it with these observations. There is

a tradition behind all such protests, authentic and ancient, a desire to keep religion simple and free, a personal relationship between each person and the Lord. The revivals themselves, although they did more than any other one movement to build up church membership, were very much a protest against "coldness" and "formality" within the churches.

One of the greatest of pre-Civil War evangelists was brought up in the same up-State New York district where both Millerism and Mormonism had first come to light. Charles G. Finney was not himself converted in a revival, however. He set out to be a lawyer, and checked the Bible, as a source of the common law, against Blackstone until he developed a personal knowledge of Scripture and a firm logic. He was converted alone one day in the woods; convincing himself of the fullness of the atonement, he entered the forest vowing to himself, "I will accept today or die in the attempt!" There he felt after long striving that his sin was infinite. "It broke me down before the Lord," he said. He returned to his law office to pray, and had a personal vision of Christ. "It did not occur to me then, nor did it for sometime afterwards, that it was wholly a mental state. On the contrary, it seemed to me that I saw Him as I would see any other man. He said nothing, but looked at me in such a manner as to break me right down at his feet. . . ."

Finney set out at once to preach and was ordained in 1824. He did not spare the Hell; yet he marked a progression from the frontier. He was the inventor of the "immediate decision," inviting sinners to stand in their seats as a token of surrender, and then come down the aisle to the forward bench, a more orderly method than the wholesale slaughters at Cane Ridge. And over the years he grew in stature, placing less emphasis on the fear of Hell and more upon the love of God; historians say that wherever Finney went, he left behind scores of earnest young men "emancipated from sin and Calvinism and overflowing with benevolence for unsaved mankind." From 1830 to 1860, when he was at the height of his power, hundreds of American philanthropic movements were started, with admiring laymen like John Wanamaker on their boards of directors. Societies were founded to promote foreign missions, temperance, education, and Sunday-Schools, to colonize the Negroes in Africa, to fight tobacco, prostitution, or bad language, to improve the diet, the prisons, and the insane asylums, to advance women's rights and world peace, and to save the sailors in the ports and along the canals. There was for most of the church people during the nineteenth century no violent opposition between "practical Christianity" and the old-time religion. Finney had both. Once, seeing a proud New York woman at a meeting eye him with cool insolence night after night, he prepared a sermon on the Devil as a destroying archer, drew a figurative bow, and let fly an arrow which pierced her heart so that she rolled senseless in the aisle. In his later years he took the presidency of Oberlin College, in Ohio, on the condition that none be barred because of race or color.

Finney converted one man who carried reforms farther than the evangelist could have anticipated; John Humphrey Noyes, in 1834, announced himself as "morally perfect," and after various experiments in freedom from sin, established the community of Oneida Perfectionists. Of all the by-products of the revivals, it was one of the most interesting: a high-minded and serious effort to achieve love without lust, do away with sexual jealousy, and carry out a communal plan of eugenics or selective breeding. The Oneida Perfectionists lived as one large family, guided by each other's mutual criticism, and in business matters they were exceptionally able. After a storm of gossip and threatened legal action broke up the community in 1881, their descendants organized a stock company which still manufactures a well-known silver plate, a popular gift for the American bride.

The old-time religion has always had its offshoots on the left as well as the right; and early in the nineteenth century many of the New England Congregationalists, who had generally remained true to Calvinism, began to leap directly from the blazing flames of Jonathan Edwards into the cool Unitarian Heaven. The effect was intoxicating. According to Van Wyck Brooks, it was a sudden change from preoccupation with the affairs of the next world to an interest in the affairs of this, which inspired the flowering of New England culture, and with it a passion for reform. Sometimes the followers of the "Boston religion" departed church life altogether; Ralph Waldo Emerson is the most famous example of a Protestant saint and prophet who walked in the woods on Sunday morning. An interaction between the "conservatives" and the "liberals" has gone on ever since and is one of the most interesting aspects of our subject, although so vast and subtle in its effects that it cannot be traced or argued.

The New England liberals soon began to call loudly for the freeing of the slaves.

Anti-slavery feeling in the orthodox churches was old and

spontaneous. New York Presbyterians in 1783 called for abolition; and all Methodists, upon the organization of their church in 1784, were at first required to free their slaves. (It is reported that, perhaps for this reason, an exasperated North Carolina planter put a mustard plaster to his wife to cure her of Methodism.) Five years later, the Baptists of Virginia urged laws to "extirpate this horrid evil from the land." Francis Asbury called on General Washington to ask his signature to an anti-slavery petition; Washington refused to sign, but told Asbury that he shared his sentiments, and would support anti-slavery legislation if it came up in the Assembly.

The failure of the early movement for emancipation was one of the unfortunate near-misses in American history; for soon the cotton gin gave slavery a new economic lease on life; and Southern ministers, whose fathers and grandfathers had favored emancipation, backwatered rapidly and buttressed slavery with Bible texts. They also declared themselves true defenders of the faith, against Yankee "infidel abolitionists" like Emerson and Whittier. The deep Fundamentalism of the South, say some historians, dates essentially from this early controversy with Northern Christians. In Kansas, the Beecher Bible and Rifle Church is still standing, built in 1856 by followers of the great Congregationalist preacher, who gave each man a Bible and a rifle "to defend his faith and his ideas of freedom." Before the shooting started, the religious quarrel had divided the Methodists, Baptists, and Presbyterians into North and South; the split between the churches, dividing the country at the heart's core, made the Civil War almost inevitable. Both read the same Bible and pray to the same God, Lincoln would say sadly; but they didn't — not exactly. On either side religion took color from its surroundings; and the Northern abolitionists, whether they knew it or not, were influenced by their circumstances, too.

For outside the South, the United States had become a business and industrial civilization, a development for which religion is entitled to much of the credit or blame. Puritanism, not the formal Puritanism of New England alone but the ancient, dissenting spirit of the Baptists, Methodists, and Presbyterians, had always encouraged the virtues of thrift, industry, and plain living; and as the country prospered, many yielded to a natural temptation and believed that God rewarded His followers with earthly riches and asked them only to use them for His glory. "God gave me my money," said John D. Rockefeller, late in life. In the rural South, where the preachers had got themselves all tangled up with economics but didn't seem to know it, the people made jokes about the pious Yankees. ("John!" called the storekeeper to his son on Sunday morning. "Have you watered the milk? Have you sanded the sugar? Then come to prayers.")

The churches grew steadily with the cities. Following the railroads, church boards sometimes wangled free sites for churches or large grants of land.

Then in 1857 there was a nation-wide business panic, and with it the first revival in American history which sprang up outside the churches, and was not induced by the fear of Hell.

Prayer meetings broke out in Wall Street among the penitent and bankrupt stockbrokers. The first, apparently, was conducted by a solitary businessman named Jeremiah Lanphier, who knelt alone, day after day, although he had asked others to join him, in an upper room of the Old North Dutch Church in Fulton Street. "O Lord, what wilt Thou have me do?" prayed Mr. Lanphier. Gradually others came to join him, and the street meetings began. Business houses turned out *en masse* to sing hymns. Stevedores knelt to pray on the docks, and the sailors knelt on the decks of two hundred ships. Times were very bad; and the movement swept the country, with the aid of the telegraph companies; at certain hours of the day they carried free of charge messages from one sinner to another. Newspapers published extras as the "thousand-mile prayer meeting" struck one city after another. By 1860, almost a quarter of the American people were church members.

The 1857 Revival was as genuine as such an outbreak could be. The nation feared that it had displeased the Lord. Henry Ward Beecher, who disliked "got-up" revivals, would not attend special meetings at his church until the crowd had gathered voluntarily, night after night. But when it reached Boston, it took a "sponsored" turn. Church people there had planned to hold a city-wide revival in the previous year, in 1856, but during boom times found no one interested; now in 1857, they climbed eagerly on the bandwagon; and some of the orthodox brethren vented their spleen on the Unitarians for whom the city was famous. One zealous orator prayed that God would put a hook into the jaws of Theodore Parker, the leading liberal minister of the day.

This prayer was not answered, for the next year Parker preached a famous sermon against revivals: "I do not hear any prayer for temperance, any prayer for education, any prayer for the emancipation of slaves, for the elevation of women, for honesty, for industry, for brotherly love; any prayers against envy, suspicion, bigotry, superstition, spiritual pride, malice, and all uncharitableness. . . . The churches need a revival. No institution in America is more corrupt than her churches. No thirty thousand men and women are so bigoted and narrow as the thirty thousand ministers. . . ."

The 1857 Revival left one hymn of universal popularity. The Reverend Dudley A. Tyng, a young Episcopal minister ousted by his Philadelphia vestry for taking a stand against slavery, had opened an interdenominational meeting-hall to the revival crowds. One day, going from his study to the barn floor, he stopped to pat his mule, which was shelling corn in a treadmill; the sleeve of his gown caught in the cogs and crushed his arm. Six days later, just before dying in the hospital, Mr. Tyng sent a message to his fellow evangelists at the hall: "Tell them, Let us all stand up for Jesus!" A fellow minister wrote the last four words into a hymn which was promptly used by all the leading churches, and was a favorite with the troops in the Civil War. There were constant revivals during the war among the armies, especially in the South.

For some years after the war, there was a gradual decline in the proportion of the American public on the church rolls. It was not until 1890 that they again claimed twenty-three percent of the total population, as in 1860.

All sorts of causes were blamed by the godly. Some spoke unkindly of the European immigrants, who seemed to have no ideas of Sabbath observance; among the Lutherans, even the pastors drank beer. But the wave was only temporarily subsiding.

In part, the churches began to answer the criticism of

Theodore Parker. They turned mightily to good works. At Chautauqua, New York, during the eighteen-seventies, a Methodist preacher named John H. Vincent turned the old camp-meeting ground into a sort of extension university, beginning with Bible courses and expanding into literary and scientific subjects, including an interesting novelty, Domestic Science. Before the century ended, little Chautauquas had sprung up on camp-meeting grounds throughout the country. "Day is Dying in the West" and other famous hymns were written especially for Chautauqua. It was the symbol of a direction which the old-time religion had taken; hopeful, overflowing with sweetness and light, the sign of a generation which intended to bring about the Kingdom of Heaven on this earth. It was still inconceivable to the average citizen that religion and education were, or could be, in conflict.

In the cities, settlement houses and rescue missions absorbed some of the evangelistic energy, and gradually Sunday-Schools were beginning to take over from the revival meetings the job of making new members. Horace Bushnell, a Congregationalist divine, in 1857 had written *Christian Nurture,* advancing the revolutionary thought that it was possible for a child to grow gradually into being a Christian without any shattering emotional experience. The idea spread rapidly in a generation which had been weaned on Hell; and the churches set out to create a "Christian environment" which would make a "Christian world."

To be fair-minded, to see some of the results accomplished, it is necessary to avoid either partisanship or cynicism. It is true that from the viewpoint of many artists and writers during the latter part of the nineteenth century and the first part of the twentieth, Puritanism and hypocrisy spread over the national life like a coating of grease. Wall Street buccaneers were pillars of the church, Anthony Comstock and his friends set out to make America be good by force.

Herbert Asbury, in *Up From Methodism*, has described in bitter and vivid language a priestridden small town in the Bible Belt early in this century. The "anti-institutional" emphasis of the old-time religion had become invisible to the naked eye; some enthusiastic Presbyterians and Methodists even campaigned, unsuccessfully, for a constitutional amendment to declare Jesus Christ officially the Ruler of Nations. A Mr. George F. Baer, president of the Reading Railroad, summed up all that was wrong with the idea of "making the world Christian" in 1902. During a coal strike he declared that "The rights and interests of the laboring man will be protected and cared for not by labor agitators but by the Christian men to whom God in His infinite wisdom has given the control of the property interests of this country."

The first effort to graft temperance upon the old-time religion was made by Francis Asbury, who in 1780 persuaded a Baltimore Methodist Conference to pass a resolution against distilling. The movement for National Prohibition did not capture the churches, however, until 1913 — according to the testimony of the late Wayne B. Wheeler of the Anti-Saloon League. Seven years after the major Protestant churches were safely within the Prohibition camp, the law was passed. It could never have been enacted without church support; but it had been a long, hard struggle.

Early Baptist preachers were sometimes paid in barrels of whiskey; and many a deacon, even after the parson was forced to take a dry stand, took a dram in the kitchen now and then and wished the preacher could join him. Even John Wesley, while against whiskey, expressly advised his Methodist circuit riders after preaching to take "a little lemonade, mild ale, or candied orange peel."

It appears to be true that liquor attacked the preachers first, and they gradually retaliated. For a favorite sport of the frontier drunk was to break up meeting. The Southern mountains today show the hard-and-fast line much as it was drawn in the early days: a sociable drink or two before dinner, a bottle of beer at bedtime, is not the rule in that section; it is all or nothing, and religion and whiskey are mutually exclusive. The fact is that we are an intemperate people, immoderately drunk or dry.

The first Temperance Society was organized at Saratoga, New York, in 1808; by 1851, Maine had gone dry. But other States had an unhappy experience with Prohibition; the movement flickered and flared. It was the women who finally put it across. In 1874, the Woman's Christian Temperance Union was organized, operating in a few sensational instances with hatchets, more often with prayer meetings and *Ten Nights in a Bar-Room*, and most effectively and steadily through quiet work behind the scenes. The deacon's wife, if she could not dry up the deacon, could put pressure through him upon the minister. The women, through the W.C.T.U., began to run the churches and then the United States; for the W.C.T.U. early sponsored the women's rights movement and gave it a tremendous impetus. More important perhaps for the average man in his relationship with the churches was the virtual writing-in of total abstinence as an article of the Christian faith. It was a serious step to take, and it led to grave consequences.

Yet — except to those who for one reason or another have a grudge against the old-time religion — Prohibition and vice-crusading were not its chief American contributions to the concept of a Christian world. Somehow, from the wilderness and the generations of Hell-fire preaching, issued the basic belief that the world was *meant* to be kindly, just, and free, to live by the teachings of Jesus; over the decades from the most severe and rigorous orthodoxy the thought of an earthly Kingdom of Heaven keeps breaking out. One nineteenth-century landmark was a book by Charles M. Sheldon, called *In His Steps*, which is said to have reached a circulation of twenty-three million. "Practical Christianity" within and without the churches launched a thousand movements, from farm co-operatives to world peace. Quickly the religious label washed off most of them, as it disappeared from those started in the Finney revival before the Civil War, and from the ancient schools, colleges, and hospitals the American churches had first founded. Visiting Northern brethren today are surprised at small trade-union chapters in the South which still close their sessions with "a word of prayer." The old-time religion in part has been invisible, a leaven in the lump. It does not try to keep a cross stamped upon its ideas and institutions, but turns them loose.

> *For not with swords' loud clashing*
> *Or stirring roll of drums,*
> *But deeds of love and mercy*
> *The Heavenly Kingdom comes.*

The changed emphasis of the churches during the nineteenth century shows clearly in the hymns, always a better clue than the remarks of preachers to what the people in the pews are really thinking. Along with the strictly soul-saving hymns, the newer hymns of personal devotion and social service found a place; Americans as a whole may prefer to be vague about theology, but they made it pretty clear, by the dawn of the twentieth century, that they intended their religion to be concerned with this world as well as the next. And the concern was world-wide. Foreign missions had become an enormous enter-prise.

The missionary business, for isolated village people, was fun and excitement; the returning adventurer brought with him a breath of far places — and if he was the right sort of missionary, a sense of kinship with distant peoples whose skins might be yellow or black. The missionary impulse entered naturally — so naturally that practically all the church people supported it as a matter of course — into the world government proposed by Wilson, the Pres-byterian minister's son.

And none of this was in conflict with the revivals. In all the years between the end of the Civil War and the night when President McKinley wrestled with his Method-ist conscience and decided that it was America's duty to Christianize the Filipinos, the greatest evangelist in our history was at work. How much he contributed to the stream of philanthropy, to the shifting, broadening, mis-sionary impulse, there is no way to tell. But by 1890, the churches once more enrolled twenty-three per cent of the total population, as they had in 1860. And from 1890 to 1910, with help from Dwight L. Moody, Chautauqua, Sunday-Schools, Y.M.C.A., and all the other forces of righteousness, the proportion leaped to forty-three per cent. This was the age of Moody and Sankey.

Dwight L. Moody was not himself converted in a revival, nor — according to the record — by any such fearful and violent struggles as those we have witnessed. Brought up in New England as a Unitarian, he took to attending the Mount Vernon Congregational Sunday-School in Boston, where he worked as a shoe clerk. His Sunday-School teacher, Edward Kimball, dropped in to see him at the store one day and asked him in a few words to give his allegiance to Jesus Christ. Moody was wrapping up a pair of shoes. He paused briefly, the string tight in his fingers, said, "I will," and went on wrapping.

The quiet beginning may be significant; for Moody — although he firmly believed in Hell and was sure that he was saving sinners from it — did not *preach* Hell. He preached the love of God; and he was the most popular and successful evangelist the United States has ever known. In Chicago, during the 1857 Revival, he was greatly stirred, and began his wholesale work of salvation by starting Sunday-Schools for hardened characters in the Chicago slums.

During the Civil War, Moody went with the stretcher-bearers under fire. With few natural gifts and little training, he found that he could preach; and beginning with services in a Chicago Y.M.C.A. in 1867 and continuing to the Kansas City Convention Hall at the end of the century, he preached across this country and Great Britain, to an estimated one hundred million people. He is generally credited with a million conversions.

For his meeting at Barnum's Hippodrome in New York in 1876 the choir alone numbered twelve hundred, and five hundred ushers were needed to marshal a million and a half worshipers who stood in line, night after night. At

Chicago, he preached in the big tent during the 1893 World's Fair. Royalties on the hymnbooks of Moody and Sankey, his musical partner, amounted to a million and a quarter dollars.

With Moody and Sankey, the revival had reached the stage of big business; yet such was not Moody's intention or his desire. He did not want to institutionalize religion; his whole life was a protest against bigness, coldness, high-pressure organization in the name of Christ. A modest man, by all accounts, he genuinely hated the build-up and the committees, acknowledged there were parts of the Bible he did not understand, and died worth exactly five hundred dollars. At all hours of the day or night he asked people whom he encountered, on the street or in hotel lobbies or anywhere, his unfailing question, "Are you a Christian?" If the answer was uncertain, Moody hung on until he had made a convert.

In the twentieth century, however, the great revival, which had started as an outburst of protest against "established" religion, was ending as an established mechanism. After Moody, the evangelists fell off in a series of steadily descending peaks, each relying more and more upon organized preparation, printed cards, street-car ads, "flying squadrons," and of course slogans. "Get Right With God" was popularized by Torrey and Alexander. The evangelists, many of them, began to lean heavily on the support of business and industrial interests. It became common knowledge that Southern mill-owners sometimes subsidized revivals to head off union organizations; and the radicals exploited every link between religion and the bosses, in order to drive a deep wedge between working people and the churches.

The late Doctor Billy Sunday, an ex-ballplayer, flung strong language at his foes and shadow-boxed the Devil in the pulpit. He drew enormous crowds. At one of his New York meetings, seven thousand workers were trained to herd converts down the sawdust trail to pump Billy by the hand. His earnings were said to be in excess of one hundred thousand dollars yearly. Yet many of the churches stayed aloof. The Federal Council of Churches had been organized in 1908; its studies and research work were becoming influential; and cold-blooded experts were beginning to check on the after-effects of revivals, the number of penitents who actually joined the churches, even the cost per convert in dollars and cents compared with results obtained from other methods.

And there was a shift in feeling in the man in the street. Something like the popular skepticism of the eighteenth century was returning by the days of the First World War.

Billy Sunday, it is said, came from his great Chicago tabernacle one day and asked a newsboy the way to the postoffice. The evangelist thanked him, asked for the instructions a second time, and started off. Then he turned back with a warm smile.

"Come to my meeting tonight and I'll show you the way to Heaven."

"How can you show me the way to Heaven?" asked the newsboy, "when you don't even know the way to the postoffice?"

4. SURVIVAL OF THE FITTEST

Mr. Darwin and Mr. Darrow do a little
pruning, but the tree survives

CHARLES DARWIN had published the *Origin of Species by Natural Selection* in 1859; the American people as a whole, occupied first with a Civil War, then with several decades of enormous westward expansion and rising industrial prosperity, did not seem to pay very much attention to it. The churches had their period of most rapid growth from 1890 to 1910. Some denominations conducted heresy trials, and under the surface, in theological schools and universities, thinking about the Bible began to change. But for the most part, the transition seemed to be peaceful. If Dwight L. Moody shocked some of his friends by associating with Henry Drummond, a leading Christian evolutionist of England, the public showed all the confusing, contrary characteristics Americans have always demonstrated. The same people sometimes applauded Colonel Bob Ingersoll, the battling atheist, laughed at Mark Twain's digs at the ultra-pious, and went on following nights to hear Mr. Moody or Phillips Brooks, the great evangelist of the Episcopal Church.

Like Bishop Brooks, perhaps most of the church people were somewhere in the wide middle of the road, not too insistent upon dogma, willing to make concessions here and there. An early tenet of the old-time religion, never wholly forgotten, held that church membership was not essential to salvation; in every generation were people outside the churches — Abraham Lincoln, for example — whom religion sooner or later claimed with pride. Freedom of thought spread from the schools and colleges which the churches had themselves established. The people both supported their churches and reserved the right to make jokes about them.

As revivals became an old story, legends about them multiplied. They survived longest in the South, where still in the fall of the year, when the farmers have money in the bank, the wandering evangelist pitches his tent on the edge of town. It was in Alabama not many years ago that one aged sister held out until the last. When not even the "workers" could move her to the mourners' bench, the preacher himself came quietly up the aisle.

"What's the matter, sister? Don't you love everybody?"

"Everybody but the damn Yankees!" she exploded through clenched teeth.

The preacher had come from across the line in Mississippi.

"Bless the Lord!" he cried. "She's through!"

The churches seemed to thrive on controversy. The editor of a Texas Baptist paper summed it up inelegantly but with crushing precision: "You know how it is when you hear a horrible squawking from the alley at night and expect to find it littered with dead cats in the morning? But what happens instead is more cats."

The ten years just before the First World War, it has often been remarked, were among the happiest the United States has ever known. The world was at peace, science and education were making progress on every front, something like the Kingdom of Heaven seemed at hand.

What happened to our subject in the nineteen-twenties? Was the impact of the war so unsettling? Had religion, in National Prohibition, disastrously overreached itself? Was the theory of evolution suddenly beginning to bite? Whatever the reasons, American church membership began a sudden decline. The proportion the public enrolled dropped from forty-three per cent in 1910 to forty per cent in 1930; and in that year many of the large denominations showed an actual loss. The simplest explanation was in a popular phrase, "the acids of modernity." The jokes ceased to be good-natured. The non-church-going male who, in 1920, took off his hat when he passed a church, by 1930 kept his hat on, and more than likely considered the local parson as a figure of fun.

It was about this time that the general public became conscious of a distinctly "old-time" religion. For the average American during the eighteenth and nineteenth centuries there had been no such adjective. There was just religion, take it or leave it. There had always been radical offshoots and conservative reactions, but during the nineteen-twenties, for the first time, the doings of those who wanted to stop the clock became national news. Americans gradually became aware that besides the average church on the corner, where religion adapted itself gradually and quietly to its circumstances and the preacher belonged to Rotary or Kiwanis, there was something which called itself "the old-time religion," denouncing "Modernism" and claiming to be the genuine article.

Here is where I came in. Remembering the uproar of the nineteen-twenties, a quarter of a century later I visited some of the scenes of the conflicts which had made headlines in my boyhood.

The only passenger for Zion, I dismounted from a Chicago and Northwestern commuting train at a large, empty brick station, set in the midst of empty fields. There was no human habitation in sight, only the prairie. This is the place where, during the nineteen-twenties, it was officially decided that the earth was flat. Certainly it looked flat, now. I followed the road, on foot. After a quarter of a mile, still without reaching civilization, it made a great asphalt circle around a sweet-smelling hayfield. The scene was lonely, Druidic, almost terrifying. In the exact center of the circle were concrete foundations, and these, I learned later, marked the site of Zion Tabernacle, which the Devil had burned in 1937, annoyed by preparations for a Passion Day.

I knew a little of Zion's history. In the late nineteenth century, Doctor John Alexander Dowie, a native of Scotland and a Congregational minister, became convinced that he had the gift of Divine healing, and assumed the title of Elijah III. In this capacity he created an immense sensation in Chicago and was hailed by the late Judge Elbert Gary, among others. But after taking off for New York in six special trains, Dowie flopped in Madison Square Garden; and even in Chicago he was opposed by the established churches and the medical profession, and was arrested more than one hundred times for his healing labors. Organizing his followers into the Christian Apostolic Church, he announced on the last night of the nineteenth century his plan for a new city of Zion. Here liquor, tobacco, playing-cards, oysters, pork, and clams would be prohibited, and no trains would stop on Sunday. Even the railroad tracks, as I now observed, had been kept at a safe distance.

Dowie's successor, Wilbur Glenn Voliva, industrialized

Zion with a number of communistic enterprises, all owned by the church. Mr. Voliva also announced his revelation that the earth was flat, a view in which he persisted even after a trip around the world. He explained that he just traveled around the edge.

I reached the inhabited portion of Zion at last. A three-story frame hotel bore the legend "Zion Old People's Home" and the encouraging sign "Dining-Room." But a Middle-Western couple with Grant Wood faces, rocking on the porch, said it was only open Sundays. In the next block Zion became godless, with neon lights and chain stores. The first drugstore, out of respect for the old tradition, did not sell cigarettes, but recommended the barbecue stand across the street.

Over the din of a juke-box arose the sound of a street meeting, and gulping my barbecue I hastened back to the line of duty.

Fifteen or twenty citizens listened without excitement to a Gospel quartet and a master of ceremonies, who introduced each speaker. A pleasant woman waiting for the bus with an armload of packages recommended the next attraction. "He's good. He started to commit suicide leaning against the bank on Saturday night, when a still small voice told him to go see the preacher." As a young man recounted this experience, she explained that the meeting was conducted by one of the offshoots of the Christian Apostolic Church.

"I go along with the church people all right, but I use my own judgment about what they tell you. You know. Like Mr. Voliva, who said you'd go to Hell if you ate pork. We've already got a bowling alley, and they just voted to have a movie. It's a nice place to live." She smiled and took her bus.

Across from the Old People's Home, a building was still marked "Zion Industries." But the experiment with Christian socialism hadn't worked. The town had gone bankrupt in 1906, was redeemed in 1910, and went into receivership again in 1933. In 1939, after Voliva lost control, titles to real estate were transferred to individuals. Doctor Dowie's communistic lace factory is now used by Marshall Field to make curtains. Private capitalism also manufactures fig bars and office furniture.

The church offices in the Industries building were closed, but the caretaker, a cordial, chatty old man, opened the Overseer's Office and Council Room. The big round mahogany table had come from Europe — "Not a scratch on it!" — and he lifted the tablecloth in proof. On the wall a "living photograph" of Dowie was formed by a mass of the faithful who, arrayed in black or white robes, had climbed a huge scaffolding to form his likeness. The very beard of the prophet was there — ten feet long.

I asked about Voliva. "There weren't so many that went along with the flat-earth proposition. Some pretended to, but didn't. But my, he had the folks at the Old Folks' Home all stirred up about the Second Coming! Had 'em all dressed up, waiting up all night in the lobby. A lot of 'em went crazy," he added reflectively.

High-school kids were playing ball in the dusk across from the school building. In the school auditorium, an artist with a deeply lined, spiritual face superintended the dismantling of Palestinian scenery. He was H. J. Taylor, author and director of the Zion Passion Play, held each Sunday in April, May, and June. He had made a trip to Palestine to gather impressions for his settings. They had just now run through a special showing for the movie camera. "To check on production?" I asked. "No," he said; "so that more people can see it."

Zion is still perhaps the tract center of the United States. On the street, already laden with *The Theocrat* and *Leaves of Healing,* I was soon handed a Jehovah's Witness message, and the first stranger of whom I asked the way to the bus concluded his directions with a leaflet of hymns.

It was a surprise to see one citizen who was not saving souls. He lurched from the barbecue stand, not drunk exactly, yet his wild gray locks, his battered felt hat pushed back on his head, his rolling gait and brazen eye proclaimed the Town Sinner. We fell into step at once and over ice-cream cones at a milk bar conversed as if we had known each other always.

"I wouldn't join Voliva's church!" he shouted cheerfully. "He offered me a job in the lumber mill, at sixty cents an hour — when the regular pay was forty cents — if I'd join the church and let him check off the tithe from my wages. I told him, 'Pay me my full wages and I'll give what I feel like to the church.' It was no sale.

"Me and another fellow was the ones that busted up the no-smoking rule," he continued. "Voliva had 'em all scared to death. He arrested two men just for drivin' through town smokin' a cigarette. I held a Dowie lease on my house, that said no tobacco could be bought or sold on the premises until the Millennium; but it didn't say nothin' about *using* tobacco! Took it to law and won." He inhaled his cigarette with relish.

"I guess he's doubled up in his grave," the Sinner said with satisfaction. "You can even get liquor now at each end of town — but who cares about liquor?" He winked, and we parted.

It was a long, lonely wait at the depot in the quiet fields. At last an elderly woman, the wife of a railroad man, came to share my vigil. She had come out from Chicago to attend a Youth for Christ Rally.

"The speaker was Mr. Hendrix — he's a jeweler," she said with some pride. "But I don't like Zion. What's the sense in this big depot way off from every place? My! I'm glad to hear that train whistle! It don't seem safe down here in the dark — so many colored people around, you never know. Of course, some of them are fine people and wonderful Christians, but I met a lady from Kentucky and she told me . . . "

The train drew in.

"And I don't care much for that Passion Play either. They had a big show like that in a Chicago tabernacle — had a cow in it! Imagine, a cow in church!"

The train moved on toward Chicago. "Just give me the plain old Gospel," the lady said, "without any worldly trimmings."

Other communities got into the courts. The House of David, famous for its long-bearded baseball team, had been established at Benton Harbor, Michigan, by the late "King Benjamin" Purnell in 1903. Twenty years later, members who had turned over all their property to "King Benjamin" and worked without pay brought suit against him; a Federal District Court found that the King had deprived his followers of civil rights, instructed them how to vote, "so taught his creed and used the Bible as to cause female members of said association to have improper relations with him," and married off his victims in wholesale lots to forestall investigation. The Court also noted that "all contact with and knowledge of the outside world was systematically discouraged and no independent thinking was allowed."

Of course, there have always been eccentrics, but a much larger movement, found in all the churches, more or less, was called Fundamentalism. A World's Christian Fundamentals Association was organized in 1919, under the leadership of W. B. Riley and A. C. Dixon, to defend the Bible as they understood it against the assaults of the infidel. Throughout the nineteen-twenties in all the large churches a battle raged for control of the church machinery. Generally, the Fundamentalists lost; for many years theological seminaries had already been teaching the "historical approach" to the Bible, and the church people at large had peacefully accepted the thought that God created the world through some sort of evolutionary process. The Fundamentalists turned to the law. By 1925, movements were under way in fifteen States to forbid the teaching of evolution in the public schools. In Congress, a bill had been introduced to stop the Smithsonian Institution, in its studies of the origins of man. The more enthusiastic Fundamentalist reformers also talked of outlawing tobacco by law, now that alcoholic beverages were taboo.

Early in these travels I bought a ticket for East Tennessee, then as now the capital of the Bible Belt, and the scene of one of the greatest dramas in the history of the old-time religion.

"Last call for soft-drinks!" called the train-butcher. "Last chance to buy rattlesnakes and gold-plated chewing-gum!"

Number 41 of the Southern Railway shook to a stop at a station near Knoxville. In the next seat, a passenger with steel-rimmed glasses and a tanned, wizened face held out his newspaper cordially. I asked if he remembered the Scopes trial of 1925.

His eyes searched my face. "Sure. I saw Bryan's funeral train. Bryan was a good man, but he didn't understand the Bible. Do you believe in eternal torment?"

I said that I didn't care much for the idea.

"I don't neither." He extended his hand. "Let's go out where we can spit."

In the smoker, my friend began to quote whole chapters of Scripture at such speed, interrupted by an occasional discharge of juice, that I could hardly follow his argument. He was not a Jehovah's Witness, nor a member of any other sect.

"I started out as a Catholic, but don't seem to me any church has got the Bible right. Now take these tongue-talkers. The Bible don't say to get up in front of people and shout — it says to go in your closet and pray!"

He resumed his rapid-fire quotations, then apologized. "When I get to talkin' at the barber shop the fellows close down on me. Don't often get the chance. Now, a just God ain't a-goin' to torture his own creatures for eternity. Like the little girl said in Sunday-School, when they asked her if she wasn't scared to die without bein' saved. No, she told 'em, she'd just hide from God behind Jesus!" His view limited the period of torment to one thousand years.

The train whistled to a long bright row of lights upon a dam of the Tennessee Valley Authority. There had been many changes since John Thomas Scopes went on trial in July, 1925, for teaching the theory of evolution to high-school students at Dayton, Tennessee.

In Dayton, I registered at the Acqua Hotel, newspaper headquarters during the trial. Nowadays a visitor to the Acqua who asks, in the wrong tone of voice, "Is this Monkey Town?" will be answered, "No, but one still comes along now and then." After an enormous dinner, during a life-saving afternoon walk, I found Dayton a pleasant county-seat town like any other.

A sign at the courthouse square pointed to "Camp-Ground"; the bystander of whom I asked its meaning looked at me in alarm. Was I a preacher?

"Reason I asked," he said politely, "is that the last man who asked about that sign needed help in movin' a piano for a concert. Took me all mornin', me and two other fellows. That's just a little camp-ground for visitin' Church of God preachers." He paused, and added rather sadly, "Used to follow the holiness myself, but I kind of lost out on it during the war. Don't know what I'd do now, if a blessin' should come my way."

The country road led past a mill village, with a new brick Church of God, into the foothills. In a shaded hamlet I bought a bottle of pop at a country store, where the Chattanooga newspaper showed a headline of impending conflict.

"Looks close," said the storekeeper, an impassive mountain man with a round, bland face. "Still, this old world's meant to get worse, and I guess all we can do is to take her as she comes."

I asked if he remembered the Scopes trial. Instead of answering directly, he began to state the case for the local life. He talked slowly and without pause, as if he had been waiting years for this opportunity.

"I've lived here all my life; this was my father's store; I was born here, and only moved when I got married, and that was to a house next door. And before I was married,

I used to look out the window and say, 'We ought to plant some fruit trees on that lot.' I've never been anywhere. But I know every bluff, and creek, and spring for miles and miles around. I take my car where it sinks in to the hub caps, and I eat good ham when ham is hard to get and fryin' chickens all the time.

"I know everything that grows and is free. I know when the apples and peaches are out, I know where the fish are jumpin' and the squirrels are barkin' and where to find ginseng and hickory nuts. I know where the bee-trees are.

"Ever' two hours I take a sounding on the creek water and send it to the T.V.A. I've done it since 1934. It don't amount to much, but I like to do it. The creek rises with the season, and first I wear overshoes, then galoshes, then hip boots, and then I have to take my car up to where I can cross. And ever' mornin', rain or shine, I send the weather report to the United States at Knoxville.

"Sure, I remember the trial. We had our Sunday-School teacher on the jury, a little man with a handlebar mustache. He looked funny and all the papers wrote him up. Dayton was known to the ends of the earth. People in foreign countries would say, 'Chattanooga? Knoxville? How far is that from Dayton?' We had a great millin' around and stirrin', thousands upon thousands of people.

"I remember when them infidels got up to speak. I was so hot under the collar I could hardly contain myself. Lucky nothing bad happened and nobody got hurt. Then a little ole preacher with a clawhammer coat jumped up on top of a car and began to tear them infidels to pieces. You ought to have heard him. He tore them infidels to shreds."

He fell silent, as if afraid he had said too much. "The

trial really began," he remarked, "in Robinson's drugstore on the main street of Dayton.

In the drugstore, Bibles were on sale near the soda fountain, adjacent to the comic books, playing-cards, and dice. "Doc" Robinson came out from the prescription counter, short, white-haired, his blue eyes alert and amused behind his rimless spectacles. Writers are always wandering into Dayton after material, and "Doc" is ready for them. He gave me a match folder with a picture of the soda-fountain table at which the trial had been plotted, and we sat down at the historic table itself, where he ordered a pair of cokes.

"We were just sitting here talking, four or five of us, just like you and me today. The anti-evolution law had just recently been passed, and somebody said, 'Why not make a test of it right here in Dayton?' There was two young lawyers, Wallace Haggard and Sue K. Hicks, Johnny Scopes, the science teacher, and a mining engineer, George Rappelyea."

The discussion, over cokes after a tennis game, had been entirely friendly, partly inspired by the dawning thought of putting Dayton on the map. The boys took from a shelf of the store Hunter's *Civic Biology*, which Scopes had continued to teach, under instructions from the school board, even after the enactment of the anti-evolution law. Looking over its pages, they decided that Scopes was clearly a lawbreaker. By common consent the engineer, Rappelyea, now swore out a warrant against Scopes. The warrant was served on the spot by the local constable.

"Of course," said "Doc," "we didn't know just what it would develop into."

Rappelyea was a native New Yorker; John R. Neal, of Knoxville, a leading landowner near Dayton, a lawyer, and a teacher at the University of Tennessee, was also active in arranging for the test case. But for the most part, the trial was brought about by local men and church-workers. Teacher Scopes, a popular boy in the town, attended a Methodist Sunday-School class; and "Doc" Robinson, Cumberland Presbyterian, consulted the leading ministers of Dayton before proceeding further with the charge against Scopes.

Robinson found the preachers reluctant to be dragged into the white-hot center of the Fundamentalist-Modernist controversy already raging. They urged him to drop the whole idea, but agreed to abide by the decision of the dean of the local clergy, "Parson Charlie" Jones, a Methodist.

"Doc" therefore hunted up Parson Charlie, who was watching a track meet.

"Sure, why not?" asked Parson Charlie. "Christianity's already been on trial for two thousand years. One more trial won't hurt it."

So the switch was thrown and the wheels began to turn.

The trial, however, might have remained a strictly Tennessee matter if the Fundamentalist political movement had not coincided with the waning star of a remarkable old man.

William Jennings Bryan, three times Democratic candidate for President, had swung the nomination in 1912 to Woodrow Wilson, and had served as his Secretary of State. But by 1925, the Bryan who had set the country on fire in 1896 with his speech about the "Cross of Gold" had become hopelessly old-fashioned. At least temporarily, the United States had turned its back on all the causes for which Bryan stood. We had rejected free silver, the low tariff, pacifism, the League of Nations, and the Democrats, and we were in process of rejecting Prohibition.

Bryan settled in Florida in 1920 after the Republicans came into national power, and picked up a fortune selling real estate. But few came to hear him preach in the Miami parks except the embattled Fundamentalists. He joined their anti-evolution crusade. When the news broke of Scopes' arrest, Bryan had already proposed to carry the fight into the North and West until he could secure an anti-evolution amendment to the Federal Constitution. Although he had not practiced law for thirty-six years, he now offered his services to the prosecution in the trial of young Mr. Scopes.

This action raised the case into national stature. The American Civil Liberties Union had planned to employ only Tennessee attorneys. But with Bryan in the lists, Clarence Darrow now telegraphed an offer of his services to the Scopes defense. Defender of Leopold and Loeb, of strikers and anarchists, the most brilliant criminal lawyer of his time, he had already baited William Jennings Bryan about Fundamentalism, endeavoring to force him to answer a list of fifty questions about the Bible.

When Bryan heard that Darrow had entered against him, he exclaimed, "It will be a duel to the death." And it was.

The first outside reporter to reach Dayton was John Moutoux, then with the Knoxville *News-Sentinel*. He saw on the ticker the news of Scopes' arrest, and although his paper was not at first impressed with the significance of the event, Moutoux went down to Dayton on his own time next weekend and interviewed the teacher. He found Scopes shy, reluctant to talk, and fearful of publicity. However, Moutoux got a story and pictures which he sold to N.E.A., a feature service. At the entry of big names into the story, his paper sent him back to Dayton, where he was joined by correspondents from the press associations and all the leading American dailies. Among them were Westbrook Pegler, Brian Bell, Raymond Clapper, and Henry L. Mencken, the sharpest critic of the Bible Belt (and author of the phrase).

Mr. Mencken came to the Dayton trial in a mood of amiability. He had not joined in the preliminary breast-beating of Northern liberals (the *New Republic* said the issue was Tennessee vs. Civilization, the *Nation,* Tennessee vs. Truth). Writing in the *Nation,* he considered the "anthropoid religion" of Tennessee more or less as a quaint survival and saw no reason why mountaineers should not be educated to be "dutiful to the local religion and docile under the local mores." Mencken pointed out that a teacher, on taking his oath of office, renounced his right of free speech as certainly as a bishop, a colonel, or an editorial writer on a newspaper.

His first newspaper dispatch from Dayton said he had expected to find "a squalid Southern village," but he found the houses surrounded by pretty gardens, with cool green lawns and stately trees, the two chief streets paved from curb to curb, and good stocks in the stores.

> *Elsewhere North or South, the combat would become bitter. Here it retains the lofty quality of the duello. I gather the notion, indeed, that the gentlemen who are most active in promoting it are precisely the most lacking in hot conviction — that it is, in its local aspects, rather a joust between neutrals than a battle between passionate believers. Is it a mere coincidence that the town clergy have been very carefully kept out of it? There are several*

> *Baptist brothers here of such powerful gifts that when*
> *they begin belaboring sinners the very rats of the alleys*
> *flee to the hills. They preach dreadfully. But they are not*
> *heard from today. By some process to me unknown they*
> *have been induced to shut up — a far harder business, I*
> *venture, than knocking out a lion with a sandbag. But*
> *the sixty thirty-second degree Masons of Dayton have*
> *somehow achieved it.*
>
> *Thus the battle joins, and the good red sun shines*
> *down. Dayton lies in a fat and luxuriant valley. The*
> *fields are green with corn, pumpkins and young*
> *orchards, and the hills are full of reliable moonshiners,*
> *all save one of them Christian men. . . .*

But within a day or two, Mr. Mencken had enough of
Dayton.

> *There is no gambling. There is no place to dance. The*
> *relatively wicked, when they would indulge themselves,*
> *go to Robinson's drugstore and debate theology. In a*
> *word, the New Jerusalem — the ideal of all soul-savers*
> *and sin-exterminators. Nine churches are scarcely enough*
> *for the 1,800 inhabitants; many of them go into the hills*
> *to shout and roll.*

No one could foresee what a multitude would jump
upon the Dayton bandwagon, for the literal meaning of
Genesis, for freedom of thought, or for cash. Doctor J.
Frank Norris, a Baptist from Texas, Colonel P. H. Calla-
han, a Catholic from Kentucky, offered the prosecution
help. Mountain men came down from the long ridges
which limit the western horizon, bringing their guns to
shoot for the Bible, if necessary. An original thinker from
Georgia arrived in a bungalow on wheels, distributing
tracts explaining that the Negro is not human. He did
not do much business, nor did another rolling bungalow

which came from Tampa, Florida, to sell lots. A visitor who wore a sign, "Champion Bible Expert of the World," was only one among thousands. Robinson's drugstore quickly sold its stock of Bibles and of Hunter's *Civic Biology*. The Adventists and the "Holiness" each started a revival.

From the North, Arthur Garfield Hays, Dudley Field Malone, and other famous lawyers, with a battery of scientists and one or two liberal preachers, came to help Clarence Darrow. The Attorney-General of Tennessee, as well as the members of the Dayton bar who had taken part in the preliminary talk at the Coca-Cola table, were on Bryan's side.

The monkey motif quickly got out of hand. In a good-natured spirit, the Progressive Citizens Club had ordered monkey posters for the store windows (and instructed its members not to argue religion with the visitors). J. T. Darwin's clothing store had a big street sign, DARWIN IS RIGHT — INSIDE; Bryan and Darrow, each given a civic banquet in turn, exchanged gifts of carved monkeys; children dangled toy monkeys in the streets, a circus man displayed two chimpanzees, and a Coney Island side-show offered Bozo, its prize exhibit, to the defense. Newcomers from the North greeted each other, "Brother, thy tail hangs down behind!" — often the password to a swig at a fruit-jar of corn.

A British limerick contest was won by E. J. Rackham of Southampton:

> *If we take the Daytonian mind*
> *As an average of man's, I'm inclined*
> *To ask, not if man*
> *With a monkey began*
> *But if monkeys descend from mankind.*

The townspeople took down their monkey posters.

Because the courtroom was crowded with newspaper correspondents, Judge Raulston, who was presiding, sent the jury into another room where they were kept informed of proceedings but missed all the excitement.

The prosecution stated its belief that the theory of evolution "eliminates every mystery in the Old Testament and eliminates everything supernatural." The Attorney-General, afterward Senator, Tom Stewart, raised his arms and turned his face to Heaven as he exclaimed: "Would they have me believe that I was once a worm and writhed in the dust? Will they take from me my hope of a here-after?"

At no time did Clarence Darrow attack Christianity or the Bible, which he described as a book of religion and morals rather than of science. The defense introduced a letter from the late Woodrow Wilson, a Democrat and a Presbyterian, stating that he believed in organic evolution. But the prosecution persisted in its attitude that Christianity itself was on trial; the gibes of H. L. Mencken, the reputation of Darrow as an agnostic, and his objection to the local custom of opening court each day with prayer by a visiting clergyman, no doubt helped to strengthen this point of view.

A defense scientist explained carefully, "It is not that man came from monkeys, but that man, monkeys and apes all came from a common ancestry millions of years in the past." Mencken wrote an acid description of William Jennings Bryan as he listened to the scientific testimony.

Now and then his face darkened and his eyes flashed, but he never uttered a sound. . . . The old gladiator faced his real enemy at last. . . . The old buzzard, having failed

to raise the mob against its rulers, now prepares to raise
it against its teachers. He can never be the peasants'
president, but there is still a chance to be the peasants'
pope. He leads a new crusade, his bald head glistening,
his face streaming with sweat, his chest heaving beneath
his black alpaca coat.

In Dayton, there was talk of asking Mencken into an
alley, but "Doc" Robinson and the town elders held a
tight rein. The only fight reported during the trial was
between two local men — a Methodist minister who believed in evolution and a member of the town school
board.

Bryan arose in the courtroom and rebutted the scientific testimony in a speech which has become famous.
According to Arthur Garfield Hays, he "publicly refused
to be a mammal." Bryan pointed to the offending text-
book from which Scopes had taught, wherein a diagram
classified thirty-five hundred species. "And there is man!"
the orator cried. "They left him there with 3,499 mammals, among them skunks and other animals that smell
bad."

A fourteen-year-old boy who had studied under Scopes
was put on the stand by the prosecution to testify that
he had learned in high school the nebular hypothesis of
the origin of the earth. Under cross-examination by Clarence Darrow, the youngster also said that he had learned
that whales are mammals.

"Well, you know it now," said Darrow. "It has not
done you any harm, has it?"

"No, sir."

The prosecution interrupted. "It is for the mother of

this boy to say what harm this diabolical business has done him!"

That night a reporter looked up the boy's mother. She said that her son's morals were unimpaired by the study of Hunter's *Civic Biology*, that he was a good boy and a bright one, and she wanted him to learn all that he could about evolution or anything else. She added that he was just as keen a student of the Bible as of biology.

In retrospect, it seems that this middle-of-the-road point of view was never fairly presented at the Scopes trial, while the extremists had a field day.

For example, the Irreligionists Society of Moscow, Russia, announced its plan to raise a "Scopes Fund" for science publication. Scopes' sister in Paducah, Kentucky, lost her job in the public schools at Paducah, Kentucky, because she would not "renounce evolution." Senator Cole Blease, a South Carolina statesman, favored a law in that State requiring public schoolteachers "to accept the deity of Christ."

To the case of Tennessee vs. John Thomas Scopes, all the outside tumult was clearly irrelevant. Judge Raulston soon ruled that neither Christianity nor evolution was on trial in his courtroom, and confined the proceedings to the guilt or innocence of the high-school teacher.

As he could not place more scientific experts on the stand, Clarence Darrow now asked Bryan if he would testify as an expert on the Bible; and Bryan accepted the challenge. Court was moved for this session from the dingy, crowded upstairs room, with its long black stove-pipes and overloaded spittoons, to the spacious court-house lawn, where revival meetings had been in progress all week. The unfortunate jury was thus released from its

confinement in a separate room and given a breath of
fresh air. Facing their open-air jury box was a ten-foot
sign, "Read your Bible."

Bryan sat down on a hard pedestal and began to fan
himself happily. The crowd on the lawn, as the question-
ing began, were almost wholly in his favor, shouting fervent "Amens!" to many answers.

Darrow snapped his galluses, and was even more folksy
than before. He asked Bryan if he thought that Joshua
had made the sun stand still, and Bryan replied that he
accepted the Bible literally. Bryan said that he knew
nothing of geology or other sciences, nor of the history of
ancient civilizations. He believed the age of humanity to
be six thousand years (an estimate arrived at by one
Bishop Ussher, who had long ago added together the Biblical ages of the various prophets to reach this conclusion).
To a later question, Bryan replied that the "days" in the
first chapter of Genesis might have been of indefinite
duration, and that Creation could have gone on for millions of years.

Bryan said, however, that Eve was the first woman,
and that she was taken from Adam's rib. Darrow read
aloud from Genesis the story of God's curse upon the serpent.

"Do you think that is why the serpent is compelled to
crawl upon its belly?" asked Darrow.

"I believe that," answered Bryan.

The reporters say that at this point, Darrow, a homely
old figure stripped to his undershirt in the blazing sun,
seemed to have the crowd with him. Tennesseans know
all about snakes.

"Have you any idea how the snake went before that
time?"

"No, sir," answered Bryan.

"Do you know whether he walked on his tail or not?"

"No, sir. I have no way to know."

The crowd on the lawn laughed in derision, and their laughter was directed against Bryan.

Both men now lost their tempers. Bryan cried that "The purpose of this examination is to cast ridicule upon everybody who believes the Bible," and Darrow almost screamed his reply: "We think the purpose is preventing bigots and ignoramuses from controlling the education of the United States."

The testimony was stricken from the record, although it has since been widely reprinted. Each side considered that it won. But Darrow's friends swarmed on the platform to shake his hand, amid loud cheers, while Bryan sat almost alone, fanning himself in the heat.

The clean-up of the trial was quick. The defense itself wished a verdict of guilty, so that the case could be appealed. Scopes was found guilty and fined one hundred dollars. In Nashville, the State Supreme Court held the law itself constitutional, but reversed the verdict of the lower court and ordered the "bizarre" case nol prossed. The anti-evolution law stands on the books of Tennessee today, but is not strictly enforced.

On the weekend after the trial, Bryan and Darrow went — separately — into the Great Smoky Mountains to cool off. On Sunday, in a nearby town, Bryan told his audience of his plans for a national campaign to force all teachers who taught evolution "as a fact" to resign. (But he spoke afterward to his wife of the need for guarding against intolerance.) Back in Dayton, he ate one of his enormous dinners, in spite of the heat, lay down for a nap, and died in his sleep. His friends said he died of a broken heart; his enemies, that he overate. His body lay in state in a house belonging to Mr. Rogers, the other druggist of Dayton.

"Parson Charlie" Jones, who had been with Mr. and Mrs. Bryan at the time of his death, was asked to preach a funeral sermon on the front porch. The body was to be taken to Washington after the service for burial in Arlington National Cemetery; and the local undertaker, intent upon perfection, reached over to brush a speck of soot from Mr. Bryan's white shirt. In so doing, he smudged it. The parson found a piece of white chalk in his pocket and covered up the smudge before he began to preach.

In 1948, long since retired from the active ministry, Mr. Jones operated a tourist home on a side street. He is short, slender, and white-haired, with frosty blue eyes, horn-rimmed glasses, and a quick grin.

"Been told it was the best sermon I ever preached," Parson Charlie said without conceit. "I don't know. I just shot straight off the hip. I've always talked that way at funerals. Let's go outside where we can be more comfortable." He seated himself in the porch swing and let fly tobacco juice into the honeysuckle.

The traveling cash grocery stopped in front of the tourist home. A mountain voice called, "Want any taters? Any green tomaters?"

"What'll I do with green tomatoes?" asked the preacher. "My wife don't like to bother with 'em."

"Don't care what you want to *do* with 'em," said the peddler. "I just want to *sell* 'em."

We went out to the truck. "I'm all burnt up on punkins," said the parson, examining the produce critically and introducing me to his friend. "You'll notice how these mountain boys fix their potatoes — put the littlest ones on top and the biggest ones on the bottom. In Washington, I bet it's the other way 'round."

The farmer blushed. "Wouldn't be no religion much if we didn't," he said, and drove on.

The parson continued his recollections.

"I heard that when Clarence Darrow stood on top of Clingman's Dome in the Great Smokies, he said, 'I believe there must be a God after all.' But then Darrow wrote before he died in 1941 that he didn't believe in God — and I guess he went off that way, unless he changed his mind at the end. He was a great humanitarian, like Franklin D. Roosevelt."

According to tradition in the town, Mr. Darrow once asked, "Who is this Parson Charlie? I like him. He doesn't ram his religion down anybody's throat." On another occasion, Darrow told "Doc" Robinson at the drugstore that if in his youth he had known a preacher as broad-minded as Parson Charlie, he would have joined the church.

"That's right," said Mr. Jones. "That's the way I tried to operate, particularly with a man like that, a high-grade lawyer and a skeptic. He's a game fish and you've got to play him along."

Parson Charlie grinned. "You know, when Darrow came back to visit Dayton a year or two after the trial, he saw a big new Cumberland Presbyterian Church going up across from the hotel, and he said, 'I guess the Devil and I didn't do so much good down here after all.'"

I asked if he thought that Mr. Darrow perhaps heard too much Hell-fire preaching in his youth.

"Doubt it was that so much," said the parson seriously. "More than likely he had met up with some hypocritical church members who had turned him against religion. Like a deacon I used to know, a Baptist." Mr. Jones grinned. "He used to go on awful toots; and one night he thought he was a-dyin', and he called his wife, who was a fine woman and a Methodist. 'O Henrietta, pray for me!'

"His wife fell on her knees and prayed, 'O Lord, have mercy on my poor drunken husband!' The deacon heard her from the next room and he called out, 'No, *no*, Henrietta! Don't tell Him I'm drunk, tell Him I'm *sick!*' "

I asked about Scopes, who had been a member of Parson Charlie's Sunday-School class. With help from interested scientists outside Dayton, young Scopes had taken up graduate work and has since had a career in private industry.

"The trial ended right for him," said Mr. Jones.

Shortly before his death, Mr. Bryan had proposed building a school for mountain boys on a hill near Dayton. Fund-raising for this institution, magnified into Bryan Memorial University, was promptly started by Mr. Robinson and other public-spirited citizens. Almost a million dollars had been pledged before the 1929 business depression stopped the work. For some years the school remained a hole in the ground. By 1935, however, a new town high school had gone up, and the University was able to open modestly in the old school building where Scopes had taught biology. Gradually, with gifts from Fundamentalists all over the country and with much sweat by student labor, its own buildings have been rising on a hill near town. The site has a superb view of the mountains and the T.V.A. lake near town. A new chapel has been opened, and the cinder-block administration building partly completed.

A tall, lanky young student from the Valley of Virginia showed me through the long basement, already in use. In the science lab, a girl was running a chemistry test at the same desk which Scopes had used. Other students were at work in the laundry, kitchen, and dining-room. The library held some thirty thousand volumes, including the *Origin of Species,* by Charles Darwin, from the personal collection of William Jennings Bryan.

Bryan University, the student explained, is a liberal arts, co-educational college with a four-year course. There is no smoking, drinking, dancing, or card-playing; many of the two hundred students are candidates for the ministry. A trailer settlement on the hillside houses the married GI's. The single students share dormitory rooms. The room of my guide was lined with volumes of theology.

He pointed down the hill to an unseen asset.

"We've got — I mean the Lord's blessed us with — a new water-pump. Used to be the pressure wouldn't get up the hill between five and six, when we needed to wash before supper. Now the pressure's fine. The Lord's certainly been good to us."

To the outward eye, Dayton when I visited it had not greatly changed since it was described by the reporters of 1925. The speed limit had been raised from eight miles an hour. There were two beer-parlors, a veterans' club, and perhaps one or two bootleggers who supplied stronger waters, and a new movie house was going up. Although the suburbs have grown, within the town limits were eighteen hundred people and nine churches, as in 1925. These churches were not exactly the same nine. During the interim, two or three died or merged with others, and a Catholic Church was opened. At the time of my visit, the Four-Square Gospel was holding a revival. This is a "Holiness" or Pentecostal sect, founded by the late Aimee Semple McPherson, who at the time of the Scopes trial was just rising to fame in faraway Los Angeles.

On a Saturday night, the Four-Square Gospel people sang up and down in the street in competition with the movie. In the store windows, posters announced forthcoming menageries and political campaigns. (Mr. Estes Kefauver, a Democrat, was running for the Senate on a platform of "Peace and T.V.A.," and Mr. Roy Acuff, a Republican, sought the governorship on the Republican ticket and a platform of the Ten Commandments.) A colporteur or Bible salesman on the street told me that Dayton was the best town in his territory.

From all these outward signs, it did not seem that the "old-time religion" had been altered by the Scopes trial. As in 1925, there was reported one radical Methodist minister. He was a movie-goer and musician, who had trained a high-school fife-and-drum corps, including girls who wear knee pants. Some consider this the Devil's work, but the young people support him. On the night of a football game between Dayton High and some visiting Catholics, between the halves the fife-and-drum corps carried flashlights and formed a lighted cross upon the field, while the Bryan University Band played "Onward, Christian Soldiers."

There are still some die-hard anti-evolutionists, especially on "Bryan Hill." A pastor of a conservative church told me that he would preach about evolution fifty miles away, but not in his own pulpit.

This pastor was proud of the economic and social progress which Dayton and Rhea County had made since 1925 — largely, he thought, because of the T.V.A. There had been some changes in local attitudes. One of his members, a mill-owner who pays higher than union scales, told the pastor that he believed the generally low wages of Southern industry in the past had been a sin.

Since 1925, the nation-wide Fundamentalist movement which Mr. Bryan led has shifted its emphasis from Genesis to Revelation, from a concern with the origin of man to a preoccupation with his end. There seems less interest in legislation of any kind. Some of the extremists believe that the United Nations itself is a device through which the Anti-Christ will reign and rule. "It has always been the part of strategy for Satan to get people to compromise in order to 'come together,'" declared a postwar article in *The Voice* of the Independent Fundamental Churches of America. "God, on the other hand, has sought to keep people 'separated.'"

But not all Fundamentalists share this extreme pessimistic view. Mr. Bryan himself, it will be recalled, was the most hopeful of men. He was not only a perennial candidate for the Presidency, but a faithful champion of many good causes. He never abandoned his interest in the rights of workingmen and farmers, in world peace and international co-operation. Bryan and Darrow had more beliefs in common than the record of the trial shows.

"Doc" Robinson, mixing a prescription behind the drugstore counter, agreed.

"It made people think," he said. "Didn't do a bit of harm. And Bryan University's a good thing for the town — good for the morals, good for business."

"The kids can read their evolution outside?" I suggested.

His eyes twinkled. "That's right. They can read evolution outside. Now take even this Mencken — he didn't mean any real harm by those things he wrote about us. He was a nice guy. It was just like a man tells you that your store windows are dirty — you may not enjoy being told, but you ought to be grateful to him."

This brief historical review of our subject has given a disproportionate amount of space, perhaps, to the Scopes trial. But, as "Doc" Robinson said, it didn't kill the old-time religion.

It is the years in between which have given us a new perspective on the way we felt and thought in 1925; where the Fundamentalists did not succeed with many of their fellow citizens in placing legal authority behind the Bible story of the Fall, Adolf Hitler triumphantly convinced many doubters that there was still evil in the world, nevertheless. He opened a revelation of fearful, giant gulfs of evil within one of the world's most highly educated, "Christian" nations; and the impact on the comfortable beholder across the Atlantic was almost as unsettling as the visions of the lake of fire which caused the convulsions at Cane Ridge.

Quite independently of the Fundamentalist movement, the twentieth-century heirs of the old-time religion began to sense that faith in progress was not always justified.

The Europeans, closer to the suffering of the earlier war, felt it first; and during the nineteen-twenties, while the battle raged at Dayton, a new theology from the study of Doctor Karl Barth in Switzerland began to make its way among the American seminaries. It was called "neo-orthodoxy," and it did not depend upon the literal view of the Bible. The "rediscovery of evil" had something to do with the changed attitude of the American churches by the time of the Second World War.

During the first war, they had functioned, many of them, as red-hot recruiting centers. The Kaiser took his place as the latest Devil, along with Demon Rum and other candidates; I remember that a serious conflict was caused in Birch Avenue because a deacon of German descent wouldn't buy Liberty Bonds. The pastor finally restored peace by persuading him. Afterward, there were signs that many of the preachers felt ashamed; Doctor Harry Emerson Fosdick, for one, made an eloquent recantation. And in the Second World War certainly the churches as a whole behaved differently; perhaps it was because of a fear which so many sensitive persons felt that the blame could not be placed entirely upon the Nazis, for being human, we shared to some extent in the unspeakable evil which had overwhelmed the world. So it was that no talk was heard, during the Second World War, of calling the American Army "Battling Christians." The churches did not function as war bond salesmen or recruiting centers. Instead, they made themselves into reservoirs of spiritual strength for a time of difficulty; and many chaplains, it is reported, won high respect from the troops.

These extreme simplifications are probably dangerous and misleading, but I am trying to report the subject as it looked outside the churches, and not from a theological level. At any rate, many of us now look back with mixed emotions at the Dayton trial. The Fundamentalists cer-

tainly forgot the freedom of conscience, the complete
separation of Church and State, which had been historically
associated with their faith. But in part, they were pro-
testing against a religion which seemed to them too
shallow to meet human needs.

A fine example of well-padded Protestantism of the
Coolidge days appeared during the week of the trial.
Business and industrial leaders of East Tennessee took a
quarter-page advertisement in the Chattanooga *News* to
encourage church-going; and as the advertisement did
not mention the excitement over at Dayton or any of the
Fundamentalists' beliefs, it seemed to be meant for city
people who were currently losing interest in religion
under the influence of the times.

The Church, said this advertisement, was "the real
force that keeps men and women safe of nights, that
makes living free of constant ward and watchfulness
against the predatory." It was also claimed that the
Church was bringing about a world of peace and prosperity. This burglar-insurance view of religion would
collapse as quickly as the stock market after 1929. In the
Fundamentalist movement itself was an element of protest against it. A folksong of the period said:

> *In this world of frills and fashions*
> *Where the churches are so fine*
> *And the trademark on religion*
> *Is the classic dollar sign,*
> *There's a rule that never faileth,*
> *You will always find it true*
> *Where the dollar rules the pulpit,*
> *There the Devil rules the pew.*

From this brief and casual survey of church history I gather the impression that the free churches, like the individual Christian, sometimes take wrong directions, stumble, fall — repent, and try again. The old-time religion has been tremendously affected by the world it moves in. It has been false to its own beginnings, perhaps, and certainly least attractive to the outside observer, when it has become overbearing and has sought to enforce its views on others. And the opposite is true.

These are some of the reasons why I set out first to visit back-country churches which are, in many ways, like the living ancestors of our chief Protestant tradition. I had a good time in doing so.

PART II

SOME BRANCHES

In spite of their infinite variety, the branches — both the graceful and the grotesque — sprout from a common trunk, and a common impulse

1. PLAIN PEOPLE

*Some of the seeds which came from
Europe long ago took root in Pennsylvania
and elsewhere*

THE PENNSYLVANIA DUTCH, even those who are not
"Plain," are natural conservatives. Among many Catholic,
Lutheran, or Reformed families in the countryside, bread
frozen on Christmas Day is sometimes eaten to prevent
colds and fevers; ashes from the Good Friday fire are fed
to pigs to keep them healthy; water from the baptismal
bowl is thrown over a rosebush in the dooryard to bring
the baby rosy cheeks.

Driving out toward the Blue Ridge wall in Maryland
through rich farmland, I had instructions only to ask at
the crossroads for "the Dunkard preacher who has just
lost both hands in the farm machinery." The first house
beyond the old stone church at the crossroads belonged
to his sisters, two Old Order Dunkard ladies in matching,
high-collared taffeta dresses, capped by the prayer-veil,
from which strings depended by each rosy cheek. I asked
wherein the Old Order Dunkards differed from the rest.

"Well, to be frank about it, worldliness set in," one sister replied.

I pointed out that I had seen a number of prayer-veils in the Dunkard — or Brethren — Church in Frederick that morning.

"Yes, but how many did you see?" And her sister chimed in, "And did they have strings?"

Their brother, the pastor, his stumps still swathed in bandages, was dark-haired, serious, and smiling; he put on, I fear at some pain, the coat fastened by hooks and eyes, with its standing collar, specified in contrast to the flat or lapel collars of the world. His flock does not take part in the famous heifer project of the Church of the Brethren — early in the war this denomination began setting aside heifers to be used for world relief after hostilities — but makes its contributions through the Mennonites, to whom they now feel closer than to their apostate brethren. He looked at me, kindly yet remote, awaiting further questions across the self-erected barrier over which there could be no real communication.

He handed me a rule book explaining that the soup at the Lord's Supper "should be eaten from a common dish and not from individual plates or dishes"; forbidding the wearing of hats by women, jewelry, wrist watches; oaths, strong drink, membership in Boy Scouts or other organizations with uniform and drill. There were many rules, but none more difficult that that which the Old Order Dunkards share with the River Brethren, Mennonites, Amish, Quakers, and all other varieties of plain people: "We are to love our enemies, to overcome evil with good, and pray for them which despitefully use us and persecute us."

The Anabaptists, those early radicals who undertook to reform the Reformation, were undoubtedly "plain people." Their first signed statement of belief, dated at Schaff-hausen, Germany, in 1527, calls their association "a brotherly union of some children of God," and adopts a verse from II Corinthians, "We shall come out from among them and be separate." Taking literally even the most difficult sayings, these free congregations usually opposed war, military service, oaths, courts, capital punishments, and usury, and sometimes they advocated a community of goods. The objection to wearing buttons, which is still a feature of the stricter sects, possibly came about because buttons in the sixteenth and seventeenth centuries were a sign of wealth and fashion, lavishly used on military uniforms.

In John Bunyan's time in England the Anabaptists — many were then calling them Baptists, for short — wore clothes of plain gray, from which the Quakers, it is said, borrowed their early attire. Gradually the main body of Baptists ceased to be "plain." In the early days of Pennsylvania, the two kinds were distinguished as "hook Baptists" and "button Baptists."

In the eighteenth century word began to spread throughout Europe, among the Mennonites, Dunkards, and other groups of plain people and pietists who were persecuted from time to time, that an English Quaker, William Penn, had established a new colony in America on the principle of religious liberty; that its capital was called the City of Brotherly Love, and that the Quakers, in fact, held principles much like their own. Many of them came to settle in Pennsylvania.

In the free air and on this good soil many new sects of

plain people originated, and others constantly split off, until there are now scores of different Mennonites and Dunkards.

With one or two notable exceptions, today, even in Pennsylvania, they are gradually mixing with the rest.

A full-page ad in the Waynesboro *Record-Herald* was sponsored by the town merchants on behalf of all the churches. "The Open Bible . . . Bulwark of Freedom," said the mat and lay-out from an advertising agency. "Wherever its influence is strong, tyranny cannot thrive. Where it is read and loved and obeyed, selfishness in all its forms finds it difficult even to exist. . . . " These sentiments were endorsed by the town Ministerial Association and paid for by local merchants (Mildred and Evelyn Beauty Salon, cold waves, $10.00 to $50.00; S. Dreyfuss Co., men's clothing;" When You Think of Footwear, It's Glicks"; Mity Nice Bread, Super Enriched — 6 Vitamins, Minerals; Wise Jewelry Co.; Arthur's Quality Ice Cream; Snowberger's Radio Service; Hoffman Motor Sales; The Good Lumber Co.; "C" Glenn Fry, insurance; and the Poe Funeral Home). Clustered around the Book were notices of thirty-one churches, including Catholics and Christian Scientists, the Church of God and Latter-Day Saints, and varieties of the Mennonites, Dunkards, and River Brethren — who are still strong in this community of ten thousand souls. For the first time since the Reformation, the advertising agency had brought them all together.

On the streets of mellow red-brick houses little girls were running lickety-split, late to Sunday-School, big sister pulling the little one, hair-ribbons flying, while early returners elsewhere unloaded from the family car. I passed up the big, stocky, brick edifices of the Lutherans, the Methodists, the Reformed, and the United Brethren for the Pentecostal Tabernacle, which proclaimed on its modest sign, "The Church of the Old-Time Religion."

Between the wooden tabernacle and the neighboring residence a cement-block wall, free-standing, rose to the eaves of the church, darkening the windows on that side. I asked another late-comer on the steps to explain it.

"Well, it's like this, the fellow who lived there used to play the gramophone pretty loud and all that. We had a little trouble about it. I think it's just a spite wall, to speak plain about it."

On the other side of the wall, however, it was the old-time religion which was considered noisy.

The Pentecostal folks are an offshoot of Methodism. After church, I inquired of my acquaintance the distinction between the Pentecostal sect and the Church of God, which had opened headquarters in a store front off the Square.

"Not so much difference," he said. "About all is, they took up where the Pentecostal left down. We were the first. Now there's two Churches of God, those that tongue-talk and those that don't. And there's an Assembly of God, too. Terrible how they split, ain't it?

"Even the barn people," he went on. "They split too. Now there's a love-feast out in the country this afternoon for some of the brethren, the ones that ride in automobiles, and later in the week another for the buggy brethren, the ones with long beards that won't ride in autos. I generally goes to both of 'em," he added reflectively.

The plain people are still numerous in Waynesboro, but

are not much in evidence in the Sunday streets. They go out to their old meeting-houses in the country, where their ancestors are buried; one local church has now enrolled fifty-two descendants of the settler who gave an acre of land for the building in 1791. The soil is good and well-cared-for; Dunkards, Mennonites, River Brethren, and Amish are successful farmers. Some of their progenitors in Europe, suffering religious persecution, were driven from good land to the worse, becoming of necessity pioneers in the use of manure and in soil-conservation practices.

Almost all of the plain churches practice foot-washing (as do many of the small sects throughout the country). A zealous Mennonite of the region on a train ride, encountering an Episcopal Bishop, tried to engage him in conversation on these doctrinal points.

"We believe in foot-washing in our church," said the Mennonite. "Do you?"

"My dear sir," said the Bishop, who was trying to complete a sermon, "we not only believe in it, we insist upon it."

To varying degrees, also, they all "dress plain." Mrs. Mary E. Varner, who was in her eighties, a member of the Brethren in Christ (popularly called the River Brethren), had put on her plain black dress and prayer-cap for the love-feast at Ringgold Church that afternoon. The Eisenhower family, Brethren people of the vicinity, had produced a noted son out in Kansas, she reminded me; a good man, she felt sure, although unfortunately a man of war. A charming old lady, and far from dogmatic, she was still shocked that I did not know the reason for the prayer-cap. "Is it comely or befitting to pray unto God uncovered?"

We divided for the preaching, women and men, and buckled down to three full-sized sermons. The last, and most earnest, of the preachers chided those who had come wearing neckties. "Should women bear the cross alone?" he asked gravely. "And men alone go free?" They were all to be separate from the world. And woe unto any who had come to the love-feast solely for the food. Nevertheless, having been properly invited, I filed downstairs at the appointed time and filled a tin tray with prunes, apricots, beans, bread-and-applebutter, and coffee.

We finished the love-feast and returned to the green lawn, where I said good-bye to old Mrs. Varney. Five thousand used to attend the love-feast, she said; it lasted for days, with singing by choir after choir; people camped in the fields, and slept in the attic of the church. Her mind slipped farther back into the old days — "People aren't strict like they were then. I remember a farmer with a beard so long that he tied it behind his back so it wouldn't get caught in the fodder when he was working. And the plain people split up something scandalous. Time and again you'll see two churches of plain people standing side by each."

The River Brethren sprang up after a revival in Lancaster County in 1770 among the local Lutherans, Mennonites, and Baptists, who were all "grieved at what they considered the formalism which then characterized the churches." Afterward there was a little difference of opinion among the converts about the merits of the new "triple" or trine immersion. Those who favored it settled near the river.

"Have you seen the graves?" asked Mrs. Varney.

She showed me her family plot, and her face lit at the

memory of a small brother and sister — five and three years old — three-quarters of a century dead. "We used to call them Adam and Eve," she said. "We'd have a real good crowd today if it wasn't corn-planting time," she added, looking about her. She held out her hand. "Here's where I started out this way — and here's where I'll — " She left the rest unfinished.

Across the table at the love-feast I had met a young River Brother lately returned from service in a conscientious objectors' camp, confused by the religions he had seen. The objectors had come from every Christian denomination (there were also a few Jews, Orthodox Parsees, Hindus, Taoists, and at least one Mazdaznam, Moslem, and Buddhist). Scores of little-known sects were uncovered by the registration: the Russian Molokan or Christian Spiritual Jumpers, the Church of Radiant Life, God's Bible School, Triumph Church of the New Age, Church of the Four Leaf Clover, Church of the People, and — a title which cannot be tied — The Church. In the list of objectors Mr. Walking Jerusalem, of Divine Lodge, Samsonville, New York, a farmer and follower of Father Divine, came after Mr. Julian C. Haynes, of West Newton, Massachusetts, a psychologist and a Unitarian.

The returned River Brother at the love-feast was puzzled. "There were two fellows from the North Woods who called themselves the True Followers of Christ, but they weren't a bit plain. They talked rough, and took a little wine for their stomach's sake on Saturday night."

Only one rather small group of plain people has held strictly to itself since the seventeenth century, because of a split among the Mennonites in Switzerland a long, long time ago.

The original quarrel arose over the subject of "shunning." The great Menno Simons, in the sixteenth century had favored the practice of shunning a backslidden brother or sister, even in the marriage bed. But a century later, a bishop, Jacob Ammon, found that many Swiss had eased up on the shunning; they still turned away a backslider from the communion, but did not break up homes or friendships. Ammon, a natural Fundamentalist, also found that some of the people had begun to wear buttons and shave off their beards, and others even claimed that the "true-hearted" could somehow be saved from the fires of Hell, without making an open profession of faith. He began his work as a reformer in 1693. After an historic gathering held in a barn, he excommunicated those who would not return to the old ways; and in 1711 some of his followers, called the Amish, decided to emigrate to Pennsylvania.

But they would not share a ship for the voyage down the Rhine with other Mennonites bound for Pennsylvania, where, side by side, the two have remained separate ever since. The Amish in Europe have long since died out, but they have survived in the United States.

The "house Amish" worship in barns, or more frequently in each other's homes, because Saint Paul speaks of "the church in the house." They choose their ministers, who are not paid, by lot, just as Matthias was chosen to fill a vacancy among the Apostles (Acts 1:23–26). The men and women nominate candidates, and anyone receiving three votes or more is "in the lot." A slip of paper with a text is placed in one of several identical Bibles which are stacked upon a table; the candidates walk by, each chooses a Bible, and the one who finds the slip is God's choice. He will be ordained to one of three orders, a full minister, a preacher, or a deacon (minister to the poor).

In other ways the Amish are far less Protestant than the surrounding community. They do not hold revival services nor advertise their meetings, to which strangers, in fact, are not invited. They keep many festivals of the Old Church; an Amish farmer, asked what brings him to town, may answer casually, "Didn't you know? It's Ascension Day." At their services they use an ancient prayer-book, and do not favor impromptu prayer because "it encourages a minister to show off." They fast until noon before their communion service, held at three in the afternoon, the hour of the Crucifixion; and genuflect at the name of Christ.

A little too much has been written about the Amish as freaks and tourist bait, and nowadays they are apt to be withdrawn.

Among the fat fields and the weathered brick houses of Lancaster County I passed a text nailed to a tree, and drove back to the farmhouse to ask the way to New Holland. The proprietor, a lean, sallow Mennonite in ordinary working clothes, was talking with his tenant, a young Amish farmer waiting for the bus. His four-year-old son, in miniature costume complete with wide-brimmed black hat, looked on in a silent agony of hope at the prospect of a ride to town. The Amish, although they may not own automobiles, can ride in them.

"I'll go with you to New Holland, if you have no objection," said the young farmer. "My off is on."

He climbed into the front seat, his little boy darting quickly into the back, and offered me a big cigar. The Amish raise tobacco. (But he frowned slightly as I lit a cigarette.) He was going to the horse sale in New

Holland, he said. We watched a jeep plowing a neighbor's field.

"They'll never give any manure," said the Amish man contentedly. "I can plow my whole farm without hitting a stone."

I asked if he had placed the religious sign on the tree; no, the landlord had done that. We passed through the hamlet of Baresville, where everyone seemed amply clad. He smiled at this trite observation.

"Yes, such kind of clothes as they wear nowadays."

This was a Monday, and the women were hanging the wash beside the big two- and three-family houses; the black clothes of the men contrasted sharply with dresses of purple, magenta, blue, or green. Brilliant flower gardens burst over the white-painted fences and blue gates. (A blue gate does *not* signify a marriageable daughter; the Amish just like blue.) They disallow mixed prints, patterns or ready-made dresses, flowered carpets or curtains; but their dishes, quilts, and towels are very gay. Anything useful can be made beautiful; it is only objects of vanity that are forbidden.

My acquaintance did not wear any objects of vanity. His "barn-door" or "broad-fall" trousers opened at the side. Amish clothes last for generations and never go out of style.

He was agreeable enough, yet hard to talk to. His fleshy, unlined face, a boyish pink under his bobbed haircut, seemed too young for his black beard and parenthood.

"Fine car," he said politely. "You are a good driver."

Why were they forbidden to own tractors or automobiles?

He spat off the end of his cigar; the silent little boy in

the back seat was all ears. "Well," said papa slowly, "the way our young men drive the horses so fast, if they had automobiles hardly anybody would be safe on the road."

We had reached New Holland and my two friends dismounted. "Four more boys and a girl at home," papa said with unexpected warmth, pulling out his wallet. "What's my bill for the ride?"

We parted, the farmer directing me to the People's Restaurant, the one that doesn't sell beer. Farther down the street a house bore a sign, "Religious Mottoes, Books and Postcards (of all kinds) sold here." The bell tinkled, and Mrs. Spangler, a Mennonite lady in a rather gay red bonnet, showed me her stock. The "Jesus Never Fails Egg-Timer" operated on the hourglass principle. The "God Is My All" zipper wallet and "The Lord Is My Shepherd" hot plate offered spiritual consolation for a flat purse or a burned finger.

There were no Amish in town, she said. They lived in the country, around Blue Ball.

"How did Blue Ball get its name?" I asked at the filling station. A stranger pointed to an old tavern across the road, from which hung a large blue ball, relic of the coaching days. But there were no Amish in Blue Ball.

"People say there's no difference between the Amish and the Mennonites!" Then he added, "Why, Mennonites will wear jewelry, buy automobiles and go to Atlantic City! You ought to see some real Amish while you're here." He whipped out a writing pad. "Tell you what, I'll give you a note to my wife; she teaches the Amish children over at Intercourse."

At the door, I handed the teacher the note of introduction from her husband — signed "Your Sugar, Christ R.

Goff" — and heard the youngsters, about evenly divided between Amish and non-Amish, as they lined up under pictures of Sir Galahad and George Washington to recite, "Let me live in a house by the side of the road and be a friend to man." A flag hung on the wall, but the Supreme Court has decided the Amish need not salute it. Then they tumbled out, the little girls with bonnets and the black-hatted boys shouting, "Old pooh-pooh face!" just like the children of the world. It must also be reported that at the Intercourse filling station a six-year-old Amish hit the jackpot and stuffed his pockets with bubble-gum. "We have a lot of trouble with our young people," said a bearded prophet drinking coffee. "They grow up to be a wild lot." Even the Good Humor man meets his match in the young Amish of Intercourse; they call to him as he drives along the lane, then run and hide when he gets out to sell his wares.

An Amish man emerging from the sidewalk telephone booth — house telephones are forbidden — waved cheerfully to a young couple passing in a buggy. After marriage, the boy will grow a beard and both will ride in a gray, box-like wagon like those which lined the street. Their preliminary courting is at Sunday night sings, where five hundred young people may gather, using the benches set up for morning service. They like such hill-billy songs as "Floyd Collins"; "It may not be a sand-cave, In which we find our tomb; But at the bar of judgment, We too must meet our doom." Officially, they do not listen to the radio or go to the movies, but the word gets around somehow. They can, however, visit the circus, if it has a menagerie; it is proper to look at the different animals God has made. (The Amish in Ohio until recent years would not use mules, because God didn't make them.)

Underneath their large bonnets, the Amish women wear the prayer-veil. A city woman asked a pretty Amish girl if she didn't get tired of wearing the same clothes.

"Oh, there are bonnets and bonnets!" she said earnestly. "We have fun like other people, don't think we don't!" There is even a rumor that some of the young people stop with friends in Lancaster to change clothes en route to Philadelphia.

A deacon's daughter once broke the rules by having her picture taken in Philadelphia. On Sunday she repented and confessed before the church. That night she handed the graven image to her father. "Du cannst sie havve. Papa, burn it in the stove." He looked at it and handed it back. "It is too lifelike, I cannot put it in the stove."

On cold nights, Amish young people used to bundle. A Discipline printed in 1837 warned that sometimes "something bad happens on account of it." There is probably some bundling yet, except in Iowa; for the Iowa settlements were led by a Pennsylvania preacher who left in 1851 to establish a non-bundling church.

The Amish do things their own way. Their clocks usually run half an hour fast, so that they will never miss a bus or keep anyone waiting. Under daylight saving they must remember "fast time, slow time, and our time." They invented prefabrication. At a house-raising in a Maryland colony started in 1939, a reporter asked why they constructed sides for the houses flat on the ground, instead of in the usual way. "Oh," said the foreman, "we'll have 40 to 50 here tomorrow, the sides go up easy."

They have no life insurance or lightning rods, because these show a lack of faith, but there are no homeless

Amish. Orphans are adopted in private homes; old people are cared for by the next-of-kin.

Amish farmers generally have the latest and best of horse-drawn machinery, self-binders and cultivators. (One who bought a tractor was allowed to keep it, for special reasons, if he took off the rubber tires.) "The time will come when all the farming in the country will be done by the Amish," Lancaster people say. Every Amish family has a purpose in life, to see the daughters married to good farmers and the sons established on good farms of their own nearby.

An old couple came to the office of a Lancaster real-estate broker to settle on a farm for the youngest boy. They brought their money in a bucket, and counted it out slowly, a process which took up a large part of the morning. It came to just a few hundred dollars less than the price. The broker, moved to pity, was about to shave the difference, when the old lady spoke up quietly:

"Herman, we have brought the wrong bucket."

Outside the hotel in Lancaster, I met an Ancient Mariner with wandering gray locks and clothes of rusty black. He is the nearest approach to an Amish press agent, a correspondent for the local press and Amish newspapers in other States. We had dinner together.

"Did you know that after every service, we have dinner for everybody — free?" he asked, his mouth full of schnitz-and-knipp. "Schnitz pies — hundreds and hundreds of them."

I asked about household conveniences.

"Some have gasoline stoves and washing-machines and water in the house," he said. "But no electric. Did you know that we use the Gregorian chant in our services —

and the oldest Protestant hymnbook, printed in Switzerland in 1564?"

There are one hundred Old Order Amish churches in the United States, with about ten thousand members. In Lancaster County, there are eighteen hundred Old Order Amish, all farmers except a few carpenters, broom-makers, carpet-weavers, and harness-makers.

The Amish newspaper correspondent used to have a cheese business, and what is still more unusual, he has been around the world. I asked why.

"Wanderlust," he said; adding after a moment, "And to follow the missionary journeys of the Apostle Paul."

The Reverend Calvin G. Bachman, a minister of the Evangelical and Reformed Church who has made a scholarly and sympathetic study of the Amish, believes that they are an example of what the early Anabaptists once were like toward the dawn of the Reformation — perhaps the best such example surviving in the world.

The pietist movement, which began the first Great Awakening in America and did so much to shape the old-time religion in many ways, came a little later. Like the Anabaptists, the pietists have for the most part long since merged into the flowing stream; but here and there they have left landmarks. Bethlehem, Pennsylvania, is famous chiefly for steel; but the Moravian pietists who settled it still sing in the great Bach Festival. At Winston-Salem, North Carolina, the before-dawn Easter Service of the Moravians draws crowds from many States.

Here and there the pietists formed Protestant monasteries and nunneries.

The State of Pennsylvania has taken over the Ephrata Cloisters, a few miles from Lancaster; the last families have only recently moved away. Now on sunny weekends the curious pilgrims file through the four-story "brother house," built in 1746 of wood, clay, and straw. The Cloisters were founded in the eighteenth century by Conrad Beissel, a pietist who separated from the Church of the Brethren, or Dunkards, over the issue of the Sabbath; Beissel became a Saturday man. A gifted musician, he composed a hymn with two hundred and fifteen stanzas.

"Watch the door!" cried the guide on the day I was there. The door was only five feet high, to make us bow and be humble, and sixteen inches wide, to remind us of the straight and narrow path. A city girl, as her head struck the door-frame, giggled happily; a young Dunkard couple in transition — the husband wore a black bow tie, his wife a black bonnet and a gay printed dress — looked at each other and doubtfully smiled. We climbed the narrow winding stairs to the big room with spinning wheels; here the brothers and sisters arose at midnight to break their rest for an hour of work and prayer. The tiny, celibate cells were furnished only with a board, on which they slept again until five, when they rose for another hour of prayer, and worked until nine, the hour for breakfast. After breakfast they worked again until the second and final meal at five in the afternoon. The wounded from the Battle of Brandywine were cared for here. All this and more we learned, before we came out into the bright sun, to the tourist stand with its Amish dolls and booklets on bundling.

Another group of German pietists who sprang up at

about the same time as the Dunkards took the name of the Community of True Inspiration. They grew gradually in various parts of Germany from about 1714 to 1749. Then they openly acknowledged that the gift of inspiration had ceased among them.

Their congregations dwindled until 1817, when a peasant girl from Alsace named Barbara Heineman was recognized as inspired. The reviving sect was now persecuted by the German Government; and in 1842 Christian Hertz was inspired to lead the community to America. At first they settled on the Seneca Indian Reservation near Buffalo, taking the name of the Ebenezer Society, and building four villages — Low, Middle, Upper, and New Ebenezer. (Ebenezer means "Hitherto the Lord hath helped us.") As their numbers grew, they moved again in 1855 to the richest land in Iowa, changed their name to the Amana Society (Amana means "Believe faithfully"). They built the villages of Amana — East, Middle, High, West, and South Amana, and Homestead. A friend of mine who as a girl taught school in Iowa waited to change trains one evening on her way home for the weekend, at an empty station.

She was surprised to hear a "plain" man accost her.

"We don't like that you should wait down here by yourself," he said. "Come on up to supper."

She was taken to a charming village in which church, store, school, and homes were built alike in the gabled German style; petunias, marigolds, and hollyhocks rioted in the gardens, grapes and hops climbed the trellises on the plain, unpainted walls. Each Friday for the remainder of her school term the Amana people fetched her from the depot to their communal supper in a big farmhouse on the hill — steak, sausage, the famous bread and smoked ham which the community sells, and lebkuchen for dessert.

The Amana Community was never as extreme as some. Although celibacy was highly esteemed in the early days, lovers were allowed to marry, after a probationary period in which they lived in separate villages. Education stopped usually at grammar school, but promising youngsters were sent away at community expense to learn medicine, dentistry, and other arts needed in the community. Many of the older women still cling to German peasant dress; the young people nowadays dress like the world, and sometimes go to movies without being rebuked. They believe that since the death of Barbara Heinemann in 1883, the gift of true inspiration has again departed, and their religious meetings are quiet. They are pacifists, holding a simple form of Christian orthodoxy without any marked peculiarities.

For the better part of a century, Amana was the most successful communistic settlement in America; its products were admired up and down the Mississippi Valley, the life of the people was famous for contentment and happiness. Families were allowed private homes, which they decorated inside as they chose, but shared communal kitchens; all were expected to work as they were able, but all were assured of the necessities of life. From time to time outsiders who shared the socialist faith, but not the religious belief which made it a success, came to live in Amana. Not many were able to adapt themselves permanently. According to one authority Amana "never regarded its communism as the working out of a social theory. It claimed only to be a church brotherhood whose structure, management, and control were born of necessity and circumstance. . . . So long as the faith that had brought the members together retained its glow and living power, just so long was it possible to maintain the integrity of the Church."

In the depth of the business depression in 1932, after long discussion and prayer, the members of the community abandoned communism, established an individual household economy, and set up the business enterprises separately from church control, as a producing and marketing co-operative. Wages, time clocks, personal bank accounts were introduced. There were jobs for everyone, and everyone who would eat must work. In recent years the co-op has done an annual business of millions of dollars in farm products, woolen goods, and fine furniture — copies of old German or American originals.

The Amana Church Society was formed to carry on the spiritual life. The settlement, it is reported, still looks the same; grapevines cover the dwelling houses, schools, churches, and hotels; the old millrace flows through the pastures and villages, and "the lake with its deep border of lotus is a glory in July." There are those who say that its underlying purposes have not changed either, and will eventually prevail.

When the plain people move to town, they gradually become more worldly, even as you and I. They give up their special dress. But they cling stubbornly to the chief essentials of the love-feast and foot-washing, and it was at a Brethren church within a stone's throw of the Capitol of the United States that I was invited to one of these. The requirement for participation was simple: one must first be at peace with all one's brethren.

The minister read from the Gospel of John:

> *So after he had washed their feet and had taken his garments, and was set down again, he said unto them, Know ye what I have done to you? Ye call me Master and Lord; and ye say well; for so I am. If I then, your Lord and Master, have washed your feet; ye also ought to wash one another's feet. For I have given you an example, that ye should do as I have done to you.*

"We will now go to our rooms," the minister said, "to observe the ordinance."

The women passed through a door to the right of the pulpit, the men to the left. We removed coats and shoes, placing socks inside. Each of us then girded himself with a long, spotless towel, took a tin basin, washed and dried his neighbor's feet, and sat down to be washed in turn. It was done without haste or talking, and after the two completed the washing, they stood and kissed each other. Then the men and women returned to the church for the love-feast: a spiced-tongue sandwich and a glass of water, placed on racks in the pews. In the hushed, candlelit church the crowd ate in silence. Holy Communion was administered, the people sang "Blest Be the Tie that Binds," and went out.

After a few moments on the sidewalk, some of the men lit cigarettes. Soon from the lighted church there rose a subdued, cheerful murmur as the women cleared away the supper things.

2. *THE BUTTON BAPTISTS*

*Some Primitive Baptists, who are Calvinists,
and some Free Wills, whose pedigree is even
older, exemplify the Anglo-Saxon contribution*

THE BAPTISTS of all kinds have remained, somehow, at the center of the old-time religion, even when they build fine brick churches and universities. The Presbyterians have a strong churchly tradition reaching back to Knox and Calvin; the Methodists have an historical link with the Church of England; but there is nothing behind the Baptists except the desire of the people to take religion into their own hands. A remark of a high United States official at a dinner party in our own times explains the attitude perfectly. Asked by the British Ambassador's wife what was his religion, he answered, "I am a South Carolina Baptist."

"Low Church, isn't it?" asked her ladyship.

"Madam," he replied, "you have no idea how low."

My father, a man of catholic tastes, preached and lectured on the Greek New Testament to Protestants of just about every denomination, and among the Baptists he knew the saints at Hell-for-Sartain Church in Kentucky, although I think he felt personally closer to those at Long Hope. But for one group he felt no sympathy. The Hard-shells, or "Anti-Missionaries," who had broken away from their brethren early in the nineteenth century, opposed missions, Prohibition, colleges, seminaries — just about everything he stood for. I was never allowed near a Hard-shell Church as a youngster; and encountered them only by chance during the nineteen-thirties, when for a local paper I covered a "singing convention" on the shoulder of Grandfather Mountain in North Carolina. The choirs who competed from all over the county were small groups of men, women, and children, clustered a few yards apart on rocks and hillocks of grass. They sang without accom-paniment; before each selection a leader held up a tuning-fork to take the sound. At first the music seemed strange and monotonous, and I did not know its significance. For this was the Sacred Harp music, of the old-time religion as it was before the days of The Great Revival.

Rejecting organs along with other innovations, clinging strictly to Calvinism so that they had no use for the re-vival songs old or new, the Old School or "Anti-Mission-ary" Baptists had their music set down in print for them in 1844 in *The Sacred Harp*. Before that, country Bap-tists used to sing entirely by ear, sometimes setting the words of their old hymns to secular tunes like "Barbara Allen" which they already knew. With the coming of the singing-schools and the shaped notes, they broadened their repertory to include any more recent songs which accorded with their views, as well as the old standbys like "Amazing Grace" from across the ocean.

A marriage hymn includes the following:

When Adam was created
  He dwelt in Eden's shade,
As Moses has related,
  Before a bride was made.

He had no consolation
  But seemed as one alone
Till, to his admiration,
  He found he'd lost a bone.

This woman was not taken
  From Adam's head, we know,
And she must not rule o'er him,
  It's evidently so.

Many years after this experience, in a small red-brick meeting-house on Georgia Avenue in the District of Columbia I heard the voices of the Primitive or Old School Baptists rise in song, unaccompanied, with a strong Appalachian twang. The Elder was Mr. Ben H. Seekford, Jr., on weekdays a teacher in a Washington high school, an earnest, mild-spoken redhead with a gay, non-Calvinist necktie. We were reminded in his sermon that there had recently been an election in this country, which brought to mind, he said, another election told of in the Bible.

"In this other election, held at the foundation of the world, everyone who wants in his heart to win has already won — isn't that good news?" As an afterthought he observed, "That should comfort some of those who lost in the other election." But not a soul living, he cautioned us, was able to move another soul into the Kingdom. That is solely the work of grace.

After the sermon an aged man on the front row, his

voice weak yet firm with conviction, prayed: "Make us all into one bundle of love, through the merits of Thy Son." Letters were read from members who were out of the city, and the people were urged to write to them.

Elder Seekford, a native of Luray in the Shenandoah Valley, told me something of their customs. Having none of the usual paraphernalia of organized churches or denominations and making no effort to convert anyone, the Primitive Baptists, although steadily dwindling in numbers, persist in many parts of the South and Middle West with a quiet tenacity. One church in the Virginia foothills, dating from the eighteenth century, now has a membership of three.

They have not wholly escaped schism. The "absoluters" hold that predestination or election applies, not only to salvation, but to the smallest affairs of daily life. "It makes them a little hard to get along with sometimes," the Elder remarked. But they have been a unit in opposing Prohibition. As a Kentucky boy I had heard rumors of the "Whiskey Baptists" and I was delighted to make their acquaintance at last.

"Of course we believe in being moderate," the Elder explained. "There have been cases where churches had to discipline their members, even preachers sometimes."

As to their music, it may be heard outdoors each August in a state-wide convention of Sacred Harp singers in Alabama; and at hundreds of smaller singing conventions throughout the Appalachian uplands. The gatherings are not strictly confined to Old School Baptists and visitors are cordially welcome. The editor of *The Sacred Harp*, B. F. White, himself is said to have been a Missionary Baptist, friendly disposed toward his Old School contemporaries. White, it is said, conducted singing-schools, often without pay, throughout the South, knelt in prayer before composing a tune, and — a man of little formal education — listened to the birds to study their natural harmonies.

In the blue mountains around Asheville lies the Valley of Religion, where our family used to spend its summers when I was a child. The valley lies roughly east by west, where the Swannanoa River has carved its channel between the precipitous heights of the Craggies and the Swannanoa Mountains. At its lower end, at Old Fort, the Southern Railway puts on two engines for the climb through the Royal Gorge to Ridgecrest. These are the heavy trains Tom Wolfe heard as a boy, whistling and echoing through the tunnels, climbing the grade with long sleek Pullmans and the dining-car agleam with alien napery and silver.

Our cottage was at Blue Ridge, the assembly grounds of the Y.M.C.A., but all through the valley were gathered in the summer months the most religious people from the most religious section of the U.S.A. The Southern Presbyterians met at Montreat, just across the valley from Blue Ridge; the Southern Baptists close by at Ridgecrest. Over beyond Asheville way were the Methodists at Lake Junaluska and the Episcopalians at Kanuga Lake. In the early nineteen-twenties the Fundamentalist-Modernist controversy shook all these verandas where comfortable families from the cities sang in their rocking chairs at sunset, and recited, "I will lift up mine eyes to the hills whence cometh my help."

At Blue Ridge the emphasis in the nineteen-twenties was on the "social gospel." Here the religious inter-racial movement in the South was beginning, the fruit of co-operation among white and Negro Y.M.C.A. workers in the First World War.

The walls of the front hall were lined with the hiking-sticks of teachers and social workers, among them Doctor S. C. Mitchell's. He was an historian at the University of Richmond, married to my mother's sister Alice. Of this remarkable family, I remember especially an impatient question which one of their sons — suddenly struck with the vast importance of the practical, modern world — asked his mother one day.

"Mother, after all, what can you *do?*"

Aunt Alice thought only a moment. "Well, I'll tell you what I can do. I can spell. I can find things in the Bible. I can quote Shakespeare. And I can be reviled, and revile not again."

In 1946, on the immense porch of Robert E. Lee Hall, perhaps the noblest piazza in the world, I found Doctor Mitchell still in his usual rocker at sunset. A very old man, as he talked with one of his grandsons he looked across the valley to the six-thousand-foot wall of the Craggies, his eyes liberal, hopeful, and undimmed. Nothing at Blue Ridge had changed greatly in twenty-five years. Near Lee Hall the college students who do the work of the place pitched horseshoes and sang revival songs with a slight, affectionate edge of satire. It was the valley itself which now seemed different to me; it had become fluid and alive. Behind the white verandas of orga-nized Protestantism and social welfare were the cabins of the devout mountain people; there was a connection, but I could not put my finger on it; a telescoping of space and time.

At the abandoned toll-house of a disused toll-road was

a cabin. A woman came to the door, toothpick in hand, retreated and advanced again in the mountain manner. Was there a foot-washing church nearby, I asked.

"You just passed it." She pointed to an unpainted pine building. "We just got it built last year. Afore that, things was turrible on this mountain, young folks playin' ball on Sunday and I don't know what-all."

Prayer meeting was tonight, at Sister Snyder's house. "There's not many that gathers out, but there's a few. Come and you're welcome. Proud to have you."

The trail to the Snyders' house was steep and narrow, the night, dark. A white-faced ghost barred the way, a stubborn bull calf. Maybe it was an omen to abandon the whole project of reporting on the old-time religion. I raised a stick threateningly, renewed my reporter's vows, and the critter bounded away. Through the window of the cabin, heads were bowed around the table under the lamp.

A Presbyterian home missionary I used to know in another part of the mountains, coming upon such a scene in the course of his pastoral calls, had knocked diffidently at the door.

"I hate to disturb you," he said to the head of the family. "It's been such a long time since I've seen old-fashioned family worship."

"Oh shucks, preacher, come on in," said the mountain man. "This ain't family worship. This here's the new Sears-Roebuck catalogue."

But it was not the catalogue in the Snyders' house. As I entered, a standing circle of a dozen men and women surveyed me silently, and the silence continued after I stated my name and place of residence.

At last a tall, grim-faced man with steel glasses said slowly, "Washington, D.C. That's a long way from here." We found seats in the living-room, and the silence still held. There was a Bible on the table by the lamp, some paper-backed hymnals, no two alike and none in their prime, two rockers and four straight chairs, and a bench on which a flaxen-haired young farmer held a young baby on his knee, while his wife held the next in size. Through an open door I glimpsed sleeping children heaped in the bedroom. The pastor, a short, youngish, black-haired man with a shy smile, spoke at last.

"Here's a good old song I know we can all sing, 'There's an All-Seeing Eye Watching You.'" There is, indeed, I thought; in the steady gaze of the tall man with glasses I felt a deep scorn. "Let's kneel in prayer," said the pastor, and the tall man began to address the Throne of Grace in a loud, loud voice, as if it were a long way off.

"May them that's gathered here tonight be gathered in sincerity and truth," he said with emphasis. "We pray for all o' them that's a-goin' down to Devil's Hell. And O Lord, send thy saving Spirit in good time. Raise our children right in the way. And when all is done, let all the credit be given in Thy Name, O Jesus. Amen."

We rose, and the All-Seeing Eye fixed his glasses on me from across the room.

"Perhaps the gentleman who's come so far to worship with us would like to take charge of the meetin'," he said. "I propose we let him read us the Scripture lesson."

This was what the bull calf had tried to warn me against, I thought. It was too late now. But the pastor was a Christian. Seeing my awful plight, he handed me the big Bible and said tactfully, "Suppose we sing another

song while the brother searches the Scriptures." We sang
a song about Jerusalem. I fumbled through the pages to
I Corinthians, 13. After the reading, there was another
expectant silence.

"We'd like to hear any testimony," said Pastor Triplett
quietly.

The honest things which I could not say flashed through
my mind. "I'm here to report, folks, on religious practices
among the hill-people. Please don't mind me, just go
ahead with the service." And then my head filled suddenly with the memory of a day in Jerusalem two years
before.

The arches of the crusaders sliced the August sunshine
in the narrow, uphill street.

"What's this tour?" asked the Red Cross girl who had
been in the Junior League in Tulsa, Oklahoma. "Old or
New Testament?"

"It's all old," said a wit among the soldiers. "Churches
and more churches."

It was hot at the Station where Jesus met His mother,
and the pilgrims were restless.

"Was it for this I sweated out six months in Cairo?"
asked the Red Cross girl.

"Jesus," said a big soldier simply, wiping his brow.

"The actual Way of Our Lord, of course, is six feet
under," explained the guide, an Arab Christian. "We are
now at the Chapel of Saint Veronica. Anyone wishing to
purchase religious articles may do so here, and have them
blessed at the Holy Sepulchre. Hats off, and no smoking."

The Chapel of Saint Veronica was small, and crowded
with incense burners and shiny lamps. Beneath a large
crown of thorns in the ceiling, a life-sized statuary group

depicted Saint Veronica wiping the blood from the face of Jesus. A stand did a fair business in religious articles.

The Garden Tomb, owned by the English, is a pleasant, open garden with a warm, spicy smell of pines. On a low cliff just outside the city wall a lady guide pointed out two shadowy eye-sockets and the traces of a mouth and nose in the stone. "Traditionally," she explained, "this has always been called Golgotha, the place of a skull."

The Irish boy was not much interested; there were no signs of an authentically holy place. The big soldier nudged me angrily in the ribs. "What's she tryin' to tell us happened here?"

On the ship home, I had put together these impressions of Americans in Jerusalem and found they added up to little, except to show that for some citizens even the memory of faith had dried up. But these would not be welcome tidings at the Free-Will prayer meeting. I stumbled through a few words about Jerusalem and sat down.

Now the flaxen-haired farmer handed his baby to his wife and rose to speak, stretching out his arms, palms outspread.

"I want to say that the way of the Cross lies in between us and the Promised Land — and we've all got to travel that road. I want to say that when we see a brother stumble and fall, even if our cross is heavy, we've got to lean down and help shoulder his'n. I want to say that I want to live each day with my neighbor, so that when the sun goes down I can say, 'I done right by ever'one truly, O Lord. My dealings with 'em was fair and above-board, and what I spoke about 'em, I spoke good.'"

These things he said with a deep, terrible earnestness,

as if each sentence cost him pain. I learned soon that this was the usual mountain method of speaking to one's Lord, but the first impression is appalling. And now, with astonishing effect, the young farmer dropped to an easy, conversational tone.

"You know they tell little children stories about the Ole Devil, how he's got hoofs and horns an' a tail. I want to say that the Devil can be the prettiest thing you ever saw. He can be fixed up to look like the nicest thing you ever saw for sale in the store." Suddenly he shouted, "O Lord, help us take a-holt of common things!" He held out his clenched fists. "Plain dirt common things that's best," he ended, and sat down by his pretty wife, who had no ribbon in her hair.

"I like that what you read," she said to me. "That Paul writes pretty."

We sang "How Beautiful Heaven Will Be," and stood for a closing round, the pastor going from one to another and saying, "Anyone that isn't feeling just right, let us pray for him." I was all right, I said.

"Let's pray for our friend later," said the pastor. "He's come a long way to see us. Maybe he's heard so many different kinds of religion talked, seen so much high society religion, that it's kind of unsettled him. We'll remember him."

"Sometimes hit just comes quiet-like — by easy stages, sort of," he said to me. "Just listen and you'll hear."

"What?" I asked.

"The Holy Spirit," said Mr. Triplett.

I next encountered Mr. Triplett on the highroad where my car had stalled. He is a mechanic on weekdays, and after a little tinkering with the carburetor had me going.

I was invited to go to another of his charges, next Sunday morning, near Old Fort.

It seemed possible that the handful of faithful at the church in the woods beyond Old Fort felt more at home than they would have in the stylish, brick Missionary Baptist Church in town. Their own church was finished — almost — in imitation paper brick, a naked gap of pine boarding in the belfry testifying to the need of cash. Inside were home-made benches and a pulpit. We sang "I'll Shake Hands with Mother Up There," and went to our classes. Sunday-School quickly formed itself by age groups in different corners, not without a quick, effective paddling of one or two youngsters. The children were the "card class," using gaily colored printed lessons about the size of a playing-card. In the men's class we had only The Book, and one copy of that, which we passed around, reading a verse in turn, the farmers anxiously sweating in anticipation of getting a verse full of long, Greek names. (It was a chapter of Acts, and rough going.) A little Free-Will dog ran happily between the benches wagging his tail.

We recessed for five minutes before preaching, the men squatting on their heels under a mimosa tree, taking deep consoling draughts of home-rolled cigarettes. I was called into the pulpit to repeat the travelogue about Jerusalem, before the sermon of the day.

"What Brother Robertson says, hit's all true," observed the pastor. "We can read about ever' one of those places he mentioned in the Bible. Hit tells it all. And shame on you little chi'yern for runnin' in an' out while he was talkin'."

A visiting brother from Asheville now prayed, on the

floor; this is a mountain style, akin to the Moslem; he knelt, bowing down and slapping the floor for emphasis, and it was disconcerting to suspect that this activity was partly directed at me.

"If there be a stranger in our midst that has been to far, distant, holy places and has heard The Call, O Lord! — Let him not be like the man that hid his light under a bushel."

Mr. Triplett now dismissed us, but not with any formal benediction. The congregation and minister, standing in a ring, shook hands.

"Is ever' one at liberty?" asked Mr. Triplett quietly. "Then we can go."

Mr. Triplett and his Free-Will friends trace their own denomination to a church organized in Wales in 1701, which emigrated to Pennsylvania that same year. Receiving a tract of land as a grant, the company prospered and sent missionaries to other Colonies, including North Carolina.

Long before the other Baptists, they had broken with the old doctrine of predestination, and accepted the new teaching of Arminius, who believed that Christ died for all and that "salvation is free." After The Great Revival, as most of their American brethren swung away from strict Calvinism and became known as "Missionary Baptists," the doctrinal difference melted and many Free Willys joined with the main body. They survive independently in some rural areas, an example of the early Baptists of the British Isles.

These seem to have arisen independently of the Anabaptist movement on the Continent. They probably sprang from the ancient, underground "dissent" from the

Established Church, which can be traced back to John
Wyclif, the first English Protestant, born around 1324.
His followers, called Lollards, believed that neither the
sacraments nor the Church was essential to salvation;
passing from hand to hand the manuscript of the Bible
which Wyclif first translated into English, they made converts rapidly until at one time Lollards may have been
a third of the population. Despite persecution, they never
died out. Their roots may even go back to the ancient
split between Anglo-Saxon peasant and Norman con-
queror; and the Lollard movement had a hand in the
great English peasant revolt of the Middle Ages, with its
famous jingle: "When Adam delved and Eve span, who
was then the gentleman?" Some say that Geoffrey
Chaucer was a Lollard at heart.

As to total immersion, the early Lollards stopped at the
water's edge. But they were among the most important
ancestors of the old-time religion, stressing the right of
each man to interpret the Bible, and the right of any man
or woman to preach. Long before Calvin was heard of,
they believed in predestination (a point at which the
Free-Will Baptists were among the first to break with
their fellows). The Lollards of the Middle Ages were poor
and hard-working, "cherishing the one desire to read, so
that the Bible would be intelligible." * They opposed
the pleasures of the wealthy class which persecuted them.
Lollards were against maypoles, morris dances, cards,
and other medieval diversions. They were probably the
first Protestants to "dress plain." The Methodists, the Salvation Army, the whole main stream of the old-time religion, derives in large part from them. And in America

---

* *The Religious Background of American Culture,* by Thomas Cuming
Hall. Little, Brown and Company, 1930.

their descendants among the plain, dissenting stock in Virginia and New England met with common people of European ancestry holding similar views.

I did not see the Free Wills again for several days, while I visited the Presbyterians in their comfortable, if Calvinist, hotel at Montreat. Nothing here had changed since my boyhood; down at the lake the young people splashed and shouted, a Scout troop with blanket rolls prepared the overnight conquest of Mt. Mitchell, and in the auditorium a lecturer told a story I had heard my father tell from that platform. "Had it been a good year?" asked the visiting minister of the president of the Women's Auxiliary. "Terrible," the good lady replied, "but thank God the Methodists haven't done any better."

The discourse rambled on to tithing. A Presbyterian businessman lived next to a Jew. They agreed one week to visit each other's churches.

On Friday night at the synagogue the Jew took from his wallet $17.50 for the collection.

"Do you give this much every week?" asked his Presbyterian friend.

"Oh, no. But this was a good week and I put in just ten per cent, rain or shine."

Next Sunday the Presbyterian placed his sealed envelope in the plate.

"How do you determine what to give?" asked the Jew. "I just pledge whatever I can afford each year," said his neighbor.

"Almost," said the Jew, "thou persuadest me to be a Christian."

Walking down the road to buy a pack of cigarettes at the nearest outpost of ungodliness, I was delighted to see my Free-Will friends high-tailing along in a small pick-up truck: Preacher Triplett, his wife and assorted babies, and Mr. Jenkins, the tall, lean brother with glasses who had given me such a stern inspection at the prayer meeting. It was a gay, lively party. They were on their way to a family reunion down off the mountain and I must go along. They had plenty of cigarettes.

As we swung around the curves, Mr. Jenkins chatted cozily. "You should have heard the preacher this mornin'. Preached the sweetest sermon you ever heard. It was like honey in a deep dish. Hit cut some so deep they couldn't speak. Yonder's Swannanoa Mountain," he said, pointing to an abrupt change of subject. "Been yarbin' there many a time after bloodroot and sang. If a child gets diarrhea in the spring, a dose will sometimes cure him up, save a big doctor bill.

"I don't go yarbin' just for the money," he continued. "Hit's partly that. But the Government's made an appeal. They need more yarbs for the boys overseas. Feller says to me the Government ought to do this. I says what *is* the Government? Hits us! We make the depressions, the booms and the wars!"

From this robust, Free-Will position he now shifted slightly toward the Calvinist view.

"Still and all, other things is comin', else it wouldn't be foretold like it is in the Book of Revelation. The last things is near, and all we can hope is that the young 'uns'll be better prepared for it than if it had come when we was young." He brushed a sticky, unprepared youngster off his knee.

There had been a disagreement in the church over the election of a pastor.

"Some folks insist that people see things just their way.

I say there ought to be agreement just on the big essentials — don't matter *what* church people belong to; if they're followers of Christ they'll find themselves comin' together at the point that matters.

" 'Bout the only difference between us and the Missionary Baptists, is that we invite ever'body to the Sacraments, and then we have the foot-washing."

Now the truck followed a winding lane through endless folds of the foothills to a wide clearing, where a long table was spread in the shade by a tarpaper shack, the summer home of Mrs. Triplett's parents, the Reverend and Mrs. Barney Clemson. The family reunion was in their honor. Inside the one-room house, Mr. Clemson, an old mountain preacher of the Missionary persuasion, held court, a bald-headed eagle with a rock jaw, a shrewd, quick smile, and eyes of love. On the two beds the pillows were crocheted "Father" and "Mother." We were late to the feast, and the old people were uneasy until we had been fed. ("Ain't there a Scripture verse about he that cometh at the eleventh hour shall find as much as the first-comers?" said Mr. Jenkins, his mouth full of chicken.)

Mr. Clemson was then eighty; in middle life he had taught himself to read from the Bible. One day while hoeing corn, he said, he felt the call. A Calvinist in theology, his eyes shone with the memory of a thousand local disputations.

"You know, I have some friends among the Holiness people, the tongue-talkers. One time a daughter died and they didn't want the undertaker to do his work — said it warn't necessary. But the undertaker embalmed the body anyway, and he done right — 'cause the Bible says plain that it won't be *this* body! And then there's the Wesleyan

Methodists and their Discipline that says no gold teeth — when the Book itself says the very streets up there will be paved with gold!"

His smile flashed, his eyes gleamed with every point and he tapped me on the knee, an old man already half over Jordan, looking backward with humor and without bitterness.

"Once I had an argument with Doctor Sells, a big city preacher, mighty fine man. You know we're hard-heads up here about the perseverance of the saints. Doctor Sells asked me finally, 'Do you mean to say that a man has to *die* in order to be saved?' And I told him, 'I've never seen one go to Heaven yet that wasn't dead.' And I believe that baptism's essential. You know when Paul and Silas were in the jail-house, and the jailer found the door open, and was about to kill himself with mortification? And Paul said to him, 'What you're goin' to do? You think we're goin' to break out of this little ole jail when we haven't done anything wrong?' and the jailer answered, 'What should I do to be saved?' And Paul told him, 'Believe on the Lord Jesus Christ and be baptized, thou and thy family!'

"I had a good woman in my church who asked me to dinner and told me right out she'd voted against me in the election for sheriff. I asked her why. She said, ' 'Cause you warn't hard enough on the young folks in your preachin'.' She had a daughter that used lipstick and painted her fingernails.

"So next Sunday in the pulpit I said, 'Better not put any money in the collection plate until I preach; you might not like what I got to say.' And I gave it to 'em straight — *hit's the people that have the raisin' of the young 'uns that's responsible*. And, anyway, it ain't lipstick and painted toenails that's most important."

"They'll wash off," said Mr. Jenkins.

"Hit'll wash off, and they won't take it with 'em when they go. They just won't *need* 'em up there any more. We'll have hearts to love and tongues to praise — there'll be no more sorrow there." He stopped a minute.

"You know, preachers is always preachin' on little things. I had a brother help me once with a revival; he held forth at length about worldiness, card-playin' and so on. On our way up the mountain afterwards, he asked me if I cared what he'd told 'em. 'Of course I cared,' I said, 'they're my people.'

" 'I laid it to 'em straight tonight about their habits,' he said in a kind of satisfied way. Then he took a big plug of tobacco out'n his mouth.

" 'That there's a habit of your'n,' I said. 'Oh,' he said, 'I just take a little for my stomach's sake.' "

Mr. Clemson smiled. "You know there's them that preaches the Bible and chews tobacco, and them that chews the Bible and preaches tobacco. There was another man that wanted to argue, said God doesn't know ever'thing about us. 'Does God know I'm goin' to sit on that log?' he asked me. I told him, 'Yes.' 'Then I'll fool Him, I'll sit on this'n,' he said."

The old man laughed at the memory until tears came in his eyes. We thanked them for their hospitality.

"Sixty people and all relatives and no drunkenness or quarrels, and ever'body well behaved," he said. "Goodbye."

I did not see Mr. Clemson again. He died the following winter, full of wisdom. Pastor Triplett, his Free-Will son-in-law, has written from time to time that he hopes this book will prove a means of grace, although he does not consider that he and his flock really represent the old-time religion. That lies up another creek in an outlaw parish where even the Church of God preacher carries a gun.

3. *TONGUES AND SNAKES*

The fire of Cane Ridge still falls upon the various Churches of God, including the Church of God with Signs Following

IT IS NOT in any of its big institutional branches that we come closest to the contemporary flow of the sap in the religious liberty tree. We shall have to visit people who are quite likely to be found shouting, screaming, jumping, carrying on other activities as a co-product of religious enthusiasm, being thoroughly human and natural. The events narrated in the New Testament are still the most exciting news the human race has ever had; and for many Americans the excitement, far from wearing off, seems to be just beginning.

The census lists seven independent bodies calling themselves the Church of God. There may be dozens more in the depths of the Great Smoky Mountains. I have been told of the Runaway Church of God, so called because it fled from a pending church merger, pastored by an old man who rides a blind mule and cannot read, but knows the Bible and the Declaration of Independence. Also, there are somewhere the Church of Brother Jesus God Almighty and the awe-inspiring Church of God, Which is the House of God, Which is the Ground, the Pillar of Truth Without Controversy.

156

The Church of God and Saints of Christ was established by the late William Crowdy, a dining-car cook on the Santa Fe, who received the revelation that the Negroes are the descendants of the Lost Tribes of Israel — the other Jews having lost their color through admixture with the whites.

A few of the groups called Church of God do not tongue-talk, and are somewhat embarrassed by the new-comers. One of the first of these older groups was established by a minister of the German Reformed Church who had taken part in The Great Revival in the early part of the nineteenth century.

All the various Churches of God, together with the Assemblies of God, numerous "Full Gospel" tabernacles, and other Pentacostal or Holiness groups throughout the country, descend in spirit from the historic excitement at Cane Ridge. Here and there in the back country, the "jerks," the "unknown tongue," * and other seizures have never wholly died out in revival meetings from the year 1800 to the present day.

Soon after the Civil War great Holiness revivals sought

---

* Belief of the Holiness people that they can, at times, speak with "other tongues," or, as they commonly say, "the unknown tongue," derives from the second chapter of the Acts, in which is set forth an account of the descent of the Holy Ghost on the eleven apostles.

"And when the day of Pentecost was fully come, they were all with one accord in one place. . . . And there appeared unto them cloven tongues like as of fire, and it sat upon each of them. And they were all filled with the Holy Ghost, and began to speak with other tongues, as the Spirit gave them utterance. . . . Now when this was noised abroad, the multitude came together, and were confounded, because that every man heard them speak in his own language. And they were all amazed and marveled, saying one to another, Behold, are not all these which speak Galileans? And how hear we every man in our own tongue, wherein we were born?"

to recapture the "personal experience" of early Methodism. The Salvation Army, which originated in England,
and the Church of the Nazarene, as well as smaller offshoots like the Pillar of Fire, represent this first phase of
the movement. Generally it taught that the believer, after
the initial experience — salvation — should go on to be
sanctified by the Spirit, and thus enabled to live a holy
life. Sanctification was the "second blessing." Late in the
nineteenth century and early in the twentieth, others
began to teach the doctrine of a third blessing, the baptism of the Holy Ghost, usually manifested by "speaking
in tongues."

Such is the general background of the Pentecostal
groups, which, incidentally, include the fastest growing
denomination in the United States, the Assemblies of
God. Statistics are hard to get, but an estimate of half a
million to a million members for all the various Pentecostal
Holiness churches certainly would not be too high. They
draw largely from dissatisfied Baptists and Methodists,
who charge formality, coldness, modernism, and other
failings, or who may lack the clothes to make them feel
comfortable in the older churches.

Several Churches of God have their headquarters in
East Tennessee. At Chattanooga is the (Original) Church
of God. At Cleveland I found the headquarters of two
bodies — the Church of God and the (Tomlinson) Church
of God — resulting from a dispute which involved church
property.

The present overseer of the (Tomlinson) Church of
God, the smaller of the two bodies, received me cordially
in the church offices opposite a handsome brick tabernacle.
He is M. A. Tomlinson, a frank man of middle age, sandy-

haired, freckle-faced, with gold-rimmed glasses and a serious look. He feels greatly, he says, the responsibility which he inherited from his father, the late A. J. Tomlinson, who founded the sect.

Atop a mountain in far western North Carolina, near Ducktown and Turtletown, Tennessee, the late Mr. Tomlinson "prayed and prevailed" all through the night of June 12, 1903. He had been led by the Spirit to the mountain-top, and on the morning of June 13 he received the first vision of the Church of God of the Last Days. He thereupon left the top of the mountain and went down to the house where he had been meeting with a few members of a church called the Holiness Church of Camp Creek. He joined this group with the understanding that it was the Church of God spoken of in the Bible. His friends agreed with him that his revelation fulfilled Psalm 132:6 — "We found it in the fields of the wood."

This sylvan slogan, "fields of the wood," has been generally adopted by the (Tomlinson) Church of God. They have given the name to the mountain on which Mr. Tomlinson had his vision. The story is now related there upon a concrete marker, and the whole area has been landscaped and laid out with concrete roads and walks.

The (Tomlinson) Church of God holds its great August camp meeting in Cleveland, Tennessee. Thousands of visitors come from the surrounding hills to attend this meeting. They sleep under canvas or in hay wagons. The lame, the halt, and the blind make a procession to the altar, where the Spirit is invoked on their behalf.*

There seems no reason to doubt many remarkable cures

---

* A program of this convention once carried the notice, "Visitations of the Holy Ghost, 9 p.m. — Thursday."

reported among the Pentecostal and other small sects, and the subject may deserve a closer scrutiny by the psychosomatic division of the medical profession than it has so far received. The Holiness folk, lacking the efficient machinery of larger churches, cannot document their cures convincingly, and their best proof remains their honesty and candor. (In Charleston, South Carolina, a newspaperman in charge of the "church" page once received a notice from a Pentecostal minister that "Faith-healing will be discontinued this week, due to the illness of the pastor.")

"God laid His finger on some of the people here to-night," said a young Assembly of God minister at Dayton, Tennessee, who had held healing services at the Four-Square Gospel revival services earlier in the evening. Cancer cures had been reported by members of the congregation.

We sat in a pew during the "tarrying service," while two little girls, perhaps ten and fourteen years of age, lay stretched on the floor at the altar, their arms reaching silently toward Heaven, hoping to receive the "baptism." Their mothers had covered them with coats to keep them from catching cold.

Healing is always uppermost in the minds of some of the worshipers. As he started his sermon of the evening on the subject of sin, the preacher asked his listeners to say what they hated most, expecting such suitable replies as whiskey, movies, card-playing, and so on. But a brother in the front pew promptly answered, "Indigestion." The people laughed, their eyes on the model airplane which hung from the ceiling, with "Missions" printed on one wing.

People from the local Church of God were present, too. I asked the Assembly of God minister to explain some of the differences in belief.

"Just minor matters," he said. "We agree on essentials. But take this" — he touched his gold tie-clasp — "the Church of God folks would think it was against holiness."

In Chattanooga, I went to a (Tomlinson) Church of God revival in the company of the evangelist of the occasion, whom we shall call Brother Purvis, a short, tubby man with button-black eyes. His face filled with fear when I mentioned the Ku Klux Klan. A fiery cross had recently burned a few blocks distant from his home in an East Tennessee town. "Although it might have been on account of the union," he said. (A C.I.O. organizer had recently moved into the region.) Brother Purvis told me of his own experience with the Klan, a few years previously, in Atlanta, Georgia.

Atlanta real-estate interests had brought a lawsuit against a Church of God of which he was pastor, because its services disturbed the residents in a fashionable subdivision. Failing to win the case in court, the real-estate men, he said, enlisted the efforts of the Klan. One night, as the preacher was eating supper in a café, two strangers called for him, flashed deputy sheriff's badges, and took him for a ride in the woods, where a carload of the Klan waited.

"They beat me almost to death," he said. For three months Purvis hereafter had lived out in the woods, rapidly losing weight and seeing his family only on sneak visits at night, until Doctor Louie D. Newton, president of the Southern Baptist Convention, and other church leaders in Atlanta had come to his rescue.

We drove through Chattanooga to a nice new brick church in a working-class suburb. A meeting was in progress; it had started a few nights ago, "sort of spontaneously." The pews were sparsely filled as yet; the floor was red-carpeted; in one corner stood the national colors, in the other the (Tomlinson) Church of God flag, a red-and-white emblem with scepter, star, and crown, destined to wave over all the earth. On the platform stood the tithe-box (tithing is required for all members), and on the lower level before it was the altar, a small oblong bench at which worshipers kneel to "come through." On the pulpit hung a Roman Catholic crucifix.

The local pastor — the sort of intelligent young man with a face like a *Saturday Evening Post* cover, who might begin by working in a filling-station and end up as owner — kissed a middle-aged workman squarely on the lips. This is the "holy kiss," enjoined by Saint Paul in Timothy. The week's announcements were made and visitors were introduced. Each rose to be applauded, like strangers at a Rotary luncheon.

A sister, with a sweet, rather vague, spectacled face, asked prayers for a sick neighbor.

" 'Scuse me for bringin' this up now," she added humbly, "but I thought maybe some of you all could go an' see her."

The pastor reported that his own child, who had been ill, was much better — "only trouble we have now is keeping her in bed" — and all the parents smiled.

Now we kneeled to make individual intercessions, and pandemonium lasted until the pastor said, authoritatively, "Thank you, Jesus." As the pastor took the offering, a guitar, banjo, and piano played lively swing, and my pew neighbor, a diffident youth, asked in a whisper what church I belonged to. "Well, there's heaps of good in all churches," he said, and inquired if our church had an orchestra? No, I said, just an organ. Maybe we could have an orchestra some day, he said politely.

A young girls' quartet began to sing in close harmony. The pianist beat out the blue licks. One of the girls, as she sang "I Got Happy Down In My Heart," suddenly stiffened with cramp, her upturned face contorted with a spasm; she sobbed and cried for joy. Clapping began in noisy rhythm throughout the church.

"Hold up your hands!" shouted the pastor. Upon one and another of the worshipers the Power fell, and they began to jerk.

Brother Purvis, the preacher of the evening, now took over the pulpit, his face gleaming with excitement.

"God's coming!" he shouted. "He's here now! What is this thing we all feel?"

As the young pastor read a Bible verse about the diverse ways of the Spirit, Brother Purvis expounded. "That means we don't all get the Holy Ghost in the same way. Some of us jump up and down." He illustrated this enthusiastically, shaking like Saint Nick.) "Some of us just run around." He trotted briskly up and down the platform, calling en route to the congregation, "Don't we have a good time!" until everyone was laughing. At the first Scriptural mention of speaking tongues, he paused for breath and began to explain the essentials of the "Holiness" theology.

"The first blessing is conversion, then sanctification, when the Holy Ghost washes out our old sins and we experience the blood. *Then,* after the Old Adam is dead,

we're ready for the Baptism of the Holy Ghost, speakin'
through us in tongues. It happened at Pentecost, but it
isn't the *same* as Pentecost. Lady up North said to me"
(he mimicked her stylish tones), " 'Have you had your
Pentecost?' I said, 'No, and I haven't had my Fourth of
July!' Pentecost was just the day when this first happened!"

Brother Purvis was shouting now, sweat rolling down
his ecstatic face.

"I want you all to be happy. Raise your hands and
pray for the Holy Ghost!"

Amid the ensuing uproar, the evangelist shouted at us
encouragingly, "Some folks laugh at us for saying 'glo-glo-
glo' just to get started, but after we get started, the words
just start pouring out and can't be stopped! How do they
explain that?"

"Glory, Hallelujah!" A middle-aged woman in front of
me screamed, her body twisting, hands over her head. She
jabbered, repeating over and over — "She — min — ne —
o, she — min — ne — o"; and as soon as she stopped, others
began. The young pastor was sprinting briskly up and
down the aisle, as if warming up for the hundred-yard
dash. The solid, square-jawed workman was jumping up
and down, his sad-faced wife was having a wordless
spasm, and all the worshipers were shouting and screaming. Now Brother Purvis gave the invitation to the altar.
The first call was to the unsaved; but as no one appeared
for this purpose, he proceeded to the real business in
hand. "Anyone here would like to come to know Him
better? If so, come forward, while we sing the invitation
hymn."

The young pastor tugged gently at my sleeve; I shook
my head, but two young girls in red dresses went forward

and knelt at the altar. Others who had previously received the blessing crowded close around to help, the unsanctified remaining in the background. Upon her failure to burst out in the Unknown Tongue, one of the girls promptly gave up; but her friend hung on, straining, her head flung back, her face in the semblance of a trance. A jabbering older woman thrust her head within inches as if some spark might pass between them to ignite the reluctant Spirit.

Nearly an hour passed until most of the congregation had departed. Outside on the lawn, small children, held in leash by their parents during the meeting, were playing tag. The young pastor glanced at his watch.

"Sister, have you come through yet?" he asked quietly.

Some psychologists, in regard to the tongue-talkers, have swung around to a new position: It is good for people to let themselves go. (A *Life* article during 1948 described the new cult of the "Activists," who seem to be a sort of Holy Roller without religious or other motivation.)

Disturbed by the emotional outbreaks of the rapidly growing Pentecostal movement, onlookers like the artist Thomas Benton have wondered if some ambitious leader might not turn religious enthusiasm into a more sinister direction. It is true that the industrious Smith and Winrod circularize their ministers; and in a cabin deep in the Cumberlands, I encountered a "licensed evangelist" of "The People's Institute of Applied Religion," listed as a Communist-front organization by the Department of Justice.

In October, 1948, one independent white Church of God had gone over with Pentecostal enthusiasm to the support of Henry Wallace, then running for President with Communist backing. Mr. Wallace was invited to address its annual assembly, which I found in a combined political and religious ferment, at Dalton, Georgia. The walls were draped with Wallace banners, sound-trucks reconnoitered in front of the building, and inside the packed auditorium delegates from several Southern States listened as preachers mixed the old-time religion with the Progressive platform. "If you don't know what Jim Crow means, you'd better find out, 'cause you'll never get to Heaven if you support Jim Crow," cried one delegate.

I inquired how their beliefs differed from that of other churches.

"They believe the Devil is bound," said a tall, gloomy brother, sulking outside the hall because he had not been paid for his labor in hauling chairs.

The ruling Elder of the Church, the Reverend T. C. Pratt, confirmed this theological position. They believe that the Devil is bound; and the oratory conveyed a strong impression that unless Wallace were elected President, the Devil would get loose.

But in general, the Pentecostal groups steer clear of politics; most of them live in expectation of an early Second Coming; and a depth of feeling often underlies their "manifestations." I read with interest and respect the published testimony of a New England woman, who described a terrible calamity for readers of the Church of God *Evangel*:

> *On February 16, 1943, I lost my home by fire. I lost three children: one girl twenty-eight years old, and her little boy five; and two sons, one twenty-two and the other eighteen years. My boys died in the hospital. My*

daughter got an elderly woman and her little seven-year-old girl to the window and was overcome saving her little boy. Eight souls in all lost their lives, as I, being a trained nurse, had a convalescent home. . . . I had a son in the U.S. Army, also one in defense work in the Dutch West Indies. It cost $28 to send him a message. The Red Cross came in and sent one to him, also to the soldier. The Red Cross took care of everything. The Lord sent help when it was needed. He always comes on time, praise His sweet name. I just cannot praise Him enough. He has done so much for me. . . .

As we all prayed, the glory of the Lord filled the room. Oh, we had so many of God's people with us. It was wonderful. . . . I knelt at each casket and said a prayer. When I reached the last one, I prayed, "Not my will but Thine be done," and the Power fell. Even the undertaker said he had never witnessed anything like it. Ten preachers attended the funeral. . . . I have never questioned why all this had to come to me, but I did pray for strength to bear it.

Some remarkable people, at one time or another, have been attracted to the Pentecostal groups. Marcus Bach, the most indefatigable reporter on American religion and a minister of the Reformed Church, tells of receiving the "blessing" (and also how he lost it) in his book of travels, *Report to Protestants.* Among the students at Union Theological Seminary in New York and other intellectual centers of religion are men with a Pentecostal background.

The larger of the two Church of God groups having its headquarters at Cleveland, Tennessee, showed clear indications at the time of my visit of being on the cultural upgrade. For example, the weekly paper which contained the testimony of the trained nurse, included discussions by psychologists of child-raising, reprints by established writers such as Philip Wylie, and a scholarly discussion of the pre-Christian origins of the doctrine of the Holy Spirit, by a converted rabbi. This sect had recently purchased the Cleveland land and buildings of Bob Jones College, an expanding Fundamentalist institution which had moved elsewhere. Here they were setting up their own college; and there was also talk of merger with other Pentecostal groups.

Thus there appear to be two movements in the old-time religion, both still vigorous — toward separatism, and toward union. As a church prospers, it sets up mission boards, colleges, seminaries, and other enterprises; often its doctrines become less "literal," and it moves gradually toward closer relations with others of like views. Meanwhile, somewhere in the United States a new sect is splintering off.

Church historians say that the two movements can be traced back toward the dawn of Christianity; but in the United States, under religious freedom, they have shown most clearly, and sometimes with surprising results.

A clergyman waiting for the bus to Chattanooga introduced himself as Father Adamz, the parish priest at Sewanee, Tennessee. How were the snakes in this section, I asked casually. Father Adamz jumped.

"Why, the best I ever had!" he said. "I was out all day yesterday getting some new ones."

It was my turn to be startled at the thought of snake-handling in the Episcopal Church; but the minister, it seemed, collected rattlers only as a hobby.

We fell into relaxed conversation as the bus twisted down the steep curves; he had been converted in a Baptist Church, and had served as a Methodist and a Congregational minister before taking Episcopal orders. To show fellowship with backwoods foot-washers he had once walked twelve miles from Sewanee, only to find that his orders were not considered valid and he was allowed only as a spectator.

He recommended for my purposes the Church of God With Signs Following After.

The river road led through East Chattanooga into sparsely settled territory. In the night sky, Lookout Mountain hung brilliant with lights. Over these dark flatlands a strong breeze blew from the garbage dump. At a small Negro settlement I asked directions of a café proprietor. "I'd leave 'em alone if I was you, boss," he said.

On a rutty road several cars and trucks were parked by a two-room shack, dimly lit with oil lamps. From a small tent nearby rose a primitive flaring light and the sound of singing. Open on one side, the tent was screened by unmatched boards and torn, dirty canvas. In the outside darkness at the back, a courting couple took time out now and then to peer through a rent at the proceedings.

Those seated on the benches inside were spectators, too. A baker's dozen of the Dolly Pond Church of God With Signs Following After, who had come into town for the nightly revival, formed a sort of troupe at the front around the oil-drum pulpit. From another oil-drum at the side the flames leaped alarmingly toward the canvas roof.

The preacher was George Hensley, an able old man with a keen brown face and blue eyes which had seen much suffering.

"Hit's the rulers ever' time," he was shouting, while a woman standing at the oil-drum read the story of Christ and Nicodemus. "Hit's the rulers that persecutes the people." An old-fashioned, vigorous mountain preacher, Brother George slapped his knee and danced vigorously about. Serpents had already been handled and he was preaching now for converts.

"Now, brethering, I'm an ignorant man. I can't read nor sign my name. When they arrested me, the judge was a-feared to let the serpents come in the courtroom. But *I've* handled 'em all my life — been bit four hundred times 'till I'm speckled all over like a guinea-hen. But the judge wouldn't look at 'em!

"And he was a *learnt* man," he concluded triumphantly. "Now, read over there in Hosy. Wait a minute 'til I fix this telephone. I'm a leetle bit deaf." He paused to adjust his hearing aid.

In 1909, on White Top Mountain, near Grasshopper, Tennessee, George Hensley, already a follower of the "Holiness," had first pondered over some verses he had heard from the last chapter of the Gospel of Mark, verses 17, 18: "And these signs shall follow them that believe; In my name shall they cast out devils; they shall speak with new tongues; they shall take up serpents; and if they drink any deadly thing, it shall not hurt them; they shall lay hands on the sick, and they shall recover."

Mr. Hensley felt that the verse was a definite command from the Lord, given after His resurrection. He found a big rattlesnake under a rock, knelt and prayed for "the Power"; then with a shout, he grasped the snake and held it with trembling hands. For the rest of his life he has preached snake-handling until the cult has spread by word of mouth through the whole Appalachian region, and beyond.

Brother George now told us how, in the prime of life, he had been crushed in a Kentucky coal mine.

"They sent for the machine and pumped life into me. And for a year I lay in the bed, this arm and this leg paralyzed. They said I'd never walk again. But they carried me to a tent where I was prayed for, and right then I began to move — little by little." He pranced and pounded his knee with vigor. "This very minute there's some that call themselves Holiness, a-lyin' in the Chattanooga hospitals, talkin' in the Unknown Tongue!"

His sarcasm was understandable; for the Signs Following people do not hold with doctors or medicines. They have been known to drink poison, to walk barefoot on a mass of rattlers, and to handle fire: even to put their hands in the flame of a blow-torch.

After a Tennessee statute against snake-handling in 1947, old Brother George refused, as a matter of principle, to pay a fifty-dollar fine (although friends had offered the money), and went on a road-gang. As he began to weaken in the hot sun, his lawyers obtained an appeal to the criminal court, where the case was dismissed.

"I'll handle 'em even if they put me on the road-gang again!" the old man shouted. "Just you wait! *Now* hit's handlin' serpents that's agin' the law, but after a while hit'll be against the law to talk in tongues, and then they'll go after the Bible itself!" He waved the Book defiantly.

Four nights passed before I saw the serpents handled; meanwhile, I met several of the church members.

An elderly deacon from Dolly Pond, a remote mountain

hamlet some thirty miles from Chattanooga, explained the delay. "We've got to be perfect in love," he said seriously. He is a big man with intense eyes. "We've got to be in the Spirit. Say you're a writer? Well, you're welcome. But there's just one thing a fellow wrote about us that I didn't think was fair. He said we're poor and ignorant; and I guess we are. But we don't mean for our *children* to grow up ignorant. I've got three children and I see that they go to school. I want 'em to have it better than I've had."

Another son is dead of snake-bite. A husky young man who worked in a plant near Chattanooga, he had preached the faith to his fellow workers. The men in the plant had warned him of danger; once he had replied, "I may be bitten some day to prove to unbelievers that the serpents will kill, and that we can only handle 'em when God anoints us to handle 'em."

After his death from a snake-bite, which he received at a brush-arbor service, two thousand persons attended his funeral at Dolly Pond; at the climax of the service, six large struggling snakes, including the killer, were thrown into his coffin.

On the oil-drum lay a loaf of store bread which Brother Ramsay, the preacher of the evening, had brought for a bread-breaking. This was a new service, "right out of the Bible," as the preacher explained. He invited every Child of God present to come forward and participate. But no one sat on the front bench except a skeptical youngster, blowing a huge bubble of gum.

Brother Henry now rose and began to speak his mind about the proposed innovation. He made it clear that he could not break bread if he found any meanness in his heart toward anyone else. He intended to search his own heart first, and he advised the other members to do the same, lest they eat and drink "their own damnation, as the Bible says."

Deeply stirred, he broke out in the Unknown Tongue. Others began to talk also, some in plain English, while the preacher appealed for order.

"They've got a confusion amongst 'em," explained a spectator in a whisper. They disagreed, he said, about the words to be used at baptism. Brother Henry and his faction thought that the sacrament should be "in Jesus' name," while the others believed in pronouncing the Trinity. The dispute itself did not come out in the open, but was reflected in scraps of incoherent preaching, first by one, then another. Brother Henry, at one point, denied that he was a "Jesus only," explaining that Jesus certainly had a Father.

From time to time the church members tried to "pray it out," kneeling on the floor and speaking loudly in tongues, while some had violent jerks and convulsions. But still the "cross-up" persisted.

Now an old man among them rose and said: "I've had the Holy Ghost for twenty-eight years. Seems like there's a confusion here. 'Tain't God that causes the confusion. Let's see what we can do."

Upon this, the men began to embrace, and the women likewise; there was no embracing or kissing between the sexes, but the grizzled farmers held each other closely as in a waltz, and the women, in plain dresses without ornaments or hats, hugged and kissed.

In an effort to resolve the difficulty, they also sang: "Dust on the Bible," "I Got Happy Down in My Heart," and "The Great Speckled Bird."

But no one came to the altar that night. The bread-breaking was put off, and the snake-box stayed in the lamplit shack behind the tent.

I saw only one collection taken during the revival; it amounted to $5.40. The Signs Following Church has no paid ministers and makes few appeals for funds.

On another night, when the confusion about the baptism had been straightened out, Brother Henry preached a straight revival sermon.

Outside in the shadows, the sightseers lingered. "If I got to go to Heaven handlin' snakes, I just won't go," said a mill-hand's wife. Two boys of eight or nine had a running spit-fight on the edge of the circle of light. Deep in the shadows stood a silent, unhappy man. "They preached against me last night," he said. "All I done was sell candy-bars, but they preached against me 'cause the folks et 'em durin' meetin'."

At the oil-drum pulpit where a woman read the Scriptures, Brother Henry strummed his guitar lightly as he preached in a light cadence. "Some folks say, 'What is adultery?' I say read the Bible and you can find out if you're in it, and if you're in it and don't get out of it, you're Hell-bound. And if you find your brother in a fault, don't go to nobody else and talk about it. Go straight to him and tell him, 'Brother, I seen you in a fault.'"

He told his assistant to continue reading. "But Peter said unto him, 'Thy money perish with thee.' God don't want your money. He just wants your life. You can just put your life right on the altar and get the good blessing. Won't somebody come?

"You can get the Holy Ghost without a-bein' baptized.

You can get it bein' baptized. I've seen 'em many a time come up out of the water shoutin' to glory and speakin' in tongues. But one time they was two groups bein' baptized on opposite sides of the same river, one in the name of the Father, Son, and Holy Ghost, and one in the name of Jesus Christ, and they *both* come up shoutin'. One of them ghosts ain't holy — 'cause there's no disputation when folks has got the Holy Ghost. Don't matter how few there is, if there's only one or two, when they come together on some point or other, then they're headin' right."

His voice rose, he had stopped strumming now.

"If one verse in God's Word don't count, the others don't count! If the water baptism don't count, the Holy Ghost don't count, and if the Holy Ghost don't count, the serpents don't count!"

He broke into the Unknown Tongue, and resumed. Flames leaped to the canvas ceiling from the open stove. Brother Henry kicked and danced. "Oh, I'd do *anything* to keep from going to Hell! Wouldn't you, folks? Don't you care about your soul? Won't somebody come?

"Maybe there's somebody here tonight that's never had the Holy Ghost. May even be a sinner man or a sinner woman that ain't even been saved. Won't somebody come?

"I like to see serpents handled, I like to see anything done that's done under the power of God. But what I like best is to see sinners up here at the altar, a-strugglin' through. Someone's under conviction tonight. I'll keep on preachin' if they put me on the chain-gang. I'll stay here all night. I want some victory in God."

His voice was soft and desperate. "Won't somebody come?"

No one came to the altar that night. Brother Henry soon left for Florida to conduct meetings there.

I tried to locate the Church of God With Signs Following more definitely as a branch of the family tree. To many they seem a trifle eccentric; but their belief is certainly based on the Bible as they understand it. They are closer, in many ways, to the main stem of religious liberty than the rest of us. They not only "believe in religious freedom," they are willing to go to jail for it.

Critics of the snake-handling practice (who are numerous) suggest that part of the blame lies with the educated, high-salaried preachers of other Southern churches, who know the historical origins of the Bible but have been afraid to pass this knowledge on to the people. For example, a conservative Baptist theologian said of the snake-handlers, "Those folks base their practice on a verse that doesn't even belong in the Bible. It's in the doubtful end of Mark." Consulting a "Schofield" edition of the King James Version — an edition much favored by Fundamentalists — I found a footnote at the end of Mark explaining that these verses are not found in the oldest manuscripts.

On the last night of my sojourn among them, the church had erected a new and better tent in another part of Chattanooga. A metalworks sent a bright blast into the sky, and neighborhood Negroes stood outside the tent-flaps and murmured uneasily. Preacher Ramsay came to the door, a short, spry old man with a few white hairs on his head, rimless glasses, and a genial, shrewd face, which suggested a fox. He wore a sleeveless sweater, without a necktie.

He invited the colored people to come in.

"We're a-goin' to praise God together and preach about a place where there'll be no white or black. In Heaven when we meet up yonder we'll all be children of God."

He told me that there had been a little trouble in getting snakes. The rattlers were going back into their holes at the approach of cold weather; and the law had confiscated some which they had planned to fatten up during the winter.

"But once in a while some feller brings us one." He smiled encouragingly.

I entered the tent with the colored people, who filled all but the front benches.

As before, the Signs Following church people occupied forward seats at right angles to the pulpits. There was a real mourner's bench, T-shaped and varnished. On it throughout the evening Elaine, very pretty in pink, folded and unfolded a pink blanket, endlessly making her bed, lying down, getting up, and starting over. Elaine was nineteen months old.

"All I ask is order on the grounds," said Preacher Ramsay. (His remarks were not addressed to Elaine, who played unmolested all evening.) "I mean you colored people, and you white people too."

He issued a call to prayer for the sick.

"Any colored child of God, hit's just the same as a white child of God, come forward if you will."

No one came; the church members knelt down in a body at the altar and began to pray and burst out into a tumult of "the tongues." A handsome black-haired girl in a red dress began to jerk so violently it seemed she might dislocate a vertebra. The middle-aged woman who had read Scripture for Brother Henry jerked also, holding

her hand to her neck as if she had a toothache. Two girls
in blue began to dance; and a tall young man, who I was
told was a preacher of the sect, began to jump up and
down, wordlessly, his eyes closed, his face in a trance,
and his fingers opening and closing as if his hands were
hungry.

They sang to guitar and mandolin, "They Called My
Name on the Radio," a new popular hymn inspired by
the "give-away" programs of the time.

Gradually I learned to understand some of their other
songs:

> *When first I went to holiness,*
> *I thought it was a shame,*
> *To see the people jump and shout,*
> *In praisin' Jesus' name.*

And

> *The Devil tried to tell me*
> *My Bible was a lie,*
> *That Jesus didn't love me,*
> *And I was sure to die.*

Elaine stopped making her bed on the altar and began
to jump and clap with the cheerful tunes. Then she
turned to stuffing saw-dust down the shirt-tail of a boy
friend of like age.

Her parents turned to me and smiled, a foreman in a
local mill and his wife. She was of hill stock, with delicate
fair skin, blue eyes, and a firm set to her jaw; her husband
might have had Welsh or Irish blood, for his smile was
quicker, and his face had a round, candid mold. They
were visiting Baptists.

"Of course, we don' go along with all they do, but we think they're good people and we like to help out," he said.

Preacher Ramsay now asked Elaine's parents to sing a duet. They sang a Baptist missionary hymn, "Send the Light," while the Holiness people listened respectfully. The Signs Following band struck up, "I'm Gettin' Ready to Leave This World, I'm Gettin' Ready for Gates of Pearl."

They followed this with "What a Beautiful Thought I am Thinking." The tall man's hands opened and closed hungrily.

The preacher stretched a rope across the front. "All you unbelievers and little children, stay back." Elaine's parents pulled her to safety, as a man walked down the aisle with a small box covered with a wire mesh. The preacher took out a dry-land moccasin, not quite full-grown. His face was transported; the two girls in blue went into a dance, the girl in red began her violent jerks, the man with hungry fingers began to jump higher, higher. The preacher made the serpent into a crown for his bald head and leaned over the rope, his glasses blazing. Several of the colored people, and a white Episcopalian from the front row, left the tent.

"This makes you feel *good*, children!" the preacher shouted. "Hit's the best feelin' you ever had in your life! Hit puts you way upon a high place where you look down on ever'thing that's gone before!" He slipped the snake in his pocket, placed it under his shirt, and passed it to one of the dancing girls in blue, who coiled it closely in her hand.

A ten-year-old in my pew whispered proudly, "That's

my sister up there!" The man with the hungry fingers held the poisonous snake over his heart.

"Hit's the Word of God!" cried Preacher Ramsay. "The Bible don't say you *can* handle serpents, it says they *shall* handle serpents!"

After a few minutes the moccasin was returned to his box. (Elaine's parents held her up for a quick look.) The box was taken out into the street, where a police whistle blew.

The little boy whispered, his eyes big. "Ever' policeman that kills one of our snakes, dies."

Brother Ramsay continued to preach. He gave the altar call, but no one came.

Now he asked the Negroes if they would sing. They were silent. He picked out a buxom stolid woman on the back row and told her to lead; she began slowly, in a rich, rocking rhythm:

> *He got His eyes on you, He got His eyes on you;*
> *My Lawd settin' in de Kingdom, got His eyes on you.*

All the Negroes joined in the chorus, the rich voices warming the tent. The snake excitement was all gone.

> *You better mind, my sister, you better mind what you say,*
> *My Lawd settin' in de Kingdom, got His eyes on you.*

Now she sang slowly and solemnly, "Gimme That Old-Time Religion." The chorus grew in volume and intensity, verse by verse.

> *It will make us love one another,*
> *And it's good enough for me.*

Elaine's parents joined in.

It was good for the Hebrew Children.

The Signs Following people, their guitars silent, were singing too. The tent began to rock.

It will make me love my enemy.

"Glory to God!" shouted the preacher. "Makes me feel good to see white and colored praisin' God together!"

It was good for Paul and Silas.

Brother Ramsay leaped over the rope. "I tell you, children, if we can't work and pray together in this world, we'll never get to that world up yonder!" His face was shining.

Elaine's father turned to me, flushing slightly, "I don' care what folks say — the Lord must be with 'em — else that moccasin would have bit."

4. THE SUN DO MOVE

*The life of the Reverend John Jasper spans a
century of American religion among Southern Negroes and whites; since his death,
there have been changes among both*

T HE INTER-RACIAL MEETING in the snake tent showed no
trace of left-wing influence. It was not arranged or sponsored by anybody, in contrast to more artificial minglings
at which white and colored are painfully polite. I was reminded of a sunny Saturday on a family-sized railroad in
Virginia years ago, when I rode home in the caboose with
a mixed train crew, white and colored cracking jokes and
getting along fine.

These things happen often in the South, when people
have no fear of each other. As to the fear of the Lord
that runs deep into the emotional background of white
and black, some claim that it leads to the perfect love
which is able to cast out the other kind of fear. I suppose
that it all depends.

As to the spirituals, I don't think that hearing them in
a concert hall, night club, or over the radio really counts.
They should be heard in a small, unpainted church or revival tent. It isn't easy to understand the words; sometimes the singers don't understand them either. E.
Emmet Kennedy, in *More Mellows,* quotes Aunt Patience
Ivins: "I know de song was intend to give Gawd praise,
so I ain't got no reason to consider de words ain't straight

long as I feel sho dat Gawd kin understan' what I'm tryin' to tell Him." Aunt Patience used to sing:

> *O the sons an' daughters of Jerusalem*
> > *Left their lonesome 'tation,*
> *For to see my Lawd in the precious gift*
> > *An' close him in salvation.*

At one point before it reached her ears, it went like this:

> *The sons and daughters of Jerusalem*
> > *Left their lamentation,*
> *To receive my Lord and the precious gift,*
> > *And clothe them in salvation.*

New spirituals are being written all the time. Sometimes they get into the little paper-backed, shaped-note hymnals which are published by the hundreds each year by small printers all over the South, for use by whites and Negroes. Sometimes they are printed by the author as "ballets" on slips of paper and sold for five cents a copy, "to help the poor and sick." Here is a sample:

> *When I get in Heaven*
> > *I'm going to the sea of glass;*
> *I'll make a little inquiration*
> > *Have I got home at last.*

> *(Chorus)   I have something to tell you,*
> > *Please bear it in mind;*
> *Some of these people in this church*
> > *Is three and four months behind.*

Extreme left-wingers are sometimes solemn about the spirituals, trying to turn their symbolism into the Com-

munist Apocalypse; and, curiously enough, the Fascists
are solemn about them too, no doubt lulled by soothing
visions of Ole Massa in a white-linen suit, julep in hand,
and pious slaves to tend his every want. I don't think the
spirituals can be perverted, however, by Communist or
Ku Kluxer.

If you come from the South, you will remember the
Reverend John Jasper and "The Sun Do Move."

Jasper was born a slave at a period when his race had
just completed one of the most remarkable experiments
in history, breaking completely with its native religious
heritage and adopting the faith of its masters.

In the first century of North American settlement, many
slave-owners held an uneasy conscience about baptizing
their slaves, fearing that if made Christians, they should
then be set free. It was questioned if Negroes had souls.
After some twisting and turning by theologians, the
Bishop of London, toward the end of the seventeenth century, found that "the freedom which Christianity gives is
a freedom from the bondage of Sin and Satan" — and
nothing more. Christians, therefore, could be slaves, and
slaves could be Christians.

The Church of England was the first to undertake missionary work among the slaves, and in 1695 the first school
for Negroes was opened at Goose Creek Parish in Charleston — eleven years before the first Negro school in the
North. In the eighteenth century, The Great Awakening,
as we have seen, encouraged a strong sentiment among
Southerners for the abolition of slavery; a movement
which failed only by a narrow historical margin.

Early in the nineteenth century, as the revivals still
held sway, independent Negro churches — mostly Baptist

and Methodist — were started and large numbers of slave preachers helped in the rapid spread of Christianity. Among those in Virginia was Philip Jasper, who was allowed by his masters to preach funeral sermons and speak at various churches on invitation. His wife, Tina, was head of the workingwomen on the Peachy estate. She was noted for a gracious manner, which she imparted to her twenty-four children.

Philip died two months before John Jasper, their youngest, was born. On his deathbed he prophesied that the baby would be a boy and a great preacher. He admonished Tina to take special care in raising him.

John passed his first years on farms, and later was moved to a Williamsburg estate, where he drove the ox-cart. A bright, efficient boy, he was soon given the choice jobs of waiting at table and working in the yard.

On most well-conducted Virginia plantations, the slaves were assembled in the great house on Sunday afternoons to study the Apostles' Creed, Lord's Prayer, and Ten Commandments; sometimes the masters preached to them or engaged white ministers for the work. Young John, no doubt, heard the Gospel both from his mother and from the white people, but there is no sign that he inclined toward religion. His thoughts had turned toward a plantation maiden named Elvy. They were married while he was still a young boy; but on the next day he was hired out to a Richmond, Virginia, master and sent away without regard for his marriage.

Elvy, after a few months, wrote John a letter in which she said that she considered herself free. In later years, after John became a preacher, he showed this letter to the deacons of his church, asking their consent to a second marriage. They passed a resolution that he could marry again.

But in Richmond he was at first a handsome gay blade among the women, illiterate, wild, and pleasure-seeking. On the Fourth of July, 1839, given time off from the tobacco factory where he had been hired out to work, he wandered among the noisy crowds on Capitol Square. Here, he tells us, the Lord struck him, and he was suddenly and deeply convicted of sin. He left the Square "badly crippled," and for six weeks lay in the slough of despond.

Then one day, while stemming tobacco, in his own words he felt light as a feather. "Salvation rolled like a flood through my soul, an' I felt as if I could knock off de factory roof wid my shouts. But I sez to myself, I gwine to hol' still till dinner, an' so I cried, an' laughed, an' tore up de torbacker. Presently I looked up de table an' dar was an old man — he loved me, an' tried hard to lead me out of de darkness, an' I slip roun' to whar he was, an' I says in his ear low as I could: 'Hallelujah! My soul is redeemed!' Den I jump back quick to my work, but after I once open my mouf it was hard to keep it shet any mo!"

Soon John looked up the line of workers and saw a good old woman "that knew all my sorrers and had been prayin' fur me all de time. Dere was no use er talkin'; I had to tell her, an' so I skip along up quiet as a breeze, an' started to whisper in her ear,' but just den de holdin'-back straps of Jasper's breachin' broke, an' what I thought would be a whisper was loud enough to be hearn clean 'cross Jeems River to Manchester. One man said he thought de factory was fallin' down."

The overseer, hearing the disturbance, came up with a

whip. John Jasper got back quick to his work, explaining that he meant no harm, that "the fust taste of salvation got de better of me." The owner of the factory, however, had heard the racket, and ordered Jasper sent in to him. He was Samuel Hargrove, a member of the First (white) Baptist Church of the city. He asked John what was the matter.

John explained the trouble. "I didn't mean to make no noise, Marse Sam, but 'fore I knowed it de fires broke out in my soul, an' I jes' let go one shout to de glory of my Saviour."

Mr. Hargrove asked if he had told the other workers about his conversion. "Yes," said John. "An' I feel like tellin' everybody in de world about it."

Mr. Hargrove told him to tell it up and down the tables, and even to go upstairs and tell the hogshead men and drivers. Then he held out his hand and said to his slave, "John, I wish you mighty well. Your Saviour is mine, and we are brothers in the Lord." John Jasper had to turn around and put his arm against the wall to keep from falling, and hold his mouth to keep from shouting. Mr. Hargrove gave him the rest of the day as a holiday, and told him to go anywhere he wanted and preach.

Jasper often told this story from the pulpit long after Hargrove had died. "Farewell, my ol' marster," he ended the sermon. "When I lan' in de heavenly city, I'll call at your mansion dat de Lord had ready for you when you got dar, an' I shall say: 'Marse Sam, I did what you tol' me, an' many of 'em is comin' up here wid dere robes washed in de blood of de Lamb dat was led into de way by my preachin', an' as you started me I want you to share in de glory of dere salvation.'"

He expected that his master would reply, "John, call me marster no mo'! We're brothers now, an' we'll live forever roun' de throne of God."

Nevertheless, for many years after his conversion day, John Jasper stayed on as a slave in the tobacco factory.

In the thirty years before the Civil War, there was a gradual change in the relationship of white and Negro Christians. The liberal, anti-slavery feeling among Southern white people died down. The slaves were still instructed in religion, with especial emphasis on the duty of obedience, but some masters preferred "oral instruction," fearing that Negroes who learned to read would become dangerous. As the Cotton Kingdom rose to its Confederate climax, for the most part slave-owners preferred Negroes to worship with them under the same roof. In this way they could control the sort of preaching which they heard. Slave "galleries" were built in most churches, the original "nigger heavens." After a slave uprising in Virginia in 1831, the work of Negro preachers, such as John's father had been, was severely restricted.

Under these conditions, John Jasper began his own ministry. He had seven months' education in the evenings, from a fellow slave who taught him to read the Bible. Soon he was in great demand to preach, especially funeral sermons on outlying plantations. Those calling him out of the factory on weekdays for this purpose paid his master one dollar a day for his services.

Once a white minister who thought it dangerous for Negroes to preach took over the service, and after a long oration permitted John Jasper to lead in prayer. But John made the prayer itself into such a good sermon that afterward both Negroes and whites crowded to shake his hand,

leaving the white minister discomfited. White people
began to visit a small church at Petersburg, Virginia, of
which he was pastor; and during the war, as Richmond
filled with Confederate wounded, Jasper was often called
into the hospitals to comfort the men.

With the end of the Civil War and the beginning of Reconstruction, there was another shift in Southern customs; the Negroes generally withdrew from the white
churches and formed their own — as they had begun to do
half a century earlier.

The break was symbolic. Between white and black an
emotional chasm grew. Members of white churches during Reconstruction often said that they missed the colored
people in the gallery, their loud "Amens!" and the
chuckles, joyful cries, and wonderful singing. But for half
a century or longer after the Civil War the only substan-
tial help for Negro churches and schools came from the
North.

One Sunday in the first uneasy years of separation, it is
said, a colored man came into a white Episcopal Church
and knelt at the altar. The congregation stirred unhappily,
the moment was tense, until General Robert E. Lee left
his pew and knelt beside him.

John Jasper, in his own way, helped to bridge the gap.
He did not bring back the colored people into the white
churches, but he brought thousands of white people to
worship in his.

When Richmond fell in 1865, it was ruined. John had
seventy-three cents in his pocket, owed forty-two dollars
house rent, and was now homeless and free. He found a
job cleaning bricks for rebuilding, and as the city rose
from its ashes, he began to preach on an island in the

James River to the restless members of his race. Soon his
followers were able to buy a small Presbyterian Church,
and in 1887 he began his crowning effort, the construction
of the Sixth Mount Zion Baptist Church, a large brick tabernacle. He was also an educator for his times, establishing a large Sunday-School, and urging his flock to read
all the books they could, although he himself read little
but the Bible.

It was no doubt his lack of wider reading which led
John Jasper, like the famous William Jennings Bryan in
later years, into the conflict between a literal view of the
Bible and the findings of science. It is not that Jasper
was disturbed over evolution; it is doubtful that he ever
heard of it.

But one day Jasper heard two of his church members
engage in a friendly argument, whether or not the sun
revolved around the earth. They submitted the question
to their pastor, by this time an old man. He took it to
the Bible.

What he found there satisfied him. There was no indi-
cation that the earth revolved around the sun. On the
contrary, there was clear evidence that it was the sun
which moved. So he began to preach his most famous
sermon, "The Sun Do Move."

This event made John Jasper's reputation of national
scope. The Virginia Legislature adjourned to the Sixth
Mount Zion Church to hear him. Jasper became a famous
tourist attraction. In garbled versions "The Sun Do
Move" was reprinted and widely sold. A lecture syndicate
sent him on a tour, which was a failure. Jasper acquiesced
in this publicity, but he carried himself like a king, and
toadied to no man, black or white.

His arguments were simple. Joshua could not have made the sun stand still if it had not previously been moving; and the earth itself was flat, because in the Book of Revelation angels were seen standing on the four corners of the earth. ("'Low me to ax ef de earth is roun', whar do it keep its corners?")

The preacher pointed out that "Dar is millions of things in de Bible too deep fur Jasper, an' some of 'em too deep fur anybody." But, he went on, "I kin read de Bible an' git de things what lay on de top of de soil. Out'n de Bible I knows nuthin' extry 'bout de sun. . . . I knows dat de sun burns — oh, how it did burn in dem July days! I tell you he cooked de skin on my back many a day when I was hoein' in de cornfield. But you know all dat, an' yet dat is nothin' to de divine fire dat burns in de souls of God's chil'len. Can't you feel it, bruthrin'?"

Many of his Negro listeners — his church was always packed to the doors — fell to the floor, smitten with conviction as in the days of the frontier.

White Richmonders still remember the lavender kid gloves Jasper wore in the pulpit, and his pleasant, offhand way of acknowledging the occasional presence of a lady for whom he had once worked. She was always shown to a front pew, and at a disputatious point, John Jasper pointed at her and asked, "Aint dat so, Miss Detsie?"

The private life of Jasper was robust and honest. He frankly enjoyed both tobacco and whiskey throughout most of his ministry, although he was never a drunkard, and toward the end the Prohibition tide was rising, so he gave up both habits as an example to his flock. He was married four times. His first marriage to Elvy was broken by slavery; his second, with the consent of his church, ended in divorce. His third wife died, and his widow survived him. A Richmond woman remembers when Jasper, to silence the gossip-mongers, installed his new wife in one of the pulpit chairs, where she sat throughout the service with a wreath of flowers in her hair.

For occasional recreation, Jasper liked to fish. An aged woman of his parish recalls that often he was drawn to Capitol Square, where, in her words, "An arrow of conviction went into his proud heart an' brought him low." Here he enjoyed the cool shade of the trees, answering the questions of children and grown people, black or white, who crowded around. Many of the Richmond Jews, who liked to hear him preach, came up to ask him questions. "They called him Father Abraham and showed great good feelin' fer him. Some of 'em used to meet him in Capitol Square an' dey would have great old talks together an' he didn't mind tellin' 'em de truth. He told 'em dat dey was de chil'len of Abraham, but dat dey had gone all to pieces."

One night at the church, this old lady recalled, John Jasper told his people that he had paid all his debts, and didn't care where or when he dropped, that there was nothing left of him. He said that he wanted the church to "git together and pay off de church debt an' live together like little chil'len. He was mighty great that night, an' it looked like de powers of de worl' to come was dar."

Soon after, Jasper died. It was 1901.

In Mars Hill, North Carolina, a mountain college town, a retired white Baptist minister, the Reverend Walt Johnson, each summer holds a small retreat for whites,

Negroes, and Indians, who share common lodgings and meals. (The rest of the year, Brother Walt edits a small paper called *The Church Revitalizer.*)

In 1946, at this retreat I found the Reverend Ben Bushyhead, a Cherokee Indian and cousin of Will Rogers; the Reverend Richard Jones, pastor of two Virginia Negro churches; the Reverend W. W. Hammond, of the Church of the Brethren, Elgin, Illinois; and eight or nine laymen and women.

A white woman from the State capital told about an incident in Raleigh earlier in the summer. After a verbal brush between a white man and a Negro on a streetcar, threats crackled like sheet-lightning among the idlers on Capitol Square. Here two large Baptist churches, one white and one Negro, ever since the Civil War have confronted each other on opposite corners. The women from both churches met in joint prayer meetings until the threats died down.

Someone else brought forward a proposal for a new sort of cafeteria in a Southern city, to have three sections, for white, for colored, and for those who didn't care. I sought out a silent man who sat a little apart, smiling into space, his face brown as an Indian's.

He is J. Rufus Moseley, a white man who has no church affiliation. As if I had asked him a question, which I had not, Mr. Moseley shook hands and said pleasantly, "Just follow along in the way of loving people, doing the most loving thing, and the rest will come to you. That's the way to begin."

Then about seventy, Mr. Moseley did not look his age, nor did he look young. His face, clever and deeply lined, was tanned from work in his Georgia pecan grove. He is

a self-supporting mystic. At a "silent supper" of fish and
bread, the surplus to be sent overseas, Mr. Moseley's lips
moved occasionally as if he were about to speak under
the influence of the Spirit; but at a glance from Brother
Walt he remained silent. I do not recall anything he said
during the evening; once he rose and began to look under
the sofa cushions for his fountain pen. Afterward, from
his autobiography, *Manifest Victory*, I came to know him
better.

Moseley was born among Primitive or Hardshell Baptists in the Brushy Mountains of North Carolina, later becoming a regular Baptist and then a Christian Scientist.
As he tarried alone after a Pentecostal meeting early in
this century, a message came to him to "stop looking for
the best religion, and to give myself to seeking and doing
the will of God." Much of his free time is used in visiting
wherever he hopes to be useful; occasionally with a Congressional group which holds breakfast prayer meetings,
with Quakers and other "intellectual Christians," more
often among "Holiness" people or working-class Baptists
or Methodists. According to his book, he has helped in
the healing of many sick. On one occasion he has pre-
vented a lynching; for a number of colored boys sen-
tenced to the electric chair he has obtained reprieves, and
others he has assisted to make a joyful, shouting exit from
this world. A Negro, jailed in Georgia, caused consider-
able puzzlement to the authorities by calling himself
"God." Mr. Moseley helped obtain his release. Many
years later, the ex-prisoner came into prominence as
"Father Divine."

Moseley has studied at the University of Chicago and
Heidelberg and had been the guest of the Harvard philo-

sophical faculty in the days of Royce, James, Palmer, Everett, Münsterberg, and Santayana. He has organized his experiences and beliefs into a philosophical system which is extremely simple at its center: "Those who seek truth apart from love miss the truth, while those who seek love get love, truth, and everything."

After talking with the mystic, I sat late on the shady porch of Brother Walt Johnson's house, listening to the white students sing from across the campus. There had been a revival, with a sermon preached on the text, "He hath made of one blood all peoples," and now the boys and girls sang "A Fountain Filled with Blood," deeply and fervently. A year or so previously, a student from this place, entering the big Baptist Seminary in Louisville, Kentucky, to train for missionary work in Africa, had joined a Negro Church in Louisville. For this action he was investigated by the F.B.I.; but he was not subversive. "What's the use of going to Africa," he asked, "if I'm not sincere with colored people here?"

I made no investigation of "inter-racial activities," and report only such incidents as came to my attention on the road.

The Episcopal Diocese of South Carolina, for example, voted to admit Negro delegates to its State Convention; Baptist young people from Texas, after an all-night prayer meeting at the Ridgecrest, North Carolina, assembly grounds voted to ask Negro youth to join them the following year (a proposal overruled by the elders of the denomination); in Savannah, Georgia, the State Baptist Convention held a joint gathering with the Negro Baptists.

The Presbyterian Church at Chapel Hill, North Carolina,

voted to admit Negro members. (There was a spirited discussion, in which some white members resigned.)

In Durham, North Carolina, I attended a mixed Methodist Church in a beauty parlor in Haiti, the Negro section. Many of the congregation afterward attended a pot-luck dinner at the home of one of the Negro members.

These examples at least offset other cases in which the white religion has been used by the Ku Klux. I made no effort to look for either.

As to Negro religion itself, there have been changes since 1901. There are still John Jaspers among rural Negro preachers, but they are coming to be in the minority. Negroes still cordially welcome white people to their services, but do not feel especially honored nowadays by white attendance, since they cannot return the visit.

It seems doubtful that colored people today are more religious than white; according to a study based on the 1926 census, only forty-six per cent of Negro men attended church, compared with forty-nine per cent of the white (seventy-three per cent of Negro women attended, compared with sixty-two per cent white). Nor is it true that Negro churches, even in the country, provide simply an "emotional escape." There are some examples to the contrary.

Near Norfolk, Virginia, early in the present century, a college graduate turned down a call to a city church in order to take two small churches near a country town. When he first came, the people were impoverished, often hopeless, and only two church members owned their homes. The little Negro schoolhouse was in disrepair, and there were no buses for Negro children.

The new minister not only preached about homeownership, but bought his own house. Within twenty-five years, every family in his two churches owned its home. He helped to raise the income of his people first by preaching, then setting an example of raising vegetables for cash; he also introduced poultry-raising. He bought buses for the Negro children with his own funds; later, the county operated Negro school buses. His first appeal to the county authorities about the disreputable school-house was turned down, so he led the church people in repairing the school and adding a room. Two years later, the county board voluntarily erected a better school, of which he served as principal for more than twenty years. At the end of his quarter-century, the Negro school was the best in the county.

This exceptional minister did not suffer financially by his work. From his three jobs as pastor, teacher, and farmer, he was reported to earn more than seven thousand a year. The entire community which he served is still considered outstanding for Negro welfare and excellent race relations, and their pastor is remembered by hundreds of young people whom he had encouraged and given a good start in life. Church authorities say that there would be many more such examples if a larger percentage of Negro ministers could have seminary or college training.

In the grandstand of the Washington ballpark, a large porportion of the city's Negroes, and a small sprinkling of whites, watched the choir march single file from the dugout to their station at the pitcher's box. Men and women in ample robes of shining white silk, they swayed to the music like a jolly, angelic host.

From the pulpit, draped in red, white, and blue, Elder Michaux watched the flood-lit diamond in silence until the choir had formed a great white gleaming cross and the crowd applauded. Then he explained the meaning of baptism, to an occasional loud "Amen!" "What could be sweeter than Jesus!" exclaimed the Elder, and the band struck up a song by this title.

As he called out the initials WJSV, formerly the name of his sponsoring radio station, and explained that they stood for "Willingly Jesus Suffered for Victory," a bloc of choir singers jumped up to form each letter. The next thrill, the Elder promised, would demonstrate the quickness of the resurrection — "All in the twinkling of an eye." The trumpet blew a long, sad blast, followed by a muffled drumbeat, and the choir rose; at each succeeding blast they made a quarter-turn; bowed in unified sorrow; dropped, and then recovered, white rolls of paper; and stood upright, pointing their arms to the east. On the bleachers, beneath an ad for razor blades, shone a single light bulb, a star. Now the choir waved red handkerchiefs, and the Blood of Christ flowed in center field. Until His return to earth, the Elder said, we must work for peace. He thanked God for the United Nations.

The Elder now promised "another thrill." Jesus, he said, was crucified and buried as the King of the Jews, but rose from the grave as the King of all nations. The choir unfurled at its center the flags of the Big Five countries, whose foreign ministers were then in session; next they waved the flags of *all* the nations, a magnificent flaming confusion, and sang "Victory With Christ."

In the joy of the Spirit three or four stout, satiny sisters in the choir began to jump up and down to the music.

It was now ten o'clock, and the Elder began his sermon from the first chapter of Revelation.

The choir leader read a text in a high, clear voice: "And there shall be no more pain," and the Elder interpreted in his deep, resonant baritone, "No more arthritis! No more neuritis! No more any kind of itis!" There was enthusiastic laughter and applause. At the women in the audience he hurled a challenging definition: "If your man goes off after another lady, and you can say in your heart, 'If she wants him, she's welcome — I love him, and so I want him to be happy' — that's real love!" (There were rich female cries, "Ain't it the truf!")

The Elder resumed his theological line. He ordered his assistant to read from the Book of Daniel Nebuchadnezzar's dream of Four Kingdoms. The last Kingdom of iron and clay represented the union of all the nations; and this, too, he reminded us, would be succeeded by the everlasting Kingdom. The warlords of earth with their big iron guns would fall.

"There's Churchill — out of power. Hitler — dead! Roosevelt — dead! Il Duce — dead! Stalin — the only one in power! Tojo — already tried to kill himself! Now put them together — CHRIST!" Now that we have split the atom, "The smallest thing there is, millions of times smaller and tinier than an inch," and "set the elements on fire," may it not be "time for the Coming?"

Two lady assistants laid out a suitcase of bathtowels by the side of the big baptismal tank over first base and a deacon tested the water with a thermometer. From the opposite fence a long file of humanity began to move across the field; clad in white sheets and headdresses, they looked distinctly Arabic; a gap showed here and there as small followers of Christ toddled between their parents. The grandstand broke spontaneously into "Lead Me to the Waters," an old chorus from the country days at the riverside, as the Elder baptized each candidate in turn.

On a Friday night in Georgetown, D.C., the First Baptist Church (colored) was lit up for choir rehearsal and the colored Methodist ladies nearby were meeting to arrange a pie sale. But another meeting-house bore a cross above the legend: "This leads to slavery, suffering, death." Under a star and crescent on the same sign was the explanation: "This leads to peace, prosperity, justice."

A well-dressed Negro with a polite but sardonic manner stood outside. As a few worshipers entered, I asked his explanation.

"Why, it's true, isn't it?" he asked. "Isn't that what the Cross always means? Now that's the religion of the East" — he pointed to the star and crescent — "where the wise men are."

I asked if his church followed the Koran. "That's right. A wonderful book. It's in the Congressional Library."

A former Baptist, he had been stationed in India during the war. He now summoned the Prophet Ali, a dark-skinned man in younger middle age. "This is the old religion, the true religion," he said, pointing to the Moslem sign. "It's fourteen hundred years old."

Before I could remark that Christianity is even older, he continued, "Well, there's nothing older than the moon and stars, is there? It's the religion of half the world. Christianity for the white people, Islam for the Moors. There will be peace when each has its own religion."

I was not allowed to enter. For a further account of

the Moors, we are indebted to Mr. Arthur Fauset, a graduate student at the University of Pennsylvania, who investigated several Negro cults of Philadelphia. In their meetings, the Moors sometimes sing, "Moslem's that old-time religion." They have broken completely with Christianity. Nor does the religion of the sect appear to be orthodox Mohammedanism. The members have been taught to believe that they are Moors descended from the Moabites and Canaanites, that they have a charter procured in the capital of Egypt, entitling them to possession of Northwest and Southwest Africa, and that before they can have a God, they must have a nationality.

The sect, however, teaches loyalty to the United States; the "Moors" believe that, although they have been stripped of their birthright by the palefaces in the name of Christianity, they should struggle on to establish "a world in which love, truth, peace, freedom, and justice will flourish."

Pride of race is also important to the Church of God or Black Jews, founded many years ago by Prophet F. S. Cherry. He was originally from the Deep South, which he refers to simply as "a hell of a place." (Among his other beliefs, Prophet Cherry holds that the Lord has given him the exclusive right to use profanity.) Mr. Fauset reports that the Black Jews hold a curiously mixed belief; they baptize members, for example, but do not observe Christmas or Easter. Prophet Cherry believes that the Negroes are the Jews mentioned in the Bible, and that Jesus was a black baby, taken to Egypt because he would be safe from Herod among people of his own color.

At the other extreme in race relations is Father Divine,

who does not draw a color line; many white people have joined his movement, and lived with Negroes at the various Peace Missions. Celibacy is practiced and married people who enter live as brother and sister.

Father Divine's activities have been intensively studied by various authorities, including the Bureau of Internal Revenue, which is no wiser than before. In a week at an "extension" outside of Kingston, New York, Mr. Fauset paid two dollars for lodging, and fifteen cents per meal; everything else was absolutely free. Communion, observed when Father is present, is a feast (at which every dish on which food is placed passes at least once through Father's hands). At one Communion, Mr. Fauset observed on the table ham, roast beef, lamb, roast chicken, fried chicken, sliced white meat of chicken, filling, fish, white rice, mashed potatoes, macaroni, beets, corn on the cob, greens, cabbage, string beans, cauliflower, carrots, coleslaw, bologna, tongue, another kind of beets, corn bread, white bread, whole-wheat bread, pumpernickel, raisin bread, rye bread, rolls, crackers, pineapple salad, sliced tomatoes and lettuce, platters of celery, pickles and relishes, jellies, various kinds of layer cakes, iced tea, iced coffee, chocolate, lemonade, cheese, fruit, fruit cup, nuts, jello with whipped cream, ice cream.

It was at such a board, during the depression years, that Father Divine observed, "I have mastered the economic situation!"

No collections are taken at Father Divine meetings; and although some of his followers become "angels," turning over to Father Divine their worldly income and living their lives completely in accordance with his instructions, others who subscribe to the faith continue to live normally as members of their communities. Their beliefs center around the revelation that Father Divine is God. Some of their practices stem directly from the "Holiness" movement; shouts, jumpings, and "tongues" are displayed by members when Father Divine enters the hall. His teachings are based on Christian ethics, but to an increasing extent his newspaper, *New Day*, is the scripture cited by his followers.

New Day carries advertisements from big houses like Woolworth, Fuller Brush, McCrory, and Lerner Shops (all with the injunction, "Peace!" or, sometimes, "Thank you, Father"), and also statements from Father himself:

"IF YOU HAPPEN TO BE A LAW VIOLATER, A LAW-BREAKER, AND A PROFANE PERSON, MY SPIRIT, MY LOVE, AND MY MIND WILL GO OUT AND GET YOU."

I am indebted to a good friend whom we can call Sadie for her account of the services held by Daddy Grace, another well-known prophet, perhaps second only to Father Divine in his big-city following. Sadie is religious, like many of us, in a haphazard, off-and-on fashion. During thunderstorms at our house she always disappeared quietly, explaining afterward that "The Lord might take aim at some bad person and miss." She was brought up a Baptist on a Virginia farm.

Daddy Grace comes to Washington occasionally, baptizing his converts, by special arrangement with the authorities, through the means of a fire-hose. He does not claim to be God, but some of his followers hold that he is the identical Grace mentioned so often in the Bible. Sadie was not impressed by his service, although she admitted that "He's got something up there under that long hair of his." But she objected to the gambling. I asked for details.

"He put a Bible down and said, anybody wants a blessing from the Lord come and put a quarter on it. Then he put down a great big Bible and said, anybody wants a bigger blessing come and put down fifty cents."

She attended a funeral at the Daddy Grace Temple. In the absence of Bishop Grace, another pastor arose and, pointing to the corpse, declared that the soul of the deceased could not cross over Jordan until Daddy Grace returned and gave the word.

"Come on, let's get out of here," said Sadie to her friends at this point. "Seems to me God gave us the Bible so we wouldn't be bothered with any such foolishness."

Most Negroes are still Baptists, with Methodists next, and a sprinkling of other denominations. On a Sunday night in Cleveland, Tennessee, I noticed a colored Cumberland Presbyterian Church.

This is an offshoot of The Great Revivals. The Presbyterians disagreed over the merits of the historic outburst at Cane Ridge, many who favored revivals forming a separate presbytery, the Cumberland; and after the Civil War, the Negro Cumberland Presbyterians withdrew to form their own communion. It is now a small, conservative body with no special peculiarities. Their daily vacation Bible schools have classes in weaving and other handicrafts, the products being sold for missions.

At the door a Negro cordially invited me in. The church was finished in plain white wallboard; except for a large mural of the Valley of the Jordan, which covered the entire chancel wall. It had been painted by Lightning, the porter at the Cherokee Hotel.

The Elder, janitor at the leading bank of Cleveland, was reading the Scripture. To his left on the platform sat an old man with a shiny white wisp of hair above his beaming face, to the right was his grandson, a twenty-year-old boy wearing rimless glasses, and a new blue suit with a discharge button.

We sang, "Amazing Grace, How Sweet the Sound." The Elder announced that the young man on the platform would leave Cleveland next day to begin his theological studies in the North. "He's just a baby in the ministry, but we'll do all we can to help him. Brothers and Sisters, we will now hear from Brother Sharp."

Brother Sharp rose, and held on to the pulpit. His face was determined as he began his first sermon.

"I will preach tonight on God's love," he said firmly. He began to read the parable of the Prodigal Son, finishing in his own words. "Maybe he decided to leave his folks and go up North where he heard things was better. He didn't have no money, so he hoboed on a freight train." A chorus of responses from the older men and women filled in the pauses. His own voice began to rise and fall.

"Things didn't go so good," he went on, "so he took a job down in the hog-pens; didn't even have corn to eat, just the husks." (Sweet Jesus! Well Said! Ain't It So!) "But when he came home his father fell on his neck and kissed him." (Amen!) "And that's the way with God's love. It's waitin'! It's waitin'! It's waitin'!" From the pews a woman's voice chanted an obbligato, "waitin'! . . . waitin'! . . . waitin'!"

Mr. Sharp now reminded us of other episodes in the Old Testament and New Testament. The woman who lost her shilling, the ninety-and nine sheep, old Jonah sent to preach the Word. He repeated after each, "God's love is like that — it's waitin'"; and the responses of the people tied them all together.

The Elder now began to say "Amen!" more and more often, with a distinctly warning emphasis; but Brother Sharp went on. "When I was overseas," he continued, "it was just God's love that kept me a-goin'." He began on the Twenty-Third Psalm, with spontaneous gestures, anointing his scalp with oil, kneeling on the floor to spread the table prepared in the presence of his enemies. With an effective, quiet drop of his voice he ended suddenly: "Because God is love — that's all He is."

5. THE LOST CHORD

*Homesick people in Los Angeles have given
the old-time religion some unusual twists
and turns*

THE TREE OF RELIGIOUS LIBERTY, if it bears good fruit,
also continues to sprout many new branches. Some of the
new offshoots may seem rather strange, but it is well to
remember that a belief which today may seem utterly
eccentric, after a century or so may become ripe, mellow,
and recognizable as "the old-time religion after all."

On a recent trip to the west coast, I stopped at Salt
Lake City with the other tourists, and remembering the
early beginnings of the Mormon faith during the time of
the great revivals, I admired the greatness of their accom-
plishments and the practicality of their brotherly love.
Then I moved on to Los Angeles, which for many years
has been recognized as the chief birthplace of new religions. In this city a boy evangelist is advertised as
"Little David, Sixty-Five Pounds of Holy Ghost Fire,"
and a four-year-old child, ordained a minister of Old
Time Faith, Incorporated, performs a marriage ceremony.
We expect these things of Southern California.

My introduction to these churches came through a Los
Angeles stenographer who was living in Washington during the war. We asked her how she liked the East.

"Oh, it's all right," she said. "But I can't understand all these funny old religions you have around here."

"What?" we asked.

"Oh, you know — Baptists, Methodists, Presbyterians — things like that. We don't have those much in California any more."

On Saturday morning, in the city of angels, I looked first in the telephone book. Churches, Miscellaneous, took up more than a page. Should it be the Church of Spiritual and Mental Science, the Institute of the Cosmos, Ltd., the Haven of Rest, the Infinite Science Church, the Psychosomatic Institute, the Universal Temple of Peace, the Ancient Christian Fellowship, the Assembly of God, or the Assembly of Man?

I dialed the number of a picturesque name. An angry female voice answered, "No I am *not* a Firebrand for Jesus! The telephone's changed!" — and hung up.

The Nuptial Feast Ecclesiae didn't answer. The voice at the Great I Am Temple seemed slightly puzzled at a query about morning service.

"Well, we have an *activity* at ten o'clock."

I went for a swim in the reassuring sea. A businesslike mermaid roamed the beach, pencil and notebook in hand. When had I last gone to school, and what was my last grade? And what did I think of the following titles, being considered for a new movie? They were all wonderful, I told her. She gave me a sour look and a free ticket to a sneak preview. Without warning, a strange young man resting on the sand began to discuss his love-life in a loud voice; he also wanted my opinion about it. I abandoned the beach for Pershing Square.

The difficulty was not a scarcity of human interest, but

a dismaying surplus. Stranger after stranger corners the visitor on a bench and tells all, heedless of the soapbox orators always at work under the palms. "We had a good offer for the farm in 1935, and my daughter was settled out here so we just sold out and came on." The daughter? "Oh, she got a divorce, and married a dentist in Denver. But we stayed on. Not much point going back to Iowa at our time of life. So many friends have passed on or moved away. But our grandchildren come out for a visit every fall. Let me show you their pictures."

The photographs of the distant children in Colorado somehow seemed more alive than the living grandparents on the bench.

Los Angeles is largely built up with stucco bungalows in a "Spanish" or "mission" style, white, orange, pink, or green; with advancing age, they have begun to look like fly-blown squares of grocery-store cake. At night, from the hills nearby, the enormous city under the stars glows like a reddish firmament; the suggestion of a neon Hell is not wholly removed by two or three big churches outlined in tubular lighting, and a big red "Jesus Saves" atop a leading tabernacle. In the wealthier subdivisions, the cakes are larger and the icing fresher.

Typically the tourists seemed to keep their fingers crossed about religion; yet on the Santa Monica promenade the middle-aged couples listened approvingly as the municipal band played "The Lost Chord," a comforting reminder of solemnity in the hazy, theatrical sunshine.

"See this bench?" asked a man with thin, graying hair and a vague, kindly, anonymous face. "The same man used to sit here every evening for twenty years to watch the sunset. We call it the old-timer's bench."

"We used to come just for the winter," said his wife. "But Harry — that's my husband — all his folks' lungs were delicate, so along about 1940 we decided to stay here, what with the war and all. He was a florist in Kansas City," she added with pride.

"Miss it, sometimes," said Harry. "Don't seem much point in having florists out here, does it?" He pointed to the poinsettias in symmetrical beds. "Don't look now, but this fellow waiting to talk with you, he's nuts about religion."

We strolled down the promenade to escape the nut, toward a row of fourteen wooden boxes, shaped like church windows and stuffed with literature. They had been erected by the municipality in an effort to reduce the waste paper which litters all parks and vacant lots. Harry watched indulgently as his wife ran her fingers down the line; the Presbyterian and Unitarian boxes would have been empty, except for a generous overflow from the Seventh Day Adventists. One small tract, "An Awful Calamity Coming Soon and How to Escape It," had yellowed with age; it had apparently been printed during the First World War, because it cited Spanish influenza rather than the atomic bomb as a sign of the times. Otherwise it was perfectly serviceable, but the lady refused it, with a slight frown.

"Nothing new," she said. "There hasn't been anything new for weeks." She put back a Christian Science leaflet and took one on Unity.

"We were Presbyterians back in Kansas City," she volunteered. "At least I was. Harry's people were Lutherans. But you have to keep up with things out here. I believe in having a young mind. It doesn't matter how old you are if you have a young mind."

Next morning was Sunday. I found the white stuccoed temple of The Great I Am on a downtown street. It looked stale and dingy; and the white-painted chairs inside were only sparsely filled; but an immense hubbub was going on. Worshipers clad in white were chanting loudly and moving about an altar-like arrangement; waves of violet light rippled over large rectangular screens at either side of a large chart of the human figure, from which a fleur-de-lis and something like a Mazda light bulb were sprouting. A woman now came up and asked briskly and firmly if I belonged; the Activity was for members only, I should have to see Mr. Stone downstairs. In the office, meanwhile, the Activity continued to reach us through a loudspeaker; Mrs. Guy W. Ballard, widow of the founder, was speaking in a vibrant voice of vibrations, ascensions, electronic tubes, and other matters. If you could only manage to vibrate at just the right rate, pouf! — up you go. "Keep me in the presence of the Mighty I am Saint German!" she chanted, "surrounded within and without by a wall of blue flame!"

Mr. Stone, suave in white palm beach, explained that I could attend an evening service for neophytes, after reading the beginner's books. They were five dollars a set.

I continued my researches in the free public library, where I found a book entitled *Psychic Dictatorship in America,* by Gerald B. Bryan. Across the table sat a man with long hair, tanned face, and a T-shirt on which was pinned a simple wooden sign in block letters: PROPHET. He escaped before I could make his acquaintance. I read on about the Great I Am; the late Mr. Ballard was indicted in 1929 for fraudulent gold-mine promotion. He took in an estimated three million dollars from the cult before his ascension in 1940. At one time during the nineteen-thirties, Mr. Ballard and a few close friends used to sit nightly in a hotel room, holding hands and looking intently at a gilded goblet containing a few gold trinkets and coins. Upon this subject was placed a blacklist of names, headed by those of the President of the United States and his wife. Thrusting their hands rhythmically back and forth, they then chanted a Decree: "Stiffen on the cross of blue flame all those who oppose this Light! Blast! Blast! Blast! their carcasses from the face of the earth forever!"

The late Aimee Semple McPherson died in 1944 from an overdose of sleeping-powder. She was reported to be a warmhearted and friendly person, who made strangers feel at home. Her spectacular scenes are still remembered — Sister Aimee in football togs, carrying the ball of the Four-Square Gospel for a touchdown; or speeding down the ramp to the front of the auditorium on a motorcycle, dressed as a cop, slamming on the brakes, blowing a whistle and raising her white-gloved hand to the congregation: "Stop! You're speeding to Hell!" For her sermon on "The Merry-Go-Round Broke Down," she draped her great temple in canvas like a circus tent. The merry-go-round was civilization and Sister Aimee appeared dressed as a mechanic to fix it up.

She was a beautiful woman, noted for her love affairs, which became public property.

In 1922, Sister Aimee had arrived in Los Angeles with one hundred dollars and a battered automobile. Within four years she had built her one and one-half million dollar Angelus Temple with its five thousand seats and become the most famous evangelist of her time. It was in 1926 that she disappeared. Last seen in a bathing-suit on the beach near Ocean Park, it was thought at first that she had drowned. Thousands gathered to pray on the beach, an airplane dropped flowers on the waters, and at a great memorial meeting in Angelus Temple thirty-five thousand dollars was collected. A young man drowned, trying to find Sister Aimee in the ocean.

After three days, Sister Aimee reappeared. The wire services filed ninety-five thousand words a day from Los Angeles on the event, airplanes showered roses upon her railroad train and she walked out of the depot on a carpet of flowers. She said that she had been kidnapped; but apparently she had passed the time in a cottage with a former operator at the Temple radio station known as "Goggles." Her followers did not care. When she was placed on trial for giving false information designed to interfere with the orderly processes of the law, they gathered in the Temple and shouted:

> *Identifications may come,*
> *Identifications may go,*
> *Goggles may come,*
> *Goggles may go,*
> *But are we down-hearted?*
> *No! No! No!*

She wrote newspaper articles about her various marriages, and continued to direct her church, with two hundred and fifty local branches throughout this country and abroad. After her death in 1944, for nearly a week, as she lay in state, a thousand people had passed her bier each hour. As she was buried in Forest Lawn, the acres of flowers, the six-hundred-foot floral cross, and the great procession were photographed from the air.

Aimee's Gospel was of the usual Pentecostal or "Holiness" variety, emphasizing faith healing, the "baptism of the Holy Ghost," or speaking in "unknown tongues," and the Second Coming.

A rather different influence seems to spread from some of the pulpits of the city since her death.

On Sunday afternoon I encountered a short, rabbity little man puffing along beside me toward the Shrine Civic Auditorium. He was a clerk in the city postoffice, he said; and his eyes, timid behind thick glasses, kept looking at his wrist watch in apprehension. We were both a little late for the service of Doctor Clem Davies' Prophetic Ministry, Incorporated.

"There's nobody like Aimee," he said. "You should have come while Aimee was here."

I asked about the prophet we were going to hear. "Oh, he's good, all right. Inside stuff you don't get other places."

On the sidewalk by the Shrine Auditorium agents of a rival orator passed out yellow handbills advertising the return to the city of Doctor Joe Jeffers, Brilliant Authority on Bible Prophecy and Occult Revelations. (Doctor Jeffers, I learned later, had been in retreat under Federal auspices, a matter connected with the theft of his ex-wife's automobile.) We hurried on into the enormous, softly lit, carpeted hall. It was more than two-thirds filled with comfortable people, tending toward middle age, who relaxed in theater seats after a bout of hymn-singing. The collection was in progress.

Doctor Davies, in appearance a thin-faced, successful businessman, stood behind a pulpit at the left of the stage. An attractive young woman, her legs crossed, sat at the right. In center stage a large metal cross was flanked by electric torches on standards.

As the plates were passed, the prophet discussed with us his plans for stepping-up the kilowatts; his broadcasts already brought mail from Texas and the Pacific Northwest. The basket was taken behind a velvet curtain for counting; more than three hundred dollars had been raised. There was then a second collection for "church expenses," not otherwise explained. He now read the twenty-eighth chapter of Isaiah, interjecting a remark about the poor morals of the "Communists, aliens, and international bankers" now enjoying American hospitality.

Morgan, Mellon, and Kühn Loeb, he said, had just bought a local radio station and "thrown the evangelical Christians off the air." His own approach to his subject, this afternoon, seemed notably cautious. He referred to a well-known businessmen's weekly letter which a "kind friend" had sent him. "Even these . . . Babylonian lads" (the tiniest pause before he pronounced the word "Babylonian" brought harsh, cackling laughter) admitted, he said, that war was likely within five or ten years. "That's what the merchant princes say, the wise guys, the slap-happy Babylonian boys!" Sure now what he meant, the audience laughed loudly.

He needled other causes of middle-class discontent. The City of Los Angeles had raised taxes again; he advised his listeners not to pay taxes for improvements which would be obsolete upon the collapse of "The System." He shouted that "we're paying three to four times too much for telephones." He read a list of the leading in-

vestment houses of the country; before the name of Gold-
man, Sachs and Company he interpolated quickly, softly,
"I wonder who this is."

"Unless the Lord comes," he said, "you'll find that the
soldier boys will not look at the situation calmly. Look
what happened down in Tennessee." (There had recently
been a race riot there.) "Don't forget there are thirteen
million veterans. God help The System if they ever get
together!"

In the adjoining seat my friend the postoffice clerk
sucked in his breath sharply. His eyes shone with pleas-
urable fright.

Now Doctor Davies exclaimed with virtuous anger,
"The trouble is that then the agitators will come out!"

When I left, he had been talking two hours, and was
still going strong. I missed the little postoffice clerk, but
on the bus I fell into talk with another departing worshiper.

She was the counterpart of the young-minded lady
from Kansas I had already met on the Santa Monica
promenade: a woman of indeterminate age and marital
status, with carefully bleached hair.

"That's the Mulligan mansion," she said, pointing out
the sights from the bus window. "They say it cost four
million dollars, and the inside is gorgeous. A friend of
mine went there once."

She was divorced, and liked Southern California because there were so many interesting things to do on a
small income. She had formerly been a Methodist, and
then a Christian Scientist.

"I'm really not anything now. Isn't that awful? But I
believe in being broad-minded. What do you think of
Mr. Davies?"

It wasn't the plain old Gospel, I said; and she looked at me doubtfully. "There doesn't seem much brotherly love in it, does there?" she remarked. "You ought to have been here while Aimee was alive."

Doctor Clem Davies' Prophetic Ministry is typical of half a dozen Sunday afternoon services in Los Angeles, all to varying degrees nationalistic and anti-Jewish. They draw larger crowds than the "Reverend" Gerald L. K. Smith, the most noted worker in the Fascist vineyard.

Before his meetings, Smith sometimes circulates among the audience, asking such pious questions as, "Do you believe in Jesus Christ?" or, "Do you believe in prayer?" and inviting those who say Yes to sit on the platform. By this means he has garnered a number of innocent ministers, especially of the Pentecostal or Holiness sects, who have not yet learned what Smith, Winrod, and their Ku Klux Klan affiliates are up to.

A Fundamentalist Baptist minister, of Scotch ancestry, and a devout believer in the imminent Second Coming of Christ, once stood up boldly to the Fascist version of the old-time religion and its "Bible Prophecies." He told a large congregation in a downtown tabernacle that those who hate the Jews lie under the curse of Almighty God, in His promise to Abraham.

On his return to town, Gerald Smith called a meeting which the old preacher attended; he heard himself described as a Jewish tool of the Communists, who was paid one thousand dollars for each attack upon "Christian Nationalism."

Several blocks back from the sea, I heard the hill twang mingle with the flat tones of the Middle West, in a weeknight meeting of the Santa Monica Assembly of God.

Their small, flat-topped stucco building had theater
seats, which seem to be gradually displacing the pew in
Los Angeles. On the wall behind the rostrum, the sort of
raised, flowing script one associates with a cocktail lounge
or department store spelled, "My Redeemer Liveth." But
these were country people come to town. They clapped
hands merrily as they sang "Traveling On"; the piano
player leaned back with a wide, zany smile; a mother on
the back row cuffed her little boy because after the music
stopped he kept on clapping. The preacher gibed at the
people for their lack of enthusiasm: "Come on now, folks,
if you aren't careful you might get Pentecostal! Hallelujah! Watch out or you might get a blessing."

A woman in the front row popped up promptly, raised
her arms in a trancelike position, and began to speak "in
tongues." The preacher asked, "Can anyone translate?
Hallelujah!"

No one translated; and he launched into his sermon on
the themes of Hiroshima, Nagasaki, Sodom and Gomorrah,
and the approaching End. "Jesus is coming," he said.
"Not with an Indian love call, but with a shout!"

All religion in Los Angeles seemed to take on the
special coloration of Southern California, a unique blend
of homesickness and high-pressure advertising. An Episcopal Church has a sign on the street, "The Little Country
Church of Hollywood." I was less struck by the new religions than by what seems to be happening to the old
one. Of course, there are excellent churches and sound
preaching in Los Angeles; but the tourist is more likely to
hear bigotry and prejudice on the one hand, and on the
other a sort of marshmallow Christianity, on the level of

Santa Claus and the Easter Bunny. The marshmallow aspect has been thoroughly blistered by Evelyn Waugh in his novel on local burial customs, *The Loved One*.

It is also possible, I thought, that enough satire has been written about it, and that charity is called for. It would be a becoming virtue for an American observer in any case, for whatever is wrong with Los Angeles essentially is wrong with the rest of us.

As I crossed Pershing Square on the way back to Santa Monica from a Youth for Christ revival meeting, it was a fine night, and the old men were out in force. In one corner the farmers from the Middle West, packed shoulder to shoulder, listened to a barber-shop quartet sing, "On the Banks of the Wabash Far Away." Across the square the lean-faced men from the South clustered wordlessly around a "git-tar" band playing "The Wreck of the Old 97." The moon rode high, and on their faces was a look of almost fierce, clanlike devotion.

I bought a ticket for home.

PART III

THE FRUIT OF THE TREE

*The people are still at work deciding
what the Bible means to them, and
no one can truly say which branches
bear the sweetest fruit*

1. RESCUE THE PERISHING!

*The revivalist impulse to rescue the perish-
ing takes many shapes: some older examples
in New Bedford and Chicago, a new one in
Carrollton, Georgia*

Evangelism is certainly not one of the "branches" of
the religious liberty tree; it is more like the sap itself.
But I was curious, after a brief amount of historical reading, to see how some of the offshoots, begun in the frontier
enthusiasm long ago, had fared with the passage of time.

In some of the older places the early fruits of the old-
time revivals linger on almost untouched, as they appeared a century or more ago — a small "church college,"
or orphanage, or rescue mission. In search of such an
enterprise I scouted through the back streets of New
Bedford, Massachusetts, where the Portuguese mingled
with the Anglo-Saxon minority. A ship-chandler's sign
talked New York language: "Let Us Solve Your Canvas
Problems." A boat whistled as a crowd of dark-skinned
people waited to embark; the enormous breasts of the
women shook with mirth and love; the slightest whisper
from the men made them laugh.

"It's a feast day," a Portuguese explained. "We have a
parade in honor of the Holy Ghost on Martha's Vineyard."
He offered a sandwich and a glass of beer and invited me
to attend.

On the heights of the town behind us the Puritan bells rang from the beautiful white steeples — Congregational, Baptist, Unitarian. Local ladies in white dresses, white gloves, white parasols, and white hats headed toward the white churches in the cool sunshine. A slim scattering of casually dressed summer people entered the Episcopal Church. Under the sign "Veteran Firemen's Association," I found an old man in a faded blue uniform, tilting his chair against the wheels of an ancient, hand-pulled engine. His eyes were tired, his voice querulous. "Not so many goes to church, any more. The Odd Fellows have taken over the Adventist Church now. The Catholics are doin' all right. And the Seamen's Bethel, sure, that's always open. Right across from the Whaling Museum."

Halfway down the block I heard him call defiantly, "They still let us know up here, every time they have a fire!"

Seamen's Bethel stands on Johnny Cake Hill, gaunt wooden Gothic built in 1832; it is the Whalers' Chapel described in *Moby Dick*. Here Father Mapple brought his congregation to order by shouting, "Starboard gangway, there! Side away to larboard — larboard gangway to starboard! Midships! Midships!" — and preached the best of all sermons on Jonah and the whale.

At the adjoining lodging-house for seamen, the chaplain who opened the door showed in his lean visage a Melville quality, at once fiery, wild, and kind. He was a short, white-haired parrot of an old man, a bit of a game-cock too; the Reverend Charles Thurber, unfavorably disposed toward Washington, D.C. After a full expression of his views on the late Mr. Roosevelt, his natural hospitality asserted itself, and he pulled up a rocker in the study.

Mr. Thurber had never read *Moby Dick*. "Always meant to. I've had a pretty full life as it is." He had been thirty-seven years on duty at Seamen's Bethel; before that a Methodist pastor; before that a sailor originally. His seafaring was first broken by a wife who did not want an absent husband.

"So I settled down, felt the call to the ministry, used all my savings to study theology, and spent fourteen years in one pastorate." The Bishop arranged it for him; ordinarily, Methodist preachers are shifted from port to port like sailors.

Then he went to sea again, this time in steam. "I knew the day would come when canvas sailors would walk the streets begging for bread. I worked up to chief engineer. You can boil water at sea as well as ashore."

Putting into New Bedford under steam, he called at Seamen's Bethel and was offered the post of chaplain, just fallen vacant. His wife urged him at once to accept.

"Oh, wife, haven't you had enough of these four hundred dollar a year salaries!" he cried. But during the night, in his bunk, he felt the call to see the trustees once more before sailing.

Here Mr. Thurber interrupted his story with a sudden blast at the current price of meat, for which he held the Democrats responsible.

"Come in at the end of a long cold day burying the dead or what-not and we can't have a decent bite of meat — not even a good hot stew!" He rose and stood with his back to the radiator and was reminded again of his calling.

"It's when the shipwrecked men come in, cold and wet, and stand by the warm pipes and say, 'This is Heaven!' — that's what gets you."

In the old chapel next door the pillars were still draped with colored crêpe paper from a wedding. Mr. Thurber, a bartender told me, is popular on the waterfront and performs more marriages than any other parson in New Bedford. The chaplain now pointed out the folding-back benches in the downstairs vestry, modeled after those in the old-time whaler's cabin, and an eight hundred dollar marble plaque on the wall, celebrating a whaler who walked three thousand miles over Arctic ice to save the lives of stranded shipmates. No whalers have sailed from New Bedford since 1925, but ships are still wrecked among the Portuguese fishing-fleet.

Recently a man with dungarees ripped off at the knees by the violence of the storm had come into evening service and asked if they would sing "Let the Lower Lights Be Burning." His schooner had gone aground on Gayhead Rocks and only two had been saved. Clinging to the wrecked schooner, the sailor had seen the lights ashore. "I prayed that somebody would see us," he told the chaplain. "And I thought of the old church back home and promised I'd be a different man if I ever got ashore."

In the morning, while his colleagues hold forth in the white churches on the heights, Mr. Thurber goes to the almshouse and then to the hospital. "I speak a word of comfort. I sing — well as I can — and offer up a word of prayer. When I get back to the chapel, there's nearly always some unfortunate waiting to see me." He added, with satisfaction in his voice, "Sometimes dripping wet from the sea."

Seamen's Bethel was a product of the early revival waves of the nineteenth century. At the close of the century, the great Dwight L. Moody left his name and his monetary earnings to an institution in Chicago which would train young people to carry on his work.

Outside the gray brick, Gothic administration building of the Moody Bible Institute, I encountered a middle-aged man with eyeglasses who was looping ropes about a movie projector atop his sedan, in a manner both brisk and earnest. I offered to help, and the conversation took its natural course without further effort on my part.

"A writer at heart, eh?" And did I have the old-time religion myself? Was I washed in the Blood of the Lamb? He shook his head at my equivocal answers. "You'd know it all right, if you'd been born again. No uncertainty about it."

He was a Moody Bible Institute lecturer, bound for Winona Lake, a summer gathering place where he would show the world première of a Moody film on the atom, for which the Government had granted a unique permission to photograph the inside of the atomic machinery. Still shaking his head over my doubtful status, he drove off.

Some of the frivolity of the modern world had crept into the bookstore. A game called "Bible Lotto" first caught the eye, with its companion pastime, "Bible Quotto," which as you should be able to surmise is based upon quoting Scripture. (Miss Lucy Augur held a contest of this sort in the B.Y.P.U. on Sunday nights, only she called it the Sword Drill.) I purchased a booklet adapted to my own modest requirements: *Snappy Stories that Preachers Tell*, by the Reverend Paul E. Holdcraft, S.T.D.

A Baltimore minister, says Doctor Holdcraft in this work, visited the Bible class of a rival church one Sunday morning. He was invited to lead the processional, which advanced down the aisle singing "See the mighty host advancing, Satan leading on!"

A colored preacher was asked, "Do you use notes?"

"At first I used notes," he replied. "But now I demands the cash."

The sweet child, asked by her mother to recite the text of the morning's sermon on Belshazzar's feast, said, "Meany, meany, tickle the parson." The young Methodist clergyman, asked in an emergency to conduct a Baptist funeral, wired his Bishop for instructions. The Bishop wired back, "Bury all the Baptists you can."

From the catalogue I learned that the Moody courses of study, briefer and less demanding than those in theological seminaries, train candidates for "the pastorate, the mission field, gospel music, the radio ministry, children's and young people's work." The school is tuition-free, interdenominational, and "completely Bible-centered," with the entire study body "a band of active missionaries, with sin-cursed Chicago as the mission field."

Founded in 1886 by the late Mr. Moody, the Institute is still permeated by something of his warm and kindly spirit. An article in the *Monthly* struck out strongly, on both Biblical and scientific grounds, against racial prejudice. Another writer attempted a reconciliation with psychiatry, recommending being converted as the "surest way to escape the miseries and consequences of a guilt complex."

The Dean of Men lined up three students for interviews. A black boy named Charles had walked a thousand miles through the South African bush and worked for years in a seaport city to earn money for his passage to Chicago. He planned to go back as a missionary, he said, and suggested politely that I get in touch with the Institute public relations office. Charles seemed a little tired of being written about because of his long walk, or because his skin is black.

Two white boys remained, one Northern, one Southern, both veterans. They asked my purposes and listened warily to my explanation. Then Henry, the Northerner, sprang in like a boxer, or an overeager salesman. (Henry had gone to Harvard Business School for a while before coming to Moody.) Was I a Christian? He threw text after text like hand-grenades, after each one pounding me on the knee. "There is no other Name whereby men must be saved!" It was not possible to interview Henry. I turned to his colleague, who had taken no part in the text-flinging and knee-pounding.

A quiet boy from Virginia, Jim seemed equally devout, but in a different way. His eyes were deep black and untroubled, his face at once youthful and mature. He became a Christian, he said, because his mother was a Christian, praise the Lord. This expression, which seemed to come naturally to him, accompanied most of his answers.

His ship had been torpedoed in the Pacific. He managed to climb aboard a life-raft, where he became the target of Japanese fire.

"Suddenly words just popped into my mind, 'What have I to fear, what have I to dread, leaning on the everlasting arms?' I swallowed about a quart of oil and salt water. Then I was picked up and taken aboard a destroyer, and all wrapped up in blankets and drinking hot coffee, I opened the Bible and read, 'Be of good cheer, it is I, be not afraid.'"

I asked if he had made a trade of some kind with his Lord, to become a preacher in case of rescue.

"Absolutely not!" Jim showed a touch of fire at the suggestion. Then he added as an afterthought, "I did say, 'Lord Jesus, get me out of this and I'll live for You.'"

He had five months in hospital to think it over, for he was seriously wounded on the raft, a detail which he omitted from his telling of the story. It was time for my train, and Jim walked with me through Bughouse Square, an adjacent park, frequented by soapbox orators and bums. It serves as a handy clinic for the Moody students, especially on Saturday nights.

"Lots of Communists here, too," Jim said. He added irrelevantly, "If you're grateful for something, that's a good way to begin. Praise the Lord."

But American evangelism has never been confined to formal institutions. The impulse to rescue the perishing lives in a thousand movements and organizations, from vegetarianism to United World Federalists. Certainly it is in some organizations, like Alcoholics Anonymous, which depend for their success entirely upon their divorce from organized salvation. It springs up here, there, and everywhere, with or without publicity; and the people watch, withhold judgment, and finally make up their own minds, as they have always done, about "real Christianity."

A visitor might stay for months in Carroll County, Georgia, without hearing a mention of the Carroll Service Council. It tries to link together the co-operative efforts of farmers, businessmen, teachers, preachers, and everyone interested in the county as a whole, but it has a low budget and an inconspicuous way of doing things. A small staff takes turns in sweeping out the office on the fourth floor of the People's Bank Building behind the local radio station.

Nor did I find the county itself especially colorful. It hasn't any plantations, for it was settled by yeoman stock in upland, northwestern Georgia. There is a local saying that some of the land is "just good to keep Hell from showing through," but there is also much good soil. A soil conservation co-operative has reshaped the county with terraces and turned much of it green with pastures, dotted with a hundred small, man-made lakes. Conservation, rural electrification, and the shift to livestock have done most to change the lives of the farming people. The reader is warned again that the part religion plays in this story will be exasperatingly vague.

In Carrollton, a county seat of about eight thousand, there is television from Atlanta, fifty miles away, and two movies. A Veterans' Club and the Moose, it is said, will assist a deserving stranger in dry territory. The leading Methodist and Baptist churches rival the courthouse in size and grandeur. By nine o'clock at night the lights go out even in the drugstores and the waffle shop, and the Devil seems officially licked. However, he still finds his devious routes into the human heart. For example, there was a quarrel over the schoolhouse at Sand Hill, in the late nineteen-thirties.

Sand Hill at that time centered around two stores, a scattering of homes, three Baptist churches and one Christian, and a Masonic hall which was used for school, while a new brick building stood unfinished. The two merchants had differed over how big it should be and the purchase of materials. The split spread into the homes and churches.

At the county seat there is a teachers' college. At this

time, with a grant from the Rosenwald Fund, it was choosing students who showed leadership ability during the two-year course, to spend a third year working and living in rural communities, helping people solve their problems. Sand Hill was clearly a problem.

Dean L. E. Roberts of the college was asked to come out. After thirteen tries Dean Roberts, himself a Baptist, got the Sand Hill people together at a meeting, described as of a "semi-religious nature," in the unfinished school auditorium. I should judge from this that they sang a hymn or so, and maybe somebody prayed, but nobody preached. It takes a full-scale oration to make a "fully religious" meeting in the Bible Belt. At any rate, the people agreed to try co-operation with the college and with each other. They finished the school, held a Community Day to clean up the grounds, started a co-operative cannery and school lunchroom, held an annual union service of the once-divided churches, began meeting at the school for tacky parties, box suppers, movies, and harvest festivals. Underlying these fruits of the spirit were teachers trained as community leaders, who knew how to develop leadership in local people. Sand Hill today is considered one of the best elementary schools in the United States.

About this time there was quite a wave of small, rural co-operatives in Carroll County. The co-operative movement is itself a kind of religion; and the "community leaders" sent out by the college were mostly enthusiastic believers. Co-operative sweet-potato curing-houses, canneries, mills, credit unions sprang up, until Carroll County attracted nation-wide attention. The grist mill at Tallapoosa still bears a faded, evangelistic sign: "The farmers of this community have paid for many mills, but this one they really own." During the war patriotism and gas-rationing combined to strengthen the movement. Since the war many of the small co-operatives have died. Something of their spirit, local people say, has passed into the Carroll Service Council. But the impetus for the Council came from another direction.

About the time of the quarrel out at Sand Hill, the century-old Carrollton Presbyterian Church was slowly dying on the vine — losing out to the Methodists and Baptists. Its simple brick building, with a large plain wooden cross over the rostrum, is pleasant and dignified; but the services were sparsely attended, and mostly by older people. A new minister just out of seminary was privately instructed by the presbytery to decide whether it should be kept going or allowed to die.

Dick Flinn, son of a well-known Presbyterian minister in Atlanta, had spent a dozen years wondering whether or not to enter the ministry. He began by looking over the whole county with a newcomer's eye.

Despite the new community co-operatives — indeed, partly because of them — the county was filled with divisions. Some of the manufacturers and bankers thought the young "community leaders" far too New-Dealish. An ancient suspicion still lingered between town and country people. ("Let me tell you brethren," said an exasperated cotton man to a farmer who questioned his weight, "all the thieves, murderers, and so-and-sos ain't moved to Carrollton yet.") Among the towns, Villa Rica, where the Candlers of Coca-Cola fame originated, was not on terms of brotherly love with Carrollton. There were splits in the county seat itself between mill workers and employers and between the "mill village" and the rest of town. Among the Rotarians, Lions, Kiwanis, and Jaycees, even among the churches, there was a more-than-healthy amount of competition.

Meanwhile, county roads were deep in mud, there was no county hospital nor public health services, not enough libraries, parks, or playgrounds. Negro school-children for the most part met in ramshackle lodge halls or churches. The population of the whole county had been steadily declining for years, as young people left to seek opportunity elsewhere.

Appleton Mandeville, a Presbyterian, ran the big cotton mill across the valley from the teachers' college. He had kept the mill running, sometimes at a loss, through the depression; but the mill village had a depressed, stagnant atmosphere. On its edge was an old brick toolhouse. As a "do-something" beginning, Dick asked if it could be used for a library and nursery-school. A Sunday-School teacher took out her class to scrub the floors, and the college supplied books and student playground leaders.

The young minister now asked a dozen representative citizens to meet at Mr. Mandeville's home, to analyze the situation of the whole county. Among the arch-conservatives, the word "planning" was unpleasantly associated with the New Deal; nevertheless, as Dick pointed out, planning was needed if real independence were to be saved. Unemployed, merchants, and farmers alike had formed the habit of looking to Washington for more and more aid. Others dreamed of some great superindustry to come from the North and solve all difficulties. Time and again, some local group would promote a project — often too big for it to handle — arousing a temporary wave of enthusiasm which quickly died down.

The meeting made its first business to draw up a list of the county's entire needs, and the resources available. Panels were set up on Agriculture, Industry, Welfare, Education, and Religion. (As time went by, other advisers were added to represent the various communities in the county, and its Negro citizens.) Untapped resources were found in the banks, for well-to-do citizens had been investing outside the county for lack of local opportunities. But Dick Flinn warned against calculated self-interest in raising funds to start the Council's work.

"There are some things," he said, "we ought to do for Christ's sake — for no other reason than that they are just and right. What are the things common to us all?"

The soil, for one; and here the conservation co-operative had made a good beginning. Health and schools, for another. With one thousand dollars from the Mandeville mills, and ten thousand dollars raised in the town to meet a conditional grant from a foundation, the Council staffed its office and hired a public health nurse. In the first year she treated thirty-five hundred patients, taught white and colored midwives, inoculated school-children, and started a venereal disease clinic. As the load mounted, she had a nervous breakdown. The Service Council, beginning to feel its way along, did not immediately replace her; and after a year without a public health nurse, the county hired one.

Industries were brought in; a bookmobile and playgrounds started; a new school built for Negro children; of the many activities undertaken, few are unique to Carroll County, Georgia, and most were done by individuals and existing groups rather than by the Service Council itself. The news is in the way they were strung together; with the whole picture brought in focus in a central clearing-house, it was possible for the people of the county to plan ahead.

Officers and directors were elected at an annual public meeting, wherein anyone who had ever given a dime was eligible to vote. In 1948, the Council disbursed some forty-five thousand dollars, of which about sixteen thousand dollars went for administration. The rest was spent for welfare work, the expenses of the day-nursery, for the panel on agriculture and industry (including the straight "Chamber of Commerce work"), and for the religious panel (which functions somewhat like a church federation). There was also a new venture, the employment of a full-time recreation director. Thus services, which in most communities compete for funds are brought together in a flexible budget, depending on how local needs are being met from year to year.

But there has been no miraculous transformation of Carroll County, nor was one expected.

Dick Flinn was away several years at the war; on his return, he found the town in the throes of an old-time newspaper fight. A crusading editor, F. Clyde Tuttle, set out to expose what he felt were grave sins of omission and commission by the ruling powers. The roads were still muddy, there was no hospital, many other things were wrong. His newspaper named names freely; the row quickly got into the town churches, which Mr. Tuttle said were being used as "weapons in the hands of Greed, Malice, Injustice, and Hypocrisy to oppose RIGHT and FAIR PLAY." His literary style grew more and more fevered.

The Service Council was one of the few institutions not involved in the dispute. Neither Dick Flinn (who is only an *ex-officio* member) nor anyone else found any magic formula for ending the quarrel. (Eventually, Mr. Tuttle sold out.) But the Council went to work with its previous remedy: finding things that needed doing and getting them done. A Negro library was started; more small industrial plants were located in the county seat and outlying rural districts; a successful drive raised twenty-four thousand dollars locally for a hospital.

I went to the office of County Agent John Mauldin, to see what the Service Council has done for the farmers. Although most of its funds are raised in Carrollton, eighty per cent so far has been spent outside.

"I'll be frank about it," said Mr. Mauldin. "I think one of the best things it's done has been to pay the salary of an assistant for 4-H Club work. That's given me more time to work on new crops and markets. But don't you write another piece about Old Devil Cotton. Cotton yields have been steadily going up, and we've started a growers' co-operative."

He went on to discuss agricultural progress: he had got pimientos started; a livestock sales barn and a broiler industry were thriving; members of the local Kiwanis Club were going to visit an elevator and flour mill in Alabama the next day, with a view to the possible building of a grain market in Carrollton. This, if completed, would fill the last gap in a chain of local farmers' markets which the Service Council had listed years ago as among the county's urgent needs.

On the street outside the agent's office, I met Dick Flinn. We crossed the square with its Confederate monument in a little less than an hour and a half, as the minister stopped every ten yards to transact some sort of business or chat with someone. In his office at the church, I said the picture was a little puzzling. There didn't seem any clear-cut line between what the Service Council did and what other agencies did.

"Maybe that's just the point," he said. "There isn't."

It could easily be just a Chamber of Commerce with sanctified trimmings, I said.

"Could be. Why don't you go out with Carson Pritchard to Mount Zion?"

With Mr. Pritchard, a serious-faced young Baptist minister who directs the panel on religion, I drove a few miles out in the country. He apologized for being late. The first issue of a county recreation guide, he explained, had almost come out with a grave misprint. (An ad for a tourist camp read, "Always Coo on Hot Summer Evenings.")

Mount Zion looked a good deal like a thousand other Mount Zions across the map. A freshly painted Methodist Church stood in a knoll crowned with tall oaks, the old Methodist Academy building, now used as a teacherage, was close by, and a W.P.A. high-school building was across the road. Mount Zion had won first award, Mr. Pritchard explained, in the Council's church improvement campaign. It had added two Sunday-School wings and started weekly services.

I asked the high-school seniors if they had heard of the Carroll Service Council. All had heard of it, but none could tell what it was. We went down to visit the vocational agriculture teacher, Bill Wright, in his basement shop.

"The Service Council? Why, the projector's getting to be a bigger thing than the school," said Mr. Wright. Carson Pritchard, he explained, had come out several times with the Council's projector, and now the school trustees had bought one for community use.

What else had the Council done?

"Well, Mr. Pritchard come out once to take a man to the hospital in Atlanta. Had the ambulance all ready. But he'd run off in the woods and when they caught him, he said he'd rather die at home."

"The way I see it," he went on, "the Service Council is a place you can call on and get help without waiting for things to run down to rock bottom. All kinds of little things, but they aren't little to us. We have basketball two nights a week now — the recreation man from Carrollton came out and got us started. And they got some businessmen to give prizes for the Future Farmers stock show. And a few miles down the road they got a wig for a little girl who'd been left bareheaded by fever and was ashamed to go to school."

Were the young people staying on the farm?

They had enough for two full ball teams at Mount Zion, he said. One young farmer has six thousand chickens, a job in the shoe factory, and plays for square dances at night.

Dick Flinn drove me out in the opposite direction, the following Sunday, to Oak Mountain, a low ridge largely grown up in scrub oak. It was famous, he said, until recently as a base for bootleggers. On this afternoon a score of adults and children were holding an interdenominational Sunday-School in the wooden schoolhouse; afterward there was a general discussion in the clearing. Oak Mountain was buzzing with news. Students at Georgia Tech had volunteered to draw plans for a new school, community building, and church at Oak Mountain. Dur-

ing the coming summer Methodist, Baptist and Quaker
students from various other colleges would come to Carroll County to help build it, and set up "work camps" for
other jobs that needed doing.

There was a discussion today about placing the church
east by west, or north by south, where the side windows
would command the view over rolling red-clay ridges to
the Blue Ridge foothills.

"If we place it that way, we can enjoy looking out the
windows," said an Elder who had offered a choice of a
thousand dollars cash or all the timber needed.

"I don't think we ought to look out the window," said
his wife. "We ought to look at the preacher."

"Suppose we leave it to Mr. Flinn to decide."

"I suggest you look first at the view," said the minister,
"then at me, and take a vote."

They decided on the view. On the way in town, Dick
Flinn said that a leading textile manufacturer from Villa
Rica had named his new mill in the Oak Mountain com-
munity the Farmer's Mill.

"That's what we're trying to do all through the county,"
said Dick. "We don't want all the industries in the county
seat, nor any one big super-plant. We'd like to see industries backed as much as possible by local capital,
working home folks in the plant, with the farms around
raising the raw materials the plant uses. That's one way
the Service Council tries to be a little different from the
usual Chamber of Commerce — it isn't a pure case of
Watch Us Grow.

"You know," he added, "you can get almost anything
done if you're willing to let other people take the credit."

I asked for an example. There had been a successful

family life conference in the county, he said, addressed by a noted psychiatrist; few people knew the Council had anything to do with it. And a plan had been worked out, without friction, which allowed the Negro youngsters to use the white high-school gym.

In the Council office I looked over some pamphlets. An expert from the Federal Council of Churches had stayed for months in the county, making a study of the churches in relation to types of soil, farm income, and other matters. On areas of poor soil, for example, the old-line churches have often yielded to the various "Holiness" sects. Everywhere churches throve or languished according to the stability of the agriculture.

Over at the soil conservation office the telephone rang just as the Government technician — a short, wiry native of South Georgia commonly called Pat — was explaining the number of terraces in Carroll County. He picked up the receiver, answered, "Yep. Cost you about fifty dollars," and hung up. A field to be terraced? "No," said Pat; "a colored woman wanted to know if she could get a divorce in Carroll Country. We try to serve the public here."

In the Government truck we headed toward the Clem community, passing lumberyards stacked with pine, the biggest cash crop in the county. A sign, "Love Your Gas Man," was not part of the general story of peace and good-will; it referred to Mr. Love's filling station, Pat said.

"There's a member of the church." The soil conservation man pointed to a hundred-and-fifty-acre farm entirely converted to dairy and woodland.

"They're going to black-top the county roads at last,"

he said. "Just voted a six hundred thousand dollar bond issue." He stopped the truck in a farmyard. "Here's another member of the church." He introduced Spencer Wood, a Negro farmer who is a pioneer member of the soil conservation co-op.

Spencer Wood's soil is not of the best, but Hell doesn't show through. He was so pleased with the result of his kudzu and sericea that he wrote Doctor H. H. Bennett, chief of the Soil Conservation Service, receiving in reply a letter of congratulation urging him to continue his attention to the soil, "the basis of all life."

I asked what he thought about the Service Council.

"I gives regularly," he said. At an annual meeting of the soil conservation co-operative (the Service Council had helped with speakers), Spencer Wood was called on to lead in prayer.

I asked if he remembered what he prayed for.

His eyes grew serious behind steel-rimmed glasses. "I prayed for the Lord to bless our deliberations and so forth and so on. And then I ended like this, 'As it is written in Thy Holy Word, United We Stand, Divided We Fall.'"

2. *AT EASE IN ZION*

*Country churches link the generations in
Loudoun County, Virginia*

S INCE 1930 there has apparently been new life in the churches as a whole. The *Christian Herald* estimated that in 1947 about 53 per cent of the total population belonged to some religious denomination, the highest percentage ever reported. Most of the major denominations reported gains. Slightly more than three-fifths of all the 77,000,000 members were Protestants, the same percentage as in 1906.

We are reporting, not a statistical subject, however, but a spirit of "free religion" found in our country from early times of American settlement to the present. I had rather not try to define it more closely than I have done.

Those who are seriously interested will find no difficulty in pursuing their own investigations, for the old-time religion is everywhere — with or without the label. I am inclined to think that those groups which advertise the unique genuineness of their faith are less typical than others who go about their business without any claim to a copyright on salvation.

Also, I recommend the country churches, which show

most clearly the threads of the national past, and shelter both the living and the dead.

Between the highway and the Washington and Old Dominion Railroad, or "Virginia Creeper" (as it is called locally), the small white Belmont Chapel shines dimly through the trees. An overgrown lane is impassable with briers. I climbed the fence and crossed the pastures of the adjoining Belmont estate. The disused church was guarded by another fence and a thick growth of under-brush. It was not outstanding for age or interest; the front wall was of crumbling stone, the side walls of wood with green shutters.

A tall shaft in front had been erected by the pupils of Margaret Mercer (1791–1846), who is buried beneath the chancel of the chapel. Margaret's father was a friend and associate of Jefferson, Madison, and Monroe, the chief architects of our constitutional religious freedom. He was a Congressman and Governor of Maryland. She grew up, says her biographer, in luxury on his Maryland estate. "Beautiful, accomplished, and occupying a high social position, she entered upon life with the brightest prospects before her, and for a time participated in the usual amusements and occupations of the period and circle in which she moved." In this respect she was like young James Finley before he crawled under the haystack, a ruined man, or John Jasper before the lightning struck him in Capitol Square. A gay and worldly youth is the orthodox beginning for a saint.

But Episcopal salvation lacks the explosive and color-ful character of the less formal religions. Margaret was always devout, in a quiet way. What struck her was the

emancipation movement which swept across Virginia in
1816. An American Colonization Society was formed by
her friend Francis Scott Key and others, to purchase
Negroes and send them to Africa. She freed her own servants, spent the proceeds from her property in purchasing
the slaves of others and sending them to Liberia, and for a
quarter of a century thereafter maintained herself by
teaching school. At the same time she argued with Northern liberals, fearing that their pressure for immediate
abolition would lead to violence.

The colonization scheme, it must be reported, was not a
success. Old letters still preserved in Loudoun County
show that many Negroes were unhappy in Africa. A
Negro whom Margaret emancipated, and had trained as
a doctor in Washington, died of consumption three years
after reaching Liberia. "We can't get no meat," wrote a
former slave to his former master. "The monkeys get so
wild. The leopards howl, and the monkeys steal. The
savages caught us, but, praise the Lord, they set us free."

Margaret had come to Loudoun County to establish
her girls' school at Belmont. It was then apparently a run-
down, undesirable neighborhood. She built the little
chapel as a community center. Rowdies used to break up
meetings, but after a while Margaret got them firmly in
hand in Sunday-School.

The underbrush around the deserted chapel was strewn
with cheap whiskey bottles. I climbed the fence and
drove into Leesburg, the county seat.

On the Sunday streets a dignified, middle-aged Negro
was walking to his duties as sexton of a white church. I
asked how many kinds of Christians there were in Leesburg. He named them off, slowly and politely.

"Well, sir, there's two-three kinds of Methodists — the Nazarenes that claims to be the original Methodists, and the regular kind; there's one white Baptist and two colored, one Presbyterian, one Episcopal. And the Full Gospel Holiness. They've got the biggest crowds of all. Bring in two busloads of Sunday-School chillen from all over the country."

He waited for further questions. Why were there so many kinds in such a small place?

"Why, it's just human nature." His eyes wore a white veil in his brown, unsmiling face. "Just like there's all different races and colors."

"But it isn't quite the same."

"Some believes there's a white and colored Heaven and Hell," he said cautiously.

The first church in Loudoun, as in most parts of Virginia, was Anglican. It was built in 1733. But the county, which is part foothills and mountains, was first settled by upland yeomen, Friends, Lutherans, and Baptists. (The Methodists grew a little later, holding their first American conference in Leesburg.) The Episcopalians did not begin to thrive until the younger sons of tidewater planters began to move in with their slaves — "one jump ahead of the sheriff," say the descendants of Loudoun's shirt-sleeve aristocracy still. The Presbyterians came with the Scotch-Irish, who were "brought in to fight the Indians." The Friends were admirable people, but the Presbyterians were better rifle-shots.

Conditions were turbulent in early Loudoun. The first court in Leesburg ordered that no one could leave the county without first posting a notice of his intended departure "three times on the church door."

There were no public schools before the Civil War. Professor McGuffey, nationally famous for his Readers, came to Leesburg to lecture on higher education in 1837. The town, which had already planned a lottery to bring water in wooden pipes from a spring, voted to let a boys' academy share in the lottery. The old academy building, at the time of my visit, was the home of General and Mrs. George Marshall.

"Scientific farming" and crop rotation were much urged also; a "Loudoun County system of agriculture" became famous. The war was a severe setback. But the hopeful spirit did not die. In Reconstruction days the Washington and Old Dominion Railroad, then called by another name, set out from Alexandria, Virginia, to climb the Blue Ridge; it couldn't quite make the grade, but served some of the towns along the way.

Religion thrived throughout the century. In Purcell-ville, in 1877, the first Bush Meeting was held, by a group called the Good Templars, largely Quakers. Revivals lasted three days and drew crowds from the whole county. Later called the Evangelical and Prohibition Association, a large hall was built for this work. Early in the twentieth century, it was turned into a Chautauqua. When the hall burned down, it was not replaced, because by this time good roads, automobiles, and movies had come along.

We also had a little war with Spain, which hardly counted, and two World Wars, which did.

Of the Leesburg churches, the yellow-brick Presbyterian Church, built in 1802, is the oldest still in use. It has been little changed, except to remove the spittoons manufactured in a local pottery.

Entering late, I found the pews crowded, and a youthful minister preaching a New Year's sermon. He asked his listeners, as they began the New Year, to "reach out in the dark and place your hands in the Hand of God." The people, many of them three times his age, listened intently and devoutly. After service, five or six dropped in at the manse, where the preacher's pretty dark-haired wife was at home with a new baby. The talk was light and social, as if the visitors had left their cares behind.

The Full Gospel Church, of white-washed cinder blocks, near the edge of town, wasn't full; there was a sense of anticlimax in the air; no Pentecostal shouts came from the people. In the pulpit, Brother Jaffrey was gleaming with sweat. "I've never known people more loyal to the cause of Christ!" he shouted intensely. "But let me tell you something else — I've never seen a place where tongues wagged more loosely. Backbiting and gossip isn't Christian! Why, you can't even say the Lord's Prayer!" A curious moan, as if the congregation were a collective animal being whipped, rose from the benches.

He came to the door afterward, his face still gleaming. "There's been trouble in the church," he explained. "That's what church work is, Brother — trouble."

A few miles from town a hundred automobiles, drawn up on intersecting highways, formed a big black cross in the green countryside. I looked for an ambulance or policeman, but there was none. The people were gathered on the banks of Goose Creek and on the bridge looking down.

"I used to be drunk every Sunday, but thank God I'm not drunk today!" shouted a man leaning over the rail. "Folks up here is stoppin' to ask if there was a accident, but I tell 'em this here's a sin-wreckin' crew. Glory, hallelujah!"

A Church of God preacher waded out carefully, feeling his way with a stick, to a point waist-deep. He left the stick for a marker and returned to lead out a big old man with a square, pert Dutch face. The Dutchman rose dripping from the water, shouting, "Glory, I'm saved, thank you, Jesus!" as a church friend clicked a camera on the bank.

There were people here from the Full Gospel and all over. "I'm United Brethren; we just sprinkle," said my neighbor. The Dutchman climbed the bank, clothes dripping, face wet and beaming, and shook hands with everyone, friends and strangers. I asked if he had been baptized before. He took on a momentary, sheepish look. "Yes, I was. In the Dunkards, a long time ago. Not just once," he added with some pride, "but three times for-'ards." A mill-worker's wife from across the West Virginia line held a very pale two-year-old boy on her lap, dangling a toy watch to amuse the baby. She was answering the questions of friends. "He was took sick Wednesday night; we prayed it through and next mornin' the fever was all gone. Praise the Lord!"

On the back road to Middleburg, near Oak Hill, President Monroe's house, a Sunday ball game was in progress in a golden field of black-eyed Susans, next to a small chapel-of-ease built a century ago on a big plantation. Until recent years landlords and tenants had still gathered here on Sundays, in the English fashion. Then the tenants — as elsewhere — took to the "Holiness" or the Full Gospel, and the chapel fell into disuse. It had recently opened again.

The church people today were holding an interdenominational Sunday-School for a handful of scrubbed and beribboned children and their elders. Twice a month the rector comes out from Leesburg to preach in the afternoon — after the ball game.

All the churches in Middleburg were mellow and old; the Baptists now occupied a "free church," erected at the time of The Great Revivals by a generous Episcopalian for use by all denominations. Outside the Methodist Church were British and American flags; inside Emanuel Episcopal the rector called my attention to Confederate flags crossed over a plaque on the wall, in defiance of the Northern fox-hunting millionaires.

A few miles away, Lincoln, Virginia, has seventy-five inhabitants, and two old Quaker meeting-houses, one at either end.

"I don't know why," said a State highway foreman, smoking his pipe on the porch in the evening cool. "Guess they split up back yonder, like the rest. But a windstorm took the roof off the furtherest one, and now they all meet together, at the one they call Orthodox. It's a nice town," he added. "Everything goes along quiet and easy here."

The farmhouses surrounding Lincoln were large, old, and beautiful, without the swank fox-hunting look (Sheridan's raiders spared the homes of Friends). Mixed herds of Holsteins and Guernseys sprinkled the lush meadows with brown, black, white, and red. Beyond a gate banked with clematis an old resident, in answer to my question about a Lincoln in Virginia, asked me in to the porch.

"Well, it goes back," he said, rocking slowly, as if that settled matters. He was Mr. Charles Waters, with vigorous white hair and a shrewd, sensitive Quaker face. "Used to be called Goose Creek," he added after a while.

I waited patiently for further light. Everyone in Lincoln seemed to have lots of time.

"It was settled before the Revolution by the Friends from Pennsylvania. My great-uncle, who used to live over there" — he pointed to a mansion across the vale — "was on the railroad."

The Washington and Old Dominion?

Mr. Waters smiled. "Oh dear, no! The Underground Railroad. The Friends would smuggle runaway slaves from one farm to another, all the way up from Georgia. My great-uncle would put 'em in the barn, until he could move 'em up the road toward Harper's Ferry, under a load of hay."

But the name?

"Oh, after the Civil War we got a postoffice, and just called it Lincoln. Have you seen my lightning rod?"

I admired the lightning rod, as old as the house.

"Now the Hardshell Baptists," said Mr. Waters, "they don't believe in lightning rods. Think they thwart God's will."

Providence had recently effected a temporary reunion between two old Baptist congregations of the neighborhood by the same drastic means employed to unite the Quakers, he told me. The wind had removed the Missionary Baptist roof, whereupon the Hardshells, fifty yards away, had invited them in.

"Even let 'em bring their piano, I understand," said Mr. Waters. "Good-bye, and come again."

From a swimming-pool not far off, where a family of younger Friends were playing tag, came a clear, girl's

voice: "Watch out, Father, or I'll kick thee in the fanny."
At the wind-wrecked meeting-house two women in work-
clothes were stacking bricks for the restoration of the
Hicksite Meeting. Next morning was First Day, and I
went to joint meeting of the Hicksites and Orthodox.

Quaker Sunday-School was much like any other, with
perhaps more emphasis on sand-boxes for the young. The
adult class quickly wandered off into a discussion of current affairs, notably a coal strike; the young people sided
with Mr. John L. Lewis, the older were opposed. Quakers
are not supposed to argue and the talk hung in the air.
At last an old lady by the window spoke up. "I don't
care," she said; "anybody who works underground *ought*
to get paid more than other people."

Meeting, which followed, was silent. (The religion of
all Friends is extremely simple; they believe that God
still speaks to those who will hear.) Through the open
windows earthly sounds gradually came in over the loud
ticking of the Orthodox wall clock; road traffic, a radio
blaring a loud Gospel hymn. A woman rose to speak.
She had been thinking, she said, of the many non-Quaker
newcomers in the community; perhaps something more
could be done through the public school to make them
feel at home. The silence resumed; a bee invaded us; one
of the two old men on the facing bench began to snore
peacefully, at ease in Zion. The old lady, still by the window, said, "This is the Sunday when Christians all over
the world are meeting at Amsterdam, to come closer together. Let us share their joy for a few minutes."

At one time the Quakers were the leading denomination
in Loudoun County. A marker in the Lincoln graveyard
says, "Here on a log in the underbrush Hannah Janney

worshipped twice weekly in 1736." The date is inaccurate, for the settlement was probably made about 1755. For some time Friends' meetings were held in private homes, then in a log church, until the brick meetinghouse — the one damaged by the windstorm — was built in 1817.

The Quakers, with their doctrine of turning the other cheek, were natural targets for the frontier godless. A famous mountain bully came down one day to attack a vigorous old Goose Creek Quaker as he hoed his garden. The bully taunted and slapped him, until the old man suddenly turned and lifted him off the ground. "William, I will not smite thee, but I will shake thee a passel," he said; and he shook William until he cried for mercy.

As to the Orthodox split, a nearby Episcopalian still remembers hearing his Quaker grandmother describe it. It was around 1828. She had come home one day shaking her head and said to her Baptist husband, "John, a strange doctrine was preached at Goose Creek this morning. Elias Hicks was there, and he preached that Christ was no more divine than any other man."

The breach was closed by a noted Quaker of the time, Samuel M. Janney. But in 1886 the Orthodox again withdrew. Now time and the windstorm had healed the breach. Only a handful of Orthodox were left.

In 1940, after a hundred and eighty-nine years, services were discontinued in Ketocktin Baptist Church, closer to the mountains. It is a plain and beautiful old church, with a graveyard. The congregation drifted to new, and rather hideous, Baptist churches in the nearby towns; but when they die, they come back to Ketocktin. In the late eighteenth century, many who gathered at Ketocktin when the bell tolled were rationalists, free-thinkers, or deists, followers of Jefferson, Franklin, and Tom Paine. These stayed on the lawn discussing local and national questions of the day until church was out and they could take part in the general sociable outdoor gathering. Until recently, tobacco spit-boxes were still in place in the Ketocktin pews.

The Lutherans and Reformed, early in the eighteenth century, were numerous in the county. New Jerusalem Church was organized in 1750, and over at Lovettsville a Reformed Church was begun in 1733. The Germans co-operated in The Great Revivals, but not in Prohibition. Eight stills were flourishing in Lovettsville, a tiny settlement, early in the nineteenth century. There was no railroad then to ship the grain, and the soldiers at Harper's Ferry and the bargemen on the Chesapeake and Ohio Canal were good customers. Eight flour and grist mills and two cotton and woolen mills made use of the local water-power.

The Lutherans believed in justification by faith, the Reformed were Calvinists, but every home made schmierkäse, sauerkraut, and applebutter, and had a big German Bible. The Germans during the Civil War formed two companies of Union partisans who fought with Mosby's Confederate partisans for four years, burning, killing, and terrifying in a local war outside the history books.

Nowadays the Pennsylvania Dutch are still numerous, but over in the Shenandoah Valley it is the Dunkards who most often catch the eye.

Moscow, Virginia, is even smaller than Lincoln, hardly a place at all, only a small white meeting-house on the hill with a sign: "Brethren Church (1852) Welcomes the Stranger." They said to go right in to the Men's Class. I squeezed into one of the four long benches, all full of countrymen, the older men relaxed but the young men sitting stiff-necked and self-conscious, looking straight ahead. The teacher was a farmer, too, a stolid man with a face like a good-natured brick. He was doing his best with a minor prophet nobody had ever heard of before.

"Them people, the old Jews, they'd come into the richest country in the world, all milk and honey, and forgot their God. They was being punished for it, the prophet says."

He looked through the sunny window at the valley, where dogwood floated like clouds come to earth. The morning paper was full of news from the other Moscow.

"We're just like them people. Maybe what we're doing is wrong, too. Even if it's our leaders that does it, the wrong will come back on us."

The air was sweet and thick as honey. "We're in the richest land in the world, and oh, we could have things *nice*, if we wanted to!" He spoke with a quiet passion in his square, brick-colored face, not mentioning Molotov, inflation, or war. "God's a kind of neighbor, and He wants us to meet Him just halfway, in justice to ever' one."

"How about all those that don't come to church?" asked a sallow-faced youth triumphantly. "Won't they bring God's vengeance on us in spite of everything? There's plenty hangin' around Harrisonburg this very minute, drinkin' beer."

The other young men squeezed their lips and intensified their silence. The teacher's eyes came back from the flowering valley, but he refused to relinquish his vision.

"Just sharing what we've got with other people," he said. "We could have it *nice* in this world if we wanted to!"

The next town we can call Little River. It is old and small, nearer the mountains, and not quite atmospheric enough to draw outside attention. Little River has two filling stations, no tea-rooms or Bible texts nailed to trees, a total of one hundred and eighty-five people and two churches, both Methodist.

This in itself is a scandal, for all the Methodists nowadays are supposed to be one. But sentiment in the county on the slavery question was sharply divided. So close to the steep mountain land, many farmers did not own slaves; and a pre-Civil-War "Northern" and a "Southern" church still stand at each end of Little River.

When Mr. Wheeler, the present minister, came to this charge ten years ago, he tried at once to bring the congregation together. Because there was no organized recreation for the young people, who fled Little River as soon as they could find jobs elsewhere, he proposed using one of the churches as a parish hall and community center. Union, he soon discovered, was still an impossible dream. An old man with a rock chin and a strong bank account informed him that his great-grandfather had helped to build his church, and here he meant to live and die. There will have to be a few more reunions in Heaven before the Methodists are united in Little River.

"I guess a stronger man would have found some way to bring them together," said Mr. Wheeler in discouragement.

We were at the home of Ed Hungerford, a Government scientist who is an enthusiastic Little River man on week-ends. Ed said: "You've done all you could. And anyway, even if that sort of local feeling is ridiculous, isn't it one of the real roots? I mean, the church is almost the only truly local thing that's left. Except the Virginia Creeper, and most people ride the Greyhound. The schools have con-solidated, the bread's baked fifty miles away, we get our thoughts from New York and Washington — everything's canned."

"Sometimes you get canned sermons, too," said Mr. Wheeler, "in case you don't know it." He smiled. "I'd better be getting back before the storm. Thanks for taking Sunday-School while I was gone."

He walked down the path with the Hungerfords, scraps of shop-talk floating back: a rummage sale at Ebenezer; the county farm agent's talk before the men's club at Mount Zion; the Every Member Canvass; and a quarterly conference on top of everything. "I shouldn't take a va-cation," I heard him say.

Mr. Wheeler, who has six churches, has all the worries of a city pastor multiplied roughly by six, and a salary divided by four or five. Here and there the larger de-nominations, worried about the seed-bed, have begun to plow back city money into country-life conferences, building-funds for country churches and active commu-nity programs; but within one recent decade, thirty thou-sand country churches have died.

Hungerford pulled down the shade and broke out a bottle of beer. "Not that Mr. Wheeler would mind es-pecially," he said, "but some of his flock might see us through a spyglass. Sometimes there seem to be just two kinds of small-town people, the ones who think you're lost if you take a drink, and the ones who stay drunk all the time."

A large part of the Lord's work in Little River centers around food, in one way or another. The women, at their circle meetings, go through a yearly cycle. Beginning with a promise to serve nothing but salted nuts, sandwiches, and coffee, from house to house the refreshments creep up through fruit salad and pastry into an overflowing meal. Then, perhaps after a missionary lesson about the starving Chinese, the women take a stern vow, cut themselves back and start all over.

"Our women work awfully hard," said Mr. Wheeler, "but I don't guess they'd quite approve of bingo."

We were on our way to the Quisenberry's, to pick up a few sweet potatoes.

Mr. and Mrs. Quisenberry are in their early sixties. They have stayed on the farm, after the children married, just because they like it. Mr. Quisenberry gave the lumber for the Negro church in the woods near Little River, but you would never know it to talk with him. The sweet potatoes were only a come-on; the preacher was loaded with a side of bacon, six jars of preserves, and a bouquet from a large disorderly flower garden which straggled up and down the mountainside behind the house. They also wanted us to see their pig, a huge, silvery, affectionate sow.

"We've got to butcher soon," said Mr. Quisenberry sadly, "if my wife will let me. We ought to kill the cow, too; she's got to be a regular pet."

Mrs. Quisenberry showed us the storehouse, lined with thousands of jars of home-canned food. "More than we'll ever eat," she said, "but it gives me something to do, and anybody comes by and wants something, they're welcome."

The parlor, with its walls of plain unvarnished wood and comfortable rockers, held an aura of furniture polish, gingerbread, and impending naps.

"Can't sit down," said the minister. "I'd never get up."

On the way to town, he told me that he augments his income with an additional thirty or forty dollars a year in marriage fees, although he will not marry runaways.

"Like a couple I heard of over in Maryland," he said. "They came in late at night, without a license, and the minister told 'em they'd have to come back Monday. The young fellow asked him, 'Couldn't you just say a few words to tide us over the weekend?'" Mr. Wheeler flushed slightly at his salty joke.

That night the fireflies lit the great oaks of Little River like Christmas trees, lightning flashed through the mountain gap, an angry telegram from God. Here it came, a real sod-buster. On Sunday morning the flowers were all broken down, just a week before the Flower Show. It was "Northern" Sunday; there was a discouraged look on many of the thirty-one Northern faces. The minister slipped quickly from pew to pew, shaking hands with everyone before the service, smiling thirty-one times and saying that he was glad to *be* back, and his wife's cold was better. Then he preached on Daniel in the lions' den.

Daniel wasn't delivered *from* his troubles, he was delivered *right in the middle of them,* before the very jaws of the hungry lions. Mr. Wheeler, slight and red-headed, with a quiet voice and rather shy blue eyes behind his glasses, made you feel that Daniel, even with all his faith, was pretty scared. Because the minister was so human, Daniel seemed more human too.

But that's the way with troubles, he went on; often-times afterward we can see that they bear fruit, and help us out in ways we couldn't possibly foresee. Like this cloudburst last night; certainly it ruined lots of flowers, and cornfields, which was even more serious, but later on in August, even if we have a dry spell, there'll be water in the soil.

He called on Mr. Quisenberry for the closing prayer. Mr. Quisenberry gave thanks for a needed rain, and also for the pastor's vacation. "He needed it and deserved it, and we thank Thee for bringing him back to us."

The service was short today, because we were all going over to Mr. Wheeler's Mount Zion Church for a joint celebration of Children's Day. The continued existence of Mount Zion was, in a way, the greatest scandal of all. It had been built in the eighteen-thirties two miles from town by Pennsylvanians of German stock, who had been caught in the Methodist net during The Great Revival. The Pfitz family, still numerous in the surrounding valley, insist on keeping Mount Zion open, and threaten to re-unite with the Lutherans if it is closed.

It is a pretty stone church, and the Pfitzes today had outdone themselves on decorations. Luckily before the storm, they had banked a mass of white hydrangeas in the chancel under the old blue window with its picture of The Book. The front pews swarmed with little children; par-ents and prompters sat to the rear.

"Lit-tle lips, be care-ful what you say!" sang the six-year-old Beginners in unison, pointing to mouthfuls of forbidden nursery words, their eyes twinkling. "A Father up a-bove is look-ing down in love." Six adolescent girls, one of them very fat, came forward quivering in misery; they made vague swinging motions and almost wept as they implored us to Come Join the Jolly Band.

"The next number's supposed to be a recitation by Ruby Pfitz," said the superintendent, "but she's gone out somewhere." The choir, an all-Pfitz quartet, jumped up and filled the breach while a search went on inside and out. Ruby was captured in the foundations of the old schoolhouse and led to the altar, where with heavy prompting she got through a humorous selection. (The stylish young lady with her new hat was late to church. As she entered, she thought the choir, singing "Halle- lujah!" was really calling, "Hardly knew ya!") Ruby's agony was shared all through the crowded church.

Mr. Wheeler now spoke, just five minutes. From the upstairs balcony, where the slaves used to sit before the Civil War, came the rustling of a Production Number. Down the aisles came the six unhappy girls again, arti- ficial flowers in crêpe paper, the fat girl looking like a double petunia among the rest.

Afterward the people visited for nearly an hour on the sunny lawn. Ed Hungerford discussed with Mr. Quisen- berry the purchase of a brown Swiss calf. Mr. Wheeler asked Ruby Pfitz about her mother. She was out in Iowa visiting, said Ruby.

"Oh, out in Iowa they've got *everything!*" exclaimed Mr. Wheeler, and you would have to be a country minis- ter with four children to know just what he meant.

"The cream's the best, Mother says."

Uncle Bob Pfitz remembered when his grandchildren were in the Beginners' class. "They got to arguin' over who could remember back the furtherest. Little boy was about six, his sister was five. He said, 'I can remember the day I was born.' His sister said, 'Oh, I can remember *way* before I was born. I can remember when God said, "Patsy, stand up so I can put your eyes in". ' "

Heedless of the risk to nylons, the women carried the flowers through the tall Queen Anne's lace to the cemetery. Hydrangeas were placed upon Methodists, Lutherans, Reformed, Hardshell and Missionary Baptists, Quakers, Presbyterians, Episcopalians, and no doubt one or two deists or free-thinkers, for there were enough for every grave.

Quarterly Conference was held at Mount Zion. District superintendent Ellicott came from the big city. A tactful man, tall and spare, he listened intently to the reports from each local church.

From Little River Northern, Mrs. Quisenberry reported total receipts for the year $391.64. Disbursed locally for Christian work, $362.25. Balance on hand, $29.34. She started to sit down.

"Hold on," said Mr. Ellicott. "You say that was all disbursed locally? Have you got it itemized?"

So Mrs. Quisenberry read the list, and it *wasn't* strictly local: two CARE packages, gifts to Church World Service, to the county home, to the Methodist missionary fund, repair of the parsonage furnace, and the Golden Cross. The superintendent explained that the Golden Cross, a Methodist hospitalization fund, had spent one thousand dollars in Little River territory during the past year, to pay the expenses of needy sick persons. "They were not all Methodists either," he added.

As to missions, he said, he had recently talked to a man

come back from China, who reported mighty little hope for the Chinese either in the Nationalist Government or in the Communist. "Educated Chinese are coming to feel that the Christian missions are the only hope their country has," said the superintendent, and for a moment, the whole world rested squarely on Little River. When he asked the people to approve a local budget calling for an increase in missions, the motion passed quietly without speeches.

There was no increase in Mr. Wheeler's salary of twenty-four hundred dollars a year.

The conference adjourned for dinner on the grounds. Here were the delectable mountains I remembered from Baptist Association meetings in childhood — heaps of fried chicken, cold sausage and sliced tomatoes, every known denomination of deviled egg, cole slaw, potato salad, and coconut cake, on long trestles beneath the trees.

A black-hatted man, with bushy eyebrows and a red, weathered neck, stood near the graveyard, eating a musk-melon. We shook hands, his eyes like blue-veined marbles searching my face. I was not a Methodist, I explained; just visiting.

"I'm not either," he said. "I'm a Baptist, but I believe it's all one church."

I asked about the ruined schoolhouse. "Church built it," he said. "Away back yonder. One of the best doctors we ever had came right from that old school. Now I don't like the way they're doin' the schools, ridin' the kids all day long over the county. I'm agin' it. It don't seem right."

A firecracker went off in his cold blue eyes.

"Now, take even the graveyard. They don't take proper

care of it. Keep diggin' 'em up and puttin' in new people. They even put a highway right through the middle of a nigger graveyard. Took 'em all up and put 'em in a box, with a little dirt. I know they was just nigger slaves, but it don't seem right."

I asked about the new pastor who was coming to take Mr. Wheeler's place. "I hope he's one-tenth as good a man. Too many pastors today is interested in the fleece more than the flock."

He moved toward Mount Zion Church, to which the congregation was returning. "Well, they asked me to ring the bell after dinner. Reckon I'm asleep on the job."

3. *SUNDAY IN BABYLON*

Sunday in the big city isn't altogether pagan.
Even in its city clothes, the old-time religion
ultimately aligns itself on the side of freedom

As I was leaving Loudoun County, on the mellow old streets of Leesburg a maiden lady called my attention to a crumbling real-estate opportunity. She asked where I came from.

"Well!" she said. "It must be like living in a pagan city, to judge from what we read in the newspapers."

I asked for details, remembering that I had seen her earlier at the Presbyterian Church.

"All those stories in the Washington Sunday *Star*," she explained. "We keep up with what's going on! Big embassy cocktail parties and receptions on the Lord's Day. Seems almost like a modern Babylon, doesn't it?"

I wondered if the *Star*, a most respectable newspaper, had spread across the nation this new and startling picture of the nation's capital as the scene of Belshazzar's Feast. Perhaps from lack of opportunity, I have had but small part in the more guilty activities and have doubtless passed more Sabbath hours in parks and museums than in houses of worship or haunts of sin. But it seemed fitting to close these travels with a brief account of Sunday in a big city.

It is, of course, a free country, and on Sunday morning we can all do as we please, provided we can find some way to amuse the children. My impression, colored largely by experience as a *paterfamilias,* is that Washington gets up rather earlier on Sunday than New York; Sunday morning trolley schedules in our neighborhood take adults and children downtown for Sunday-School and bring back members of the Wanderbirds Hiking Club or other adventurers to explore Rock Creek Park on foot or on horseback, or dangle contentedly for catfish in the Potomac or the old Chesapeake and Ohio Canal. Washington on Sunday may be heathen, but it is nice. There is even a stuffed whale in one of the lesser-known museums, big enough to take care of Jonah.

The Ice Palace is soon thronged with skaters on Sunday, and once or twice each winter, the Canal and the Potomac freeze. With the first warm break Washingtonians, an intensely suburban tribe, begin to worry about lawns and gardens. When it is really hot, the city people fan out on the Sabbath in two directions — east to the Bay, west to the mountains; as night falls, ribbons of light fifty miles long converge on the city from the salt water and the Blue Ridge. This is the Sabbath that was made for man. Even in low-lying Washington, where skyscrapers are not allowed, the church spires do not dominate the skyline, and religion has a place which is modest, diffused, almost invisible compared with its position in Carroll County, Georgia, or Loudoun County, Virginia.

Yet even in Babylon the subject is important. The importance is less in the "official Christianity" of public speeches (known to newspapermen as "God in the last paragraph") than in those tides which ebb and flow in the heart. During the New Deal, I remembered, the city had been filled with something like religious zeal. In the knowledge, or at least the faith, that they were helping to save the country and the world, even minor Government employees had found a satisfying emotional outlet. The missionary impulse steamed and bubbled over the high-balls in Georgetown, and if much of it was shallow and self-seeking, some of it, no doubt, was real. During the war which followed, salvation took a military turn, but seemed just as real and urgent. Now it was long after the war; the atomic threat hung more heavily over Baby-lon than over Leesburg; and I set forth to look at the old-time religion.

My first port-of-call was the Pillar of Fire.

In the last century, nineteen-year-old Alma White had gone from her Kentucky mountain home to the wild Montana Territory to teach public school. She wanted to preach, as well; and after marrying a Methodist minister, the Reverend Kent White, she sometimes took over his pulpit, feeling under the power of the Holy Ghost. The frontier Methodists of that day objected to a woman preacher; Alma objected to their worldly oyster suppers, and she withdrew in 1901 to recover true Holiness, found-ing the Pillar of Fire Church. She was stern, however, with some of the excesses of the other "Holiness" people. To some Southern followers who began rolling on the floor she once said, "You get right up or I'll stick a pin in you."

At eleven o'clock on a Sunday morning, I found the sign "Pillar of Fire" on a small row house in Southeast Washington; folding chairs had been set up in the bay-front parlor, where four black-garbed ladies knelt praying in the Fundamentalist fashion, backs toward the pulpit.

A red-eyed sister handed me a hymnbook, containing pic-
tures of Pillar of Fire educational institutions at Zarephath,
New Jersey, and Denver, Colorado, and a portrait of
Bishop Alma White. She had died a few days before.

It was a quiet, somber congregation this morning. A
minister in black clericals and his son, recently discharged
from the Navy, appeared; the minister played the violin
to a piano accompaniment, a sister on the back row un-
packed a mandolin, and four of us were left to sing.

Stating, in an aside for my benefit, that women in their
church have equal rights with men, the preacher now
called on Sister Priscilla for an account of her fight with
the Devil in Danville, Virginia. Tight-lipped and rather
tense, Sister Priscilla wore a blue-black uniform with
plain white ruching at the neck, and over the heart a red-
lettered Pillar of Fire badge. An atheist on the Danville
streets, she said, had asked how old the world was.

"My Bible tells me six thousand years," she had answered him. "But it doesn't matter how old the world is,
the Lord Jesus can save sinners. He was coming soon,"
she added, "with a shout." During the week she had
preached to one thousand and given out more than three
hundred pieces of Gospel literature.

Sister Mary had a milder face. She had been a "stiff
and starchy Episcopalian," she confessed, before the plain
preaching on the Pillar of Fire radio program had "turned
the light inward." She read us the New Testament story
of the miraculous delivery from jail of Paul and Silas.
That morning she had accosted on the streets two girls
with painted lips and flesh-tinted stockings to ask when
they had last read the Bible. The young ladies had replied that they were on their way to church that very

minute. Sister Mary had then rebuked them for wearing such attire to the Lord's House. They saw nothing wrong in it. "Read the Scriptures and you'll find different," she told them.

Some of their literature seemed a trifle stern. "Who are these people who have the mark of the beast in their foreheads and hands?" exclaimed an article in *The Dry Legion*. "They throng the streets. They are in the moving-picture shows; they have their ears to the radio listening to its filthy jokes. . . . They belong to this base world of the iniquitous, the wicked, the God-forsaken."

In the back room of the house was an accredited parochial school for Pillar of Fire children. They endeavor to keep separate from the world.

The minister who showed me through their establishment was mild and friendly. He was genuinely distressed at my question about racial prejudice. They have none, he assured me, nor any peculiar or unusual doctrines.

"Of course," he said, looking at me thoughtfully, "some of our people become a little worked up at times — but no tongues, no snakes." There are no salaries, either; as in many small sects, the work relies entirely on free-will offerings. "We all live here in this house," he added, "and live well."

Atomic energy has added fuel to the premillennial fire. A free-lance evangelist has filled Constitution Hall in Washington for Sunday after Sunday, and on Saturday nights the Seventh-Day Adventists, a permanent offshoot of the Miller agitation, draw sizable crowds to Meridian Hill Park. Here white and colored sit peaceably on the grass to see movies of the portentous events in Palestine and sing hymns from colored slides. The Adventists today are not only evangelists; they also conduct hospitals, schools, and other useful mission enterprises around the world. In a big house on a Georgetown corner, the Holiness folks shout in the Unknown Tongue, and from door to door the Jehovah's Witnesses, having no truck with churches, peddle their documents. I bought one, and read it carefully.

The Witnesses deserve to be a little better understood, for their position is unique. After the late Pastor Russell proclaimed the event during the First World War, the Witnesses have refused to back-track or announce a postponement; they explain that the end has in fact already started, unobserved by the general public.

On Saturday the *Washington Post* prints a church page more interesting than most. Besides the usual advertisements of Sunday services, it has all sorts of news: Some of the people at the Federal Trade Commission are meeting early in the morning for a brief period of meditation before work, sometimes with a talk by a visiting clergyman. A Unitarian started it. The Washington Breakfast Prayer Group meets at a hotel on Tuesdays, with doctors, teachers, lawyers, newspapermen, preachers, engineers, representing Christian Scientists, Mormons, Pentecostals, Congregationalists, Presbyterians, Baptists, Episcopalians, Disciples, Lutherans, Methodists, and others. There is a Congressional breakfast club with a similar purpose. Mr. Jennings Rodeffer, a bus driver for the Capitol Transit Company and member of the Church of the Brethren (Dunkards), has solved his problem of Sunday work by getting a job driving a bus to church. The church charters a bus to collect its members, and Mr. Rodeffer — it is impossible to avoid mentioning a busman's holiday — sings hymns with them, sometimes to a guitar and harmonica accompaniment, as they drive over the city streets.

The city Church Federation has published a guide, "Where to Worship in Washington, D.C." More complete than the church page, it lists thirty-seven Baptist churches, from Anacostia to Zion; two Brethren; thirty-three Catholic, from Assumption to Saint Vincent de Paul; five Christian Science, numbered One to Five; two Church of the Brethren, which are a little different from the plain Brethren; three Churches of Christ, the outgrowth of the anti-organ movement among the Disciples; one National Memorial Church of God; one Church of the New Jerusalem (Swedenborgian); four Community Churches, including one Chinese and one French; seven Congregational, seven Disciples, forty Episcopal, one Evangelical, three Evangelical and Reformed, two Friends, sixteen Jewish synagogues, nineteen Lutheran, forty Methodist, one Mormon, one Nazarene, four Orthodox, five Pentecostal (including a Full Gospel and an Assembly of God), twenty-four Presbyterian, five Salvation Army, five Seventh-Day Adventist, and one each of the Unitarians, United Brethren, and Universalists.

There were many omissions. The list did not mention the Washington churches I have already reported — the Pillar of Fire, Primitive Baptists, Elder Michaux's Church of God, and the Moors. Divine Science, Theosophists, and Spiritualists were not represented. But the Church Federation list undoubtedly included the vast majority of Washington's church people, and it includes the main cycle of growth and change.

Across the street from the Public Library, for example, is Mount Vernon Place Methodist, a leading "institutional" church. Some years ago, despite the combined elevating influences of the library and the church, the neighborhood began to run down until it is now the heart of the burlesque and shooting-gallery belt. Other congregations, under these circumstances, have often sold out and moved to the suburbs. Mount Vernon Place Methodist stayed put, and launched an enormous program of weekday activities for young and old. Among its current doings I saw a notice of a performance of *The Drunkard*, a well-known satire on the old-fashioned temperance play. The choice of *The Drunkard* by the Methodist young people did not, of course, imply that they have taken to drink, but it marked a certain change in attitude from the Methodism of a hundred or even twenty or thirty years ago.

Directly opposite on K Street, meanwhile, the Full Gospels were holding an old-fashioned Pentecostal revival.

Undoubtedly the Catholics get up first. At Our Lady of Victory on the hill crowds gather for early Mass. ("Wouldn't it be Hell," Governor Al Smith is said to have remarked to friends early one frosty Sabbath in the Executive Mansion at Albany, "if those Protestants upstairs turned out to be right, after all?")

According to the most rigid Ku Klux or Calvinist traditions, the Catholics after early Mass spend the rest of the day in riotous wassail, storing up juicy items for the next confession. Time has softened this harsh picture, so that there is just as much wassail in one house as the next, all things considered.

But the Protestants — some of them — also attend to their religious duties in the haphazard, irregular, scattering fashion which is their tradition. Little neighborhood churches of one kind or another have cake sales, bazaars, clubs for young and old; neighbors teach Sunday-School; the amateurishly decorated signs of the rummage sale in the chain grocery or slick, chromium drugstore have an endearing message even for the pagan, a touch of something genuine in the way of neighborly, community feeling.

Sometimes it seems to be the children who keep it alive. Our eldest returned from a neighborhood Sunday-School one day, informing his young sister, home with a cold, that there had been movies.

"Mickey Mouse?" she asked, her five-year-old chin quivering with jealousy.

Her brother relented. "No, just Jesus," he said.

It was his first noticeable act of Christian charity.

Over the centuries, and in geography too, the old-time religion seems to flow from something like the Pillar of Fire or the Full Gospel to something like Mount Vernon Place Methodist; from the country to the city, from the wildness of Cane Ridge to the luncheon meeting of the Washington Federation of Churches.

In its small brick building, a remodeled residence, I found the table being set for a Kiwanis-type luncheon by the ladies of Takoma Park Lutheran, whose pastor, the Reverend J. Adrian Pfeiffer, was therefore entitled to ask the blessing. The assembled clergy listened with professional unconcern. Two or three Negro ministers and social workers were seated with us. My host was Doctor Edward

H. Pruden, whose church President Truman sometimes
attends. Doctor Pruden came in breathless and a trifle
late, having ducked in at the National Presbyterian across
the street to scout a noonday Lenten service at which he
would speak later in the week. Doctor Pruden is a Baptist. He diverted the conversation with an account of an
awful happening at a church he had supplied on his last
vacation.

An important member of the congregation, unknown to
him, had returned after a long absence. A well-meaning
friend, therefore, scribbled a note and passed it forward
to the guest preacher. Unfortunately, he read it aloud
with the other notices: "Mrs. Grosvenor Thomas is back
from Europe, wearing floppy hat with white ribbons. Be
sure to notice her this morning."

The parsons settled back over coffee for the business.
Laymen reported on the work of committees: Church liai-
son with the Veterans' Information Center; a survey of
recreational opportunities for eighteen-year-olds on Saturday nights; a child day-care center to be established
with forty thousand dollars from the Community Chest;
a professional counseling service to be started in the Federation Building, at the request of city social agencies.
The numbers of the variously lost and bewildered were
swamping social workers and pastors alike. Some of the
clients, doubtless, would be referred to psychiatrists or
clinics; others advised to go back home.

With a huge population increase since 1940, there had
been no comparable increase in church-building, reported
the committee on research and planning. The Federation
consults with member churches in placing new buildings
where they will best serve their respective congregations

and the needs of the whole city. Otherwise, seven or eight half-empty churches might arise in the rapidly spreading suburban areas, leaving older areas with no churches at all. The overseas relief committee reported checks still coming in from the public at large. Bishop G. Bromley Oxnam would speak at the annual Federation dinner at the Statler. Inter-racial teams would soon visit city high schools to talk on the need for more understanding of the United Nations. At All Souls Unitarian, a meeting would discuss "Three Ways to World Government." And so on.

The work of the city minister becomes steadily more complicated. At a seminary I heard a professor of church administration remind his students of the need for planning ahead; he cited the example of a preacher who by Friday noon, when the local paper telephoned, had not yet decided on his Sunday morning sermon. He instructed his secretary, "Just tell them, 'sermon by the pastor in the morning.' At the evening service, I'll preach on the text about 'The Fool Hath Said in His Heart' — you know, make up a title and let them have it."

The paper carried the notice, "Morning: Sermon by the pastor. Evening: What the Fool Said."

There is usually much visiting around, what used to be called "sermon-tasting," before a newcomer settles down in the church of his choice. Almost any sort of accident may decide the matter — the church is convenient, the children like the Sunday-School, the minister seems agreeable.

It is so at all the leading city churches — at Foundry Methodist, where Franklin D. Roosevelt once took Winston Churchill to sing hymns on Christmas Eve of

1941, and the marble altar is awash with candlelight, more like Canterbury than Cane Ridge; at New York Avenue Presbyterian, where Lincoln used to sit alone in a side chapel, listening to the testimony at prayer meeting without disturbing the people by his presence; at the Lutheran Church of the Reformation, with its gay, red-and-gold Scandinavian ceiling; or at the little Gothic Reformed Church which Theodore Roosevelt attended, where a Zwingli Bible Class and high Slavic cheekbones are the chief reminders of the historic Reformation.

At a number of the leading churches downtown, two morning services are necessary to accommodate the crowds. Toward the First Baptist Church on Sixteenth Street the people start coming early in the morning, younger Government stenographers and minor employees walking from nearby boarding-houses, families arriving by car from the suburbs, an occasional more affluent member dismounting from a taxicab. These are not the Washington fashionables; such streaks of piety as pervade the gay world are more often found in Episcopal churches. The intellectuals, for the most part, are farther out Sixteenth Street at All Souls Unitarian (where the Reverend A. Powell Davies would object strenuously to being included in the old-time religion), or perhaps at the Friends meeting-house. These are an ordinary cross-section of respectable, white-collar humanity, with a somewhat marked Southern accent — although the First Church itself is affiliated with both Northern and Southern Baptists, and with the Federal and World Council of Churches.

They are as far removed as the Methodists in the next block from the wildness of Cane Ridge. Their choir, one of the best in the city, is robed, a bronze cross stands beside the Bible on the communion table, the minister, the Reverend Edward H. Pruden, preaches in a black gown. Is it the old-time religion?

For his text the minister chose from the Gospel of John, 11:48: "If we let him thus alone, all men will believe on him . . . " Such was the comment of the chief priests and Pharisees, who met in council after the raising of Lazarus to discuss what to do about Jesus. Clearly, he seemed a subversive character who threatened the established religion of the day.

Doctor Pruden now pointed out that, from the early days of Christianity until now, one great difficulty in seeing Jesus as He really is has been that even His own followers will not "let him alone." To each group He means something different, and too often we have sought to force our own picture of Him upon others. As examples the minister cited one large branch of the Christian Church which, he said, presents Jesus to outward view always upon a crucifix, in a dying condition, and has made of Him a Deity so august that He must be approached through His mother. Likewise, he said, some Protestant theologians have made Him a unit in a complicated apparatus. Ultra-liberals, on the other hand, acknowledging the value of His teachings, refuse to acknowledge Him as Saviour and Lord. Many who loudly profess His name give a distorted picture of Jesus to the world by their own lack of real Christianity.

The "prophetic" school, he continued, sees in Jesus a King who will come in clouds of glory, and thus make Him appear remote from present, earthly activities. The highly emotional, hysterical groups also give a distorted picture of Jesus. Sectarians of all sorts feel that they, and they alone, have the truth about Him.

Nevertheless, the minister said, Jesus is the unifying force who draws all Christians together. He would like to be thought of, Doctor Pruden said, first of all as human, for He spoke most often of Himself as the Son of Man. He identified Himself with all humanity. He is today, as always, the champion of the underprivileged and the oppressed. Wherever religious liberty is denied, wherever men are persecuted for nationality or race, Jesus is at their side.

"He would say today if He were living, 'If there is anyone you consider not good enough to eat with, you would not consider Me good enough to eat with. If there is anyone you consider not good enough to have as a neighbor, you would object to having Me as a neighbor.'"

Doctor Pruden is no orator. He spoke these words in his calm, rather thin voice, raising it only slightly for emphasis at this point. Through the crowded church of Southern Baptists there was a silent, yet perceptible, feeling of shock. The minister himself is from Virginia.

He ended his sermon in his matter-of-fact delivery. Jesus is also the Teacher. We learn from Him, continually, the truth of His teachings; sometimes by bitter experience, when men and nations go contrary to them. And Jesus wants to be recognized as the Incarnation of God, Whom everyone may know. He asks for each of us to approach Him with open minds and accept Him as Saviour and Lord. "If we let Him alone, all men will believe on Him." The minister extended the usual Baptist invitation to members of the congregation to accept the Saviour. During the closing hymn a number of new members, mostly from small Southern towns, came forward to the front pew, which is always left vacant for this purpose. Their names were read aloud to the congregation, before the benediction.

Parents collected small children from the nursery. A line formed downstairs to greet the preacher and his wife and the new members, and outside, on the sidewalk, the young people stood visiting, discussing plans for the afternoon.

The job of the ministers is to help sinners be reconciled to God; a sinful and secular reporter can claim no such mission. But in conclusion, some of the minor barriers between the wayward heirs of the old-time religion and their inheritance can be noted. There are those whose estrangement goes far too deep for casual comment. But some of the barriers are pretty small potatoes.

The fact that some Americans chew gum during divine service may be deplorable but is surely not too important in the sight of God.

Other barriers go back into American religious history. The outer forms of religion, under freedom, are in constant process of change, but sometimes there are cultural clashes and cross-currents while the change goes on. For example, revivalism as an institution somewhat overstayed its time — and offended many.

Still other barriers arise from time to time. The beating of the Gospel drum by powerful publishers and business interests offends some. If their only purpose in stacking up Christianity against Communism is to save their own shirts, surely the Devil will get them, after all. Meanwhile, the ostentatious parade of the high and mighty to the mourners' bench is bad for religion. (So, at least, the dean of a conservative Episcopal seminary told me.)

Yet another barrier is the fear of succumbing to nostalgia, of making a "mother image" out of Jesus. This is a real fear, based on good principles. Certainly it would be painful if people began to "take up" the old-time religion as a quaint old American custom, like square dancing. But that wouldn't be the old-time religion. You don't take it up; it takes you.

A good deal of what passes for religion is certainly just a vague fear or homesickness.

For example, I recall a white-haired gentleman with whom I shared a pew in a typical, middle-class Methodist Church in Tennessee. The minister, a young college graduate, preached an earnest sermon on the familiar theme of atomic energy and the desperate need of our times for the spirit of Jesus. The congregation listened intently; Oak Ridge was nearby. But I noticed that the old gentleman in my pew had an individual reaction. Whenever the preacher mentioned Jesus as Our Lord or as Saviour, my pew neighbor uttered a loud, approving Amen! At other times during the sermon, he was silent and downcast. After the service he introduced himself and apologized for being noisy.

"I can't help it," he said. "It's the way I was brought up. You know, I fight against this Modernism thing whenever I see it."

This old warrior represented one horn of the dilemma on which the old-time religion continually finds itself. In its concern for the faith it is apt to forget the freedom, or in its concern for the freedom it may dilute its faith into ordinary, secular liberalism. Yet if we look back over two hundred years we can see that the dilemma is not as fatal as it looks. We manage to work out of it, somehow. We are promised help, if we seriously try.

In its first American beginning, our subject was an experiment and an adventure. The purpose of those who brought "free religion" to this continent was radical: to make it possible for all men and women to know the Christ; to interpret and follow His teachings according to the dictates of their own consciences, free from official interference. For this purpose no established ecclesiastical machinery or stated form of belief was considered essential.

In fact, with Roger Williams the use of force in saving souls was specifically forsworn, as contrary to the spirit of the Lord.

As it froze into patterns of formal behavior — as when the spontaneous revivals of the early days became a definite kind of ritual — our subject lost much of its appeal for free and independent minds. And when, as in Prohibition and the anti-evolution laws, it tried to force its standards upon others, Americans rebelled. But under these superficial events the old-time religion was still there, as deep as it is simple: the personal search, under freedom, for "real Christianity."

For a number of reasons this tradition seems especially suited to the needs of Americans.

One practical reason is that we already have it. The combination of faith and freedom is found even in such churches as the Episcopal or Lutheran, which seem closest in background to ritualism and churchly authority. The tradition runs through the whole range of Protestantism, from right to left. It is in the Unitarians as surely as in the snake-handling Church of God With Signs Following After.

Between these two extremes, undoubtedly, most of the church people are found. It is a futile effort, I am afraid, to try to reconcile all the many forms of the old-time religion and its offshoots in America; and such attempts seem essentially lacking in humor and in faith. Just as political democracy must stand or fall on its belief that people are able to govern themselves, so this religious experiment still rests on its original proposition that the people are competent to interpret the Bible.

True or false? Time itself, moment by moment in the accumulating influences of all our lives, is ripening the fruit of the tree.

THE END